For my Mother and Father

THE CAULIFLOWER CHRONICLES

A Grappler's Tale of Self-Discovery and Island Living

by Marshal D Carper

LAS VEGAS

First Published in 2010 by Victory Belt Publishing.

Copyright © 2010 Marshal D Carper

ISBN 10: 0-9825658-7-9

ISBN 13: 978-0-9825658-7-2

Printed in The United States

TABLE OF CONTENTS

Part 1:
Jumping Guard

Part 2:
Controlling Posture

Part 3:
Improving Position

Part 4:
Setting Up The Submission

Part 5:
Getting The Tap

PART ONE:
JUMPING GUARD

"What lies behind us and what lies before us are tiny matters compared to what lies within us."

—Ralph Waldo Emerson

BROKEN BONES

he referee looked down at the white belt tied around my waist, its outline pale against the dingy brown background of my tattered gi.

"You're in the blue belt division?" he asked, confused as to why I was fighting up a division.

"Yeah," I replied, ashamed of the white fabric. "It's a long story."

He shrugged and waved my opponent and me to our starting positions at opposite ends of the blue mat. As the referee conferred with the judges table, I assessed my opponent.

He was taller but skinnier. I decided that the overall strength and size advantage was mine. His black gi was baggy and thin. Gripping his collar or pants would be easy. He rocked on his heels and toes, his arms glued to his sides. He did not look at me. Instead, he glanced about the convention center: to the crowd surrounding the mats, seated in folding chairs beyond a velvet rope, to the grapplers seated on the inside of the rope, some with their mouth guards hooked over their cauliflower ears, some bouncing to keep their muscles warm. My opponent looked to his paunchy, bearded coach. His eyes met mine. He looked at his feet. He adjusted the knot on his belt.

He was nerdy, awkward, and fearful. He reminded me of myself as I used to be.

At my first competition, which was in the same venue a year ago, I almost lost my first match because I was not mentally prepared to harm my opponent to win. Granted, I would not be punching or kicking (doing so is illegal in submission grappling tournaments), but the reality of a fight is still there; the winner is whoever makes the other quit. If a submission does not come by choke, it comes by pain, a joint lock that threatens the integrity of bones and ligaments and tendons. Going into that match, I expected my opponent to tap long before there was significant damage. I was wrong.

In that first fight a year earlier, I had locked my opponent into an armbar, a submission that hyperextends the elbow joint. I applied the pressure, expecting the quick frantic taps like my training partners had used to signal that they had had enough. Instead, my opponent's arm bent beyond its limit. The adrenaline ringing in my ears kept me from hearing the sound of his elbow beginning to break, the pop pop of tendons straining, and the shattering of the little doorstop piece of bone that keeps the arm from bending too far. Spectators said that they heard the snap, and, sure enough, when I watched the video of the match, the sound was distinct, like a sapling bent until the bark separates and the yellow-green meat splinters.

The video also captured the sound of my grandmother hunched forward in her wheel chair shaking her clenched fists and yelling, "Get him! Get him!" Until that day, she had never seen or heard of grappling. She did not know the rules. She did not know grappling strategy. All she knew was that her grandson was in a fight, and that was enough to bring fire to her eyes.

My opponent never tapped. I was dumbfounded and horrified.

"It's going to break," I said, imploring the referee leaning over our interlaced bodies to step in and stop the fight.

The referee shrugged. "Break it," he said.

I sat back, tightened my grip, and cranked the arm with every bit of strength I could muster. The arm bent against the joint an extra forty-five degrees, loose, like the limb of a Stretch Armstrong toy. My opponent tapped and cradled his arm. The color drained from his face and his lips moved noiselessly when he tried to speak. He was in shock.

When I stood up to fight my next match that day, my legs were wobbly, like I had just finished a marathon. My hands tingled like they had fallen asleep. My arms were heavy. Fighters call it an adrenaline dump. My nervousness combined with the stress of the previous match had expended most of my energy. I stepped into the fight with nothing left to give, and I ended up tapping to a sloppy shoulder lock. Watching video of the match afterward, I could see the openings I had missed. I saw the specific moment where I gave up my dominant position and ended up on the bottom in a headlock. I lost because I wanted to. I did not want to fight anymore. I hung my arm out for him to take and tapped when I could have kept fighting. My first fight spooked and exhausted me, and I had no desire to relive that moment.

I never made that mistake again. From that tournament on, I was comfortable with breaking someone's arm or choking them unconscious.

My opponent rechecked the knot on his belt and pulled his shaggy blond hair from his eyes.

His coach grunted from the sidelines, "You got this. Stick to your game plan, and you'll win the fight no problem."

I disagreed.

I had just returned from five months of training at the BJ Penn Academy in Hilo, Hawaii. I trained twice a day, five days a week with world-champion fighters and world-renowned black belts. Nobody, especially my opponent, was more prepared for this tournament than me. My skills were sharp. My body was fit. This fight had been on my mind since my first day of training in Hawaii. After all of the money, time, and emotion I had invested, losing now would be an embarrassment, especially with my family watching expectantly from the crowd.

Standing there, waiting for the referee to start the match, I was ready to methodically break every bone in my opponent's body. My heart beat was slow. My eyes were steady. My mind was focused entirely on the next six minutes.

We leaned in and shook hands.

The referee signaled the start of the match with a chop of his hand and backed away.

I stepped forward, reached through my opponent's hands, and gripped his lapel. I jerked him forward and jumped up, wrapping my legs around his waist, establishing my guard and dragging him to the ground.

As my shoulders bounced off the mat and I began setting up a submission, my mind flashed back to the Big Island, to the mat room, to the hours I'd spent sweating and fighting. Everything I had experienced and done in Hawaii was a buildup to this moment, to this fight.

NO RAIN, NO RAINBOW

66How about Alaska?" she asked.

"I'm not going anywhere with snow."

Hilary sighed and propped her elbow on her desk, dropping her head in her hand. I was lying on her dorm room bed, flipping through a text book on teaching writing. Hilary had stumbled upon a program called the National Student Exchange. We could go to any state college in the United States and pay their in-state tuition. She suggested California, the Virgin Islands, Florida, Puerto Rico, or Colorado.

And I was not really interested in leaving Pennsylvania. For the first time in my life, I felt like I belonged. The friendship I had with my girlfriend had become serious. I had a close group of friends. Leaving my home to live in a strange place seemed to threaten the stability that I had found in college.

I grew up an outcast. I spent my elementary years in a tiny Christian school where my bowl cut, disorganized teeth, and stutter were the punch lines to jokes told by the sons and daughters of deacons and pastors. I retreated into books and video games, much preferring the world of Narnia and Final Fantasy VII to the real one. On school day mornings, I gripped a PlayStation controller with white knuckles and tearfully begged my mother to let me stay home.

Once, when I happened upon a book on Buddhism in seventh grade, I asked a teacher how we knew that the Christian way was the right way. TJ and Billy, my worst tormentors, leaned over my shoulder from the back row. The smell of the mousse holding TJ's black hair erect stung my nostrils. The two gold chains clasped around Billy's throbbing neck jingled in my ear.

"Don't you want to go to heaven?" TJ asked, his whisper spritzing my neck with saliva.

"What a faggot," Billy added insightfully.

I was silent. Their breath was warm and heavy against my neck.

"Why would I want to go to heaven if people like you are going to be there?" I responded.

They grunted a nervous laugh and leaned back. Billy kicked my chair.

Braces and a decent haircut made public high school bearable, but I did not escape ridicule completely. The football team enjoyed poking and prodding me with insults. They mocked my Vans shoes, my baggy pants, and my books. They knew that I would never muster the courage to confront them. Even if I did, I only weighed 115 pounds. I was weak and frail. I did not know how to fight. I always stared straight forward, trying my hardest not to flinch when they made a sudden movement. Hilary was the only good thing to come out of high school. She fell in love with my charm and my intelligence. I fell in love with her smile and punkish world view.

Since neither of us particularly enjoyed high school, we avoided it as much as possible. We never went to football games. We did not go to homecoming or to prom. And, as often as we could get away with it, we skipped school. One time, in the middle of December, when the roads were still frosted with tire-packed ice and snow, we did just that. Flakes fell like thick static, and the world was black and white except for the yellow school buses rolling up and down backcountry roads.

Hilary picked me up in the lower parking lot, out of sight from teachers and security guards, and we escaped in her white '96 Honda

Accord. We drove to her Mom's house at the West Virginia line and parked in the fairgrounds bordering her property. We hopped the fence and followed the trail through the woods and around a frozen pond. We paused at the tree line to make sure no neighbors were watching. We hustled to the porch, the snow crunching like packing peanuts beneath our feet. Hilary unlocked the door. We slipped inside.

Hilary's Mom had all but moved out of the doublewide. Dust balls lingered in the canyon-like imprints of the carpet where furniture used to be. Cardboard boxes were stacked along the wall. The kitchen cabinets hung open, their insides empty and barren. Hilary's room was the only room still furnished. The water was off. The electric was off. The heat was off. Outside, it was 15 degrees Fahrenheit. Inside, it was quite possibly colder.

We gathered every blanket, afghan, comforter, and sheet left in the house and piled them on her bed. There, beneath nine inches of cotton and wool, we found summer. We passed the day talking, laughing, and loving. We hardly moved. We did not need to and did not want to.

College was a chance to start fresh, and I took it. I started lifting weights. I tried to be more outgoing. My friends were all people I had met on campus, and I considered them to be my best friends, closer than my family. I discovered mixed martial arts, the legalized and revised version of no-holds-barred cage fighting. I began taking classes in submission grappling and started to feel some semblance of confidence.

I loved my home, my university, my friends, and Hilary. If Hilary wanted to go somewhere though, I would go with her.

"We could go to Hawaii," she said. The shouts and laughter of a snowball fight going on outside drowned out the clicks of her mouse and keyboard.

"Hawaii sounds nice," I said, not looking up, copying definitions on rhetorical theory and learning styles into a notebook.

"There are two branches on two different islands."

"What's the difference?" I asked, dreading the thought of having to write a paper on the way various rhetorical modes affect the teaching of writing.

"I don't know. One is in Manoa . . . and the other is in . . . Hilo."

I looked up. "Did you say Hilo?"

"Yeah," Hilary said as she turned to face me, the blue background of a webpage reflecting in the rectangles of her dark rimmed glasses. "Why?"

"BJ Penn lives in Hilo."

BJ Penn was the former welterweight champion of the Ultimate Fighting Championship (UFC), the world's most successful MMA organization. At the time, Penn was preparing to fight for another title shot. Though Penn was a phenom in the cage, his grappling career had earned him most of his fame.

After receiving his black belt in Brazilian jiu-jitsu in just three years, when it usually takes between ten and fifteen years to earn a black belt in that art, Penn competed in the Mundials in Rio de Janeiro, Brazil, the equivalent of the Olympics for jiu-jitsu. He became the first non-Brazilian to take gold, defeating fighters who had been training their whole lives. The feat earned him the nickname "The Prodigy." Penn headlined pay-per-views. He was in magazines. His fights were all over YouTube.

When I first saw Penn, I was watching an episode of *UFC Unleashed* at my parent's house in Pennsylvania. My parents were slamming kitchen cabinets and digging through a drawer of pots and pans, banging and clanking, trying to find something to boil potatoes in. Our chubby golden retriever and our shepherd-black lab mix (a chocolate fudge swirl of a dog) shuffled back and forth across the tile floor, their nails clicking off the ceramic. Out the bay window overlooking a backyard and pasture, a lazy summer sun was just beginning to set.

On television, pre-fight banter hyped a bout between a pudgy Hawaiian, a jiu-jitsu black belt, and the then welterweight champion, a ferociously athletic Iowan wrestler. The Hawaiian, Penn, looked grossly outmatched in comparison to the Iowan, Matt Hughes. Penn was smaller. Penn was flabbier. Although Penn's record boasted victories over talented fighters, Hughes had been bulldozing the welterweight division, amassing a record of twelve straight victories.

In less than forty-five seconds, Penn had out-struck Hughes and put the D-1 wrestler on his back.

Penn worked to pass Hughes's guard, dropping punches and elbows each time Hughes left an opening. Hughes looked lost, bewildered.

With fifty-four seconds left in the round, Hughes made a critical mistake; he let Penn stand in his guard. In one motion, Penn shucked Hughes's feet to the side and cocked his right hand back. In the next motion, Penn was airborne, his whole body following his fist flying toward the downed Hughes. From that height with that velocity, Penn's hand was a cinder block crashing into Hughes's jaw. Hughes was hurt, his eyes blinking, struggling to focus. Panicked and disoriented, he rolled to his stomach, exposing his back to the jiu-jitsu black belt. Penn dropped an elbow, then a combination of hooks. With his legs wrapped around Hughes, Penn remained securely on the champion's back. Hughes fell back on top of Penn, reaching desperately for a foot lock.

Penn slipped his arm under Hughes's neck and grabbed his own biceps. Brazilians call this choke the *mateo leon*, or lion killer. Americans call it a rear naked choke. Hughes, the once unstoppable champion, submitted to the young Hawaiian with twenty-three seconds left in the first round.

Penn was a brilliant fighter, and the chance to train under him was well worth leaving my comfort zone and coping with my fear of flying. This should be clear: willingly taking a plane anywhere was not an easy decision for me. I was not just afraid of flying; I was petrified. Just thinking about an airport got me sweating.

I was a worrier, eternally apprehensive about every detail of a situation. What time is it? Will I make it on time? Are my keys still in my pocket? How about my wallet? Better check my keys again.

What time was it again? For me, airports were torture, ninth-circle-of-hell torture.

The only time I had flown without my mother holding my hand was when I took a summer trip to California with Hilary. Our flight got cancelled, forcing us to spend the night in a cheap motel room. The following morning, we were selected for increased security screening. Being shuffled through standard security was agonizing enough. I imagined the line of people muttering under their breath about me taking too long to remove my shoes. I imagined a security guard finding a pocket knife in my carry-on, even though I had never owned a pocket knife in my life. I imagined being pulled to a back-room and harassed and water-boarded by faceless homeland security officers.

Increased screening was worse.

We were pulled to the side and directed into a machine designed to dislodge incriminating residue with sharp jets of air. Hilary did not expect the puffs of air and squealed as her blouse rippled and her hair swirled around her face. I wanted to go back and tell her that it was all right, but I was already fifteen feet down the line, watching a white gloved giant rummage through my underwear. I felt like everyone going through standard security was watching us, judging us, mocking us. I thought we were going to be late for our flight, though I knew that we had two hours to spare.

I took my frustration out on Hilary. I yelled at her, a lot. I had done the same thing when we drove to Cape May, New Jersey, and took a wrong exit into downtown Philadelphia. I did it again when we went back to New Jersey three years later and she booked a junky hotel room, though I knew she had no way of knowing what the room was like. I had made it a habit to express my deep-seated fears and insecurities as anger and hostility. I knew no other way of coping.

"So you'll go?" Hilary asked, her eyes widening, her lips suppressing a smile.

"I'm in."

Hilary leaped from her desk chair and bounded to the bed, giggling. "You can train, and I can do environmental science," she said, straddling me, her arms draped loosely around my neck. "We're going to Hawaii!"

At that moment, we were both happy and smiling. We were in love, and a trip to paradise was less than a year away. I felt like we were beneath the blankets again, living out our happiness despite the world around us.

Eight months later, Hilary called me from Wyoming where she was visiting family.

We talked about mundane details, like what we did that day and what we were doing tomorrow. The conversation dragged, punctuated by awkward silence. She sounded preoccupied, like she was looking over her shoulder away from the phone for something else to do. Her voice was flat and unenergetic. Hilary had been upset with me when she left, and I could tell that she was still irked.

A week and a half before, on August 4, I had competed in the North Atlantic Grappling Association's "Battle at the Beach" in Wildwood, New Jersey. I had spent eight weeks dieting and training. I woke up in the morning at 8 AM. I went to work as a lifeguard at 11 AM. When work was finished at 7 PM, I grappled. I was asleep by 11 PM. For my diet, I ate a serving of protein and fruits or vegetables every two hours and supplemented those mini-meals with fish oil and flax seed oil. I dedicated my summer to winning the tournament, and I lost my first match twelve to one. To Hilary, the amount of time and effort I spent grappling was not justified.

Growing tired of the silence, I began talking about how I planned to modify my training so that I would win my next competition.

"I'm sick of hearing about jiu-jitsu," Hilary said. "It's not going anywhere."

"But if I write about it," I stammered, "I can make a career out of it."

She sighed, filling my ear with static. "You're not going to make money as a writer," she said. "You're not being realistic."

"I can write articles, I can write books, I can—""

"It's stupid."

I hung up.

Seventeen days later, I hung up on Hilary for good, but I did not realize that leaving Hilary also meant leaving my friends and the life that I loved.

❈ ❈ ❈ ❈ ❈

The plane bounced, shaking me from my sleep. I lifted my head from the window. The elderly couple next to me had their head phones in, watching an Eddie Murphy movie that I had mostly slept through. Their faces were blank. Eddie Murphy's screaming visage reflected in their glasses, and his shrieking voice leaked from their head phones. The elderly couple stared at the screen, unblinking.

Out the window, the Pacific Ocean passed below the plane. At 30,000 feet, the water looked like dried acrylic paint, cracked like the bottom of a desert lake bed. From above, the clouds looked like piles of snow shoveled off of a blue sidewalk.

Snow.

It was two days after New Year's, and I was heading toward the equator. In Pittsburgh, the home I was leaving behind, snow was just beginning to fall.

From Pittsburgh to Phoenix, from Phoenix to Honolulu, from Honolulu to Hilo. The entire trip would take over sixteen hours of sitting on planes and waiting in airports. And now, as I made my way to Honolulu, seeing the Pacific was both exciting and unsettling. The expanse of water seemed infinite. If something were to happen, help was thousands of miles away. Every bit of turbulence prevailed over the usual logic of how flying is safer than driving, and how the chances of a plane crashing are slim. Suddenly, as the cabin jerked back and forth and the pilot requested that everyone remain seated, those slim chances seemed incredibly probable.

The plane pulled up and then sank down. The cabin rocked from side to side in tight, jerky motions. Trays rattled and the luggage shifted overhead.

Anxiety squeezed at my heart and stomach. My mouth filled with salt. I closed my eyes and focused on breathing. I breathed in through my nose and out through my mouth, each repetition slower than the last. In. Out. In. Out. If fighters could do this to relax before a bout, it might also work for flying, I thought. After my heart slowed and my stomach calmed, I reopened my eyes.

The sun was still shining outside. The old couple was still staring, unsmiling, at Eddie Murphy in a fat suit. I looked around the cabin at the docile faces of the other passengers, a businessman reading a newspaper, a mother cradling her infant; no one else seemed worried. I dug in my bag for BJ Penn's *The Book of Knowledge* and tried to focus on the months of training to come. I thumbed through the pages of techniques. Slipping the Cross. Basic Hip Sweep. Rear Naked Choke from the Back.

The old lady rubbing elbows with me glanced down at the book spread across my food tray. She squinted at Penn pressing a shirtless fighter into the chain link fence of a cage. She directed her squint at me, a disapproving glare in her eyes, like a mother who had just found condoms in her son's sock drawer. She looked back down at the book, back up at me, and returned to the Eddie Murphy film.

I had seen that reaction countless times before.

I wanted to explain to her that the sport has evolved far beyond its no-holds-barred roots. I wanted to explain to her that the sport is not as brutal and uncontrolled as it may look and that the fighters are actually extremely skilled, using techniques from a variety of martial arts disciplines. I could not, however, expect her to appreciate the sport when what little glimpses she had seen were likely shots of MMA's most brutal moments.

Unfortunately, major MMA organizations tend to sensationalize the violence of the sport to cater to the much-coveted eighteen-to-thirty-four-year-old male demographic. Highlight reels often feature

the bloodiest matches, in which the fighters are grappling in a growing red puddle as a gaping wound is squeezed and struck. The UFC
takes its advertisements a step further and mixes cuts of the goriest
fights with splotches of cartoon blood overlaid on chain link fence.

She had probably been flipping between *Grey's Anatomy* and *The
Sopranos* and happened upon SpikeTV. After a brief glimpse of a
knee dislodging a fighter's tooth set to a heavy metal soundtrack,
she likely formed her opinion on the sport and moved on. I could not
blame her if that opinion was negative.

I let it pass and returned to aimlessly watching the ocean pass
beneath me.

✳ ✳ ✳ ✳ ✳

The Honolulu airport was busy with tourists—pale families with full
wallets dragging trains of luggage and children. Locals were few,
mostly making up the staff running the desks and shops scattered
about the airport. Outside, palm trees lined the highways, and high-
rise buildings rose out of the steep green hills. The tropical foliage
seemed to be constantly tugging at the skirts of civilization, threatening to overtake it at any moment. The sky was blue and the clouds
were sparse, and I couldn't find my gate.

Oh god, I couldn't find my gate.

I approached an official-looking man wearing a floral patterned
button up. He looked to be Chinese and in his fifties. His black hair
was cut into a crew cut, and his tanned skin was wrinkled and flecked
with dark spots. Though he wore glasses, his eyes were pressed into
a permanent squint.

"I can't find my gate," I said.

He asked to see my ticket, studied it, and looked up with a grin.
"Go down the elevator by the Starbucks and go out the door," he
said. "You'll be under a tent."

My face must have betrayed my confusion. A tent? At an airport?

He smiled. "Now, don't freak out," he said, hanging onto his O's a bit longer than I was used to. His smile widened, so much so that his already squinted eyes pressed into slits and his glasses shifted higher up on his face to make room for the expanding crescent of white teeth. "Go under the tent and through the glass doors. That lobby is where you want to go."

Don't freak out, I thought.

Since I was by myself in Honolulu, I had no one to blame for my problems, no one to yell at. It was just me. For some reason, "Don't freak out" made more sense than the usual assurances that "Everything will be all right."

I dragged my luggage down to the elevator by the Starbucks and went down and out under the tent.

Don't freak out. Don't freak out.

I found the gate for my next flight, waited two hours for my plane to arrive, and boarded a small island-to-island plane as charcoal storm clouds moved in. A mist rode the breeze across the tarmac, and a rainbow arced through the sky.

The rainbow was an uplifting sight, but once we were airborne, the plane rocked like a lifeboat loose in a stormy sea, at the mercy of every wave. I spent my last hour of flying doubled over, hugging my stomach, concentrating entirely on not throwing up.

The Hilo airport was deserted that night, save for the handful of passengers on my flight. I made my way through the open air structure and hailed a cab. When I showed the driver the address for my new home, 525 West Lanikaula Street, he read it carefully and pushed the brim of his baseball cap up away from his forehead.

"This your first time here?" he asked. When I told him that it was, he smiled and rubbed his hands together. "Braddah, no worries," he said. "I take care a' you."

I was relieved by his smile, but the next day, once I saw Hilo in daylight, I knew what the smile was about: he had driven me around town twice before dropping me off at my dorm.

Despite its location in the middle of paradise, my dorm at the University of Hawaii at Hilo was far from luxurious. The white cinderblock walls were marred with brown and black stains from who-knows-what. The mattress was thin. The desk was battered. The blinds were broken. The light switches did not work. The lamp attached to the desk did not work. The drawstring lights above the bed and chipped mirror worked, but they flickered and flared for a few seconds before coming to life, like an old PC struggling to boot up. Back home, the same amount of room and board got me a spacious room with carpeting, dry wall, and a private bathroom.

I dropped my bags and made my first visit to the community restroom. When I turned on the lights, three shadows skittered across the blue-and-white tile floor and disappeared into the dark corners at the far end of the room. I was tired, hungry, and dehydrated, but I was still pretty sure those shadows were cockroaches.

Don't freak out.

I left the light on in the bathroom, hoping that the florescent light would keep my new floormates in their beds. I dressed my mattress and lay down. In the darkness, I stared at the ceiling. The chorus of coqui frogs leaked in through the window screen, a series of chirps and croaks, their pitch and tone varied by their distance from the window. At home, the night was enveloped in winter silence. And there, in my ratty dorm room, the reality of my situation became apparent to me.

I was alone.

I was some 4,500 miles from familiar faces and familiar streets. I was scared and already beginning to regret my decision to come to Hilo. The next morning, I was going to walk half an hour to the BJ Penn Academy and begin five months' worth of training with one of the pound-for-pound best fighters alive. The opportunity of a lifetime was a night's sleep away, but I was fixated on the past, the problems that I was running from.

If I could earn my blue belt from BJ Penn, I thought, I could be happy with my life again. I could get over breaking up with my girlfriend. I could get over her taking my friends. I could find a direction for my life. I could enter and win that year's Kumite Classic in Pittsburgh, proving to myself and everyone that had ever doubted me that I could be stronger, better than I was. Looking back on it, treating a blue belt like it was an antidote seems illogical, but at the time, I was looking for a light, any light at all, to guide me through the storm.

FRIENDS AND LIARS

A month after I broke up with Hilary, a month after that phone call that ended in her heaving sobs, a coworker approached me at work.

"I have good news for you," she said, taking my attention away from Sam Sheridan's *A Fighter's Heart*. "Hilary has a boyfriend. I guess she's been seeing him for a while now."

My stomach convulsed. My lungs turned to stone. My hands began to shake. "That's great," I said, smiling.

I excused myself and went to the restroom, locking the stall door behind me. I dry-heaved over the toilet, gripping the silver handicap railing, leaning forward like a diving hawk. My stomach spun like a hamster wheel, and my heart pounded like a fist on a prison door. For the first time since our break up, I tasted regret.

When I composed myself, I sent Hilary a text.

"Want to get coffee sometime?" I asked.

She replied, "Yes."

We met at an Eat N Park on a Sunday night. Street lamps and headlights illuminated the red and orange and yellow leaves clinging to their branches. The air nipped at bare skin, like a puppy, a preview of the vicious fangs the coming winter would bear.

Hilary had her hair up and her contacts in. Punk pins ("This is my piece of flair," a portrait of Tom Waits, and a red star on a black background) pocked her green canvas jacket. An autumn orange hoody peaked out from beneath the jacket and mostly covered her lime green and ocean blue striped belt. Her jeans had holes in the knees and the cuffs were worn to strings. Her red Converse shoes and her dragging jeans hid her socks, but I caught sight of them as she climbed out of her Silver Grand Am; one sock was rainbow striped, and the other was white with a portrait of William Shakespeare stitched just above the ankle. The cold air pushed the color of her face into red splotches, one for each cheek and one for her nose.

When we greeted each other, we didn't touch. Hilary held on to the ends of her sleeves, and I pushed my hands deeper into the pockets of my faded and cracked black leather jacket.

We sat in a booth, across from each other. I tossed my jacket in the corner. Hilary kept hers on.

I ordered a BBQ bacon burger with onion rings instead of fries. She ordered a salad with ranch dressing. I ordered a French vanilla cappuccino. She ordered a coffee. I always ordered a BBQ burger when we went out, and Hilary always made fun of me for not trying something new. And Hilary always said that she liked the idea of being a vegetarian, but she could never commit to it for more than a few weeks.

I don't remember exactly what we talked about. I only recall trying to slip in references to the happy times in our relationship: Kurt Vonnegut, Cape May, Oglebay's Good Zoo. Smiles. Laughter. No yelling. No tears. We both acted normal, but the undertone was grim, like a prisoner enjoying a last meal.

I walked Hilary to her car. She got in and started the engine. I sat in the passenger seat. A Bright Eyes CD played on the stereo. The heater was set to high. Hilary sat rigid, looking down at the dry skin on her hands.

"I made a mistake," I said, watching headlights run back and forth on the road racing between Eat N Park and a run-down JC Penny's.

"Don't say that," Hilary said, her voice creaking like the hinges of an old storm door.

I couldn't look at her. I focused on the headlights. "I miss you," I said.

"Stop," Hilary whimpered.

The music played. The heater billowed. The headlights ran back and forth, slicing the darkness.

Hilary hugged me. Her arms wrapped tightly around my limp body. Her body rose and fell, breathing tears, breathing sobs. One of her tears dripped from my jacket on to my collar bone. It traced an icy trail down my chest. For a few moments, lifting my arms to hug her back felt wrong, but eventually, I returned the grasp. I squeezed her close.

"I'm sorry," Hilary said, her voice muffled by my shoulder.

"Me too," I replied.

Hilary squeezed harder and exhaled slowly. She let go and pulled back to the driver's seat. She wiped her eyes.

"I have to go," she said.

I nodded and left the car. Hilary slammed her car into reverse, backed out of the space, shifted into drive, and pulled out of the parking lot. She wiped her eyes and adjusted the radio as she went. She didn't look at me.

I called her from my cell phone. I begged her to come back with me. She refused.

After that night, I slowly realized the full range of consequences of our break up. Following the break up, I expected to spend my new free time with my friends, at their apartments, at their parties. In the weeks following the break up, however, the steady flow of invites and text messages and phone calls began to trickle. Then they stopped completely.

I spent Friday and Saturday nights alone in my room, reading books, watching movies, aimlessly browsing the Internet. My cell phone was silent.

I started going on dates. Women I hardly knew spent the night in my twin-sized bed. Our limbs interlaced, hands and feet dangling over the edges of the mattress, the sheets and comforter barely covering our bodies. I still felt alone. I wanted the solace of my friends, my good friends, their familiar faces, their company like family. I wanted to share in the inside jokes, to talk about the same music, to play the same video games. But they weren't around, and they were always busy when I called.

At first, I thought perhaps that semester was just harder on them than the last. Maybe they were buried in schoolwork. Maybe they were working more. They couldn't be blowing me off, not my friends.

The more I listened to casual conversations held between acquaintances that my friends and I shared, the more details began to slip. They did go to that movie opening on Friday. There was a party on Saturday. I just wasn't invited. There was a time when I would have died for these people, and now I wasn't worthy of a phone call. What had I done? Had I done something wrong? Should I apologize? How could I make it up to them?

Megan was my best friend, like a sister, and she revealed the truth to me.

Our sophomore year, a mutual friend of ours, Annie, kept a kitten in her dorm room, a major violation of policy. Annie frequently brought the kitten to Megan's, so moving in and out of Megan's room was always a covert operation, lest the cat be discovered.

One Sunday morning, Megan came to my room, upset and sad; the residence hall staff had seen the kitten, and they were not happy.

"I was having a party, and we were drinking, and we were playing DDR [Dance Dance Revolution]," she said, pulling her brown curls away from her bloodshot eyes. Megan was an Elementary Education major, having an underage on her record could have serious ramifications. "So a community assistant knocked on the door around one, and we panicked. Hilary dumped the alcohol down the bathroom sink, and Annie held the kitten at the doorway, to distract them. So now Annie has to get rid of her cat."

I comforted her. Then I remembered how I spent my Saturday night: alone in my room, staring at a computer screen.

"Why didn't you invite me to the party?"

"If we invited you, Hilary wouldn't have come."

Oh.

✳ ✳ ✳ ✳ ✳

A month after our first Eat N Park rendezvous, I was back in the same booth. I sipped tentatively at a French vanilla cappuccino, making revisions to a play I had written. Two folded menus sat at the far end of the booth, next to the ketchup, mustard, and single-serving jams and single-serving butters. A cup of coffee sat directly across the table from me, its steam beginning to fade.

"Waiting on someone?" a young, tired waitress asked.

"Yeah," I said. "She'll be here soon."

The waitress smiled and shuffled to serve the elderly couple sitting in the booth behind me. They were arguing about whether or not to get the salad bar.

I looked out the window. A powdered sugar snow fell. The parking space next to my car was still empty. Each time a pair of headlights left the main road to pull into the parking lot, I tensed. No, that's not her. I took small sips from my cappuccino, not wanting my mug to be empty when she arrived. I made more revisions. My cell phone vibrated.

"I'm not coming," the text said.

I sent her a picture of the table, my cappuccino in the foreground, her coffee in the background.

"No. I can't."

After that text, she didn't respond to any more of my texts or calls. I understood her position. I did and said terrible things to her. If I were her, I wouldn't have met with me the first time.

I looked at my cappuccino, now half empty. I looked at the coffee sitting across from me; its steam was gone. I stuffed my draft into my jacket pocket and left a twenty on the table.

✳ ✳ ✳ ✳ ✳

Hilo has no shortage of 7-Elevens. Kinoole Street, one of the busier streets in Hilo, has two. I normally pride myself on eating healthy and tend to avoid the life-shortening cuisine of convenience stores and gas stations, but I was desperate. My dorm room was devoid of food, and the only water I had to drink came directly from the faucet. Jet lag had me up at six in the morning, noon by Pennsylvania time, and I hadn't eaten anything since my layover in Arizona a full twenty-two hours ago. The 7-Eleven would have to do.

I packed my training gear: a pair of black sprawl shorts, a rash guard (kind of like Under Armor), a cup, and a mouth guard. Slipping into flip-flops, a novelty worth savoring in January, I stuffed my map into my pocket and went on a quest for sustenance.

My feet were not accustomed to walking long distances in flip-flops, and by the time I reached the 7-Eleven, blisters were already beginning to form. Blisters, for most people, are only a minor inconvenience, a bit of stinging puss every now and then, but for grapplers, an open foot wound can become life threatening. Wrestling mats are notorious for breeding disease. Ringworm and other miscellaneous fungi are a nuisance but not deadly. Staph infections and MRSA are the most dangerous—flesh eating bacteria that, left untreated, eat gaping holes in their victims, strip mining through skin, muscle, and organs. If not treated, Staph and MRSA infections can, and in many cases do, lead to death.

Thinking of the mats at the BJ Penn Academy triggered my neurosis; I checked my watch. It was 9:30 am. The first grappling class of the day started at 12. The Academy was a mile away. I knew that I could easily walk a mile in that time, but my worry washed the logic away in a flood of questions: What if I get lost? What if there's traffic? What if I have a lot of paperwork to fill out? What if I sprain an ankle? I better hurry.

The bell on the glass door of the 7-Eleven dinged as I pushed inside. The merchandise was mostly what I expected, but island culture had a distinct influence. At the end of one aisle, where I would normally expect to see discount candy or a cooler, hung an assortment of lei, plastic yellow blossoms mixed with white blossoms, red and white, green and yellow.

The coolers in the back were well stocked with alcohol of all kinds, an unusual site for me (Pennsylvania does not allow minors in a store that serves alcohol, so distributors are set apart). To the left of the Krispy Kreme display was the sandwich cooler. Mixed in with the typical hoagies and salads were what looked like sushi rolls: cylinders of rice wrapped in sea weed, packed with salmon, tuna, egg, or the local favorite, spam. I vowed to never eat sushi from a 7-Eleven.

I bought two protein bars and a Sobe Life Water and hustled down Kinoole Street, toward Hilo Bay, toward my jiu-jitsu Mecca.

The homes on Kinoole Street, and in Hilo in general, were of humble island design, raised slightly off the ground, lattice work skirts covering the gap between the ground floor and the earth. The roof tops were corrugated. The exteriors were painted in simple color combinations, white and green, white and blue, red and yellow. Palm trees flourished in most yards, but some yards had coconut trees, banana trees, and guava trees. At the ends of many driveways, resting at the peaks of large stones, were round rocks wrapped in ti leaves, an offering to the gods.

I noticed a few houses were upper class: the paint fresh and a Mercedes or two in the driveway. Most, however, had peeling paint and more middle-class vehicles parked in the driveway. At first, I thought a few were abandoned. High grass and vines slowly swallowed the bathtubs and rusted lawn mowers scattered in the front yard, and the houses looked dilapidated, but cars were parked in the driveway, and I could see, through grimy windows, people moving.

Scooters and SUVs and junker Honda Accords and jacked-up pickup trucks grumbled and buzzed by. I saw only one bicyclist, and I expected to see more scooters than I did. I later learned that the frequent rain fall in Hilo, sometimes two or three times a day, discourages roofless travel. Though the traffic was relatively constant on Kinoole Street, I didn't pass any other pedestrians.

The building that housed the BJ Penn MMA Academy was fairly nondescript, and I actually walked by it at first without realizing. My obsessive map checking saved me from wandering too far.

From the outside, the Academy was bland, and with holes rusted into the siding and scraps of wood and bricks discarded haphazardly on the adjacent hillside, it even looked a bit run-down. Now painted a teal reminiscent of the 1970s, the Academy used to be a cracker factory, and locals often talked about getting cookies and crackers fresh out of the oven when they were younger. Every person I heard talk about the old cracker factory sounded as if he were recalling Grandmother's Thanksgiving cooking. They spoke with a deep nostalgia and a hint of reverence and adoration. Even BJ Penn, in a UFC All Access interview, said that from down the street "you could smell the crackers."

Inside on the first floor, the Academy looked like a modern health club. Floor-to-ceiling mirrors covered the far wall. The equipment looked new. The desk immediately to the right of the door doubled as a merchandise display, advertising BJ Penn hoodies, hats, and T-shirts.

A local woman with long hair was working the desk when I came in. She smiled and greeted me. I must have looked like a tourist. I was pale and awkward. Sweat soaked a V into the front of my T-shirt, and I had a map in my hand. I told her that I wanted to sign up for jiu-jitsu classes.

"Are you here for the day or for the week?" she said, rummaging through a folder full of paperwork.

It occurred to me that hundreds of people probably visit the Academy each month to train for two or three days on their vacation. I had deluded myself into thinking that my arrival was unique, that my presence deserved special attention.

"I'm here until May," I said.

She nodded and handed me a stack of forms.

When I signed up to come to the University of Hawaii at Hilo on exchange, I imagined that Penn would teach the majority of the jiu-jitsu classes. I dreamed of him taking me underneath his wing, becoming my Mr. Miyagi while I became his Daniel-san. I had so romanticized my journey to Hawaii to train that I was mildly offended that Penn didn't greet me at the door with an obscure gardening exercise that would unlock the secrets of jiu-jitsu.

My fantasies were interrupted when I reached the payment plan portion of the paperwork. When I called the Academy two months before my flight, the woman on the phone told me that training would cost me $100 a month. This paperwork said that the monthly fee was $150. On top of that, I had to pay a processing fee, a start-up fee, and a membership card fee. Before I left Pennsylvania, I budgeted my money very carefully for the trip, allotting myself $100 a month for training, $125 a month to eat, $100 total for pleasure spending, and $100 for an emergency. My emergency money and pleasure money were almost gone, and the extra $50 a month was going to have to come from my food money. Well, damn.

Preferring hunger to training less, I signed for the unlimited training package and handed over my credit card. It felt like my wallet was weeping, but it may have been the sweat running down my back.

"Grappling doesn't start until twelve," she said, handing me my credit card and a receipt. It was 10:30. "You can just cruise until then, if you want. The mat room is through there."

She pointed to a door in the far corner of the fitness center. The door was rickety and wooden and painted the same teal as the outside of the warehouse. Tucked in the corner of the gym, just behind a biceps curl machine, the door seemed like the path through an Italian kitchen that leads to the secret backroom where shady but powerful sorts tend to secretive business.

The door opened onto a platform almost two stories above the ground floor; the platform was also teal (I was beginning to think that whoever painted the gym really liked that color). Reggae music echoed through the room. This section was not air conditioned, but a steady draft of cool air wafted through the three warehouse-style windows on the left and an industrial-sized garage door on the right. Screens didn't cover any other windows, but oddly, the entire garage door was covered by a screen. When I inspected the garage door more closely, I saw that the screen was actually two pieces pulled shut and padlocked together—a screen door with a padlock on it.

A boxing ring was at the front of the warehouse. Japanese writing coated a blue canvas. Beyond the boxing ring lay an eight-sided cage, the same kind used by the UFC. The canvas of the cage had "Rumble on the Rock" written on it. An assortment of heavy bags, long and skinny, short and thick, and spherical hung from a metal frame to the right of the cage.

The MMA portion of the gym was more Spartan than I expected. With fighters like Randy Couture and Matt Hughes opening state-of-the art facilities filled with brand-new equipment, the BJ Penn MMA Academy seemed antiquated. But really, the gym was distinctly local. The focus was not on stuff but on training. The rugged environment was a reflection of the training philosophy: a fighter is born from hard work, not from shiny stuff. The mat is all that matters, not the color of the paint on the walls or fancy designs on the buckle pads. The gym is about bettering the people.

The music itself also reflected the local culture. The choice to play reggae instead of the usual heavy metal or alternative rock gave the gym a distinctly laid-back feel. The gym seemed like a place to relax, a sanctuary. Perhaps this really was my jiu-jitsu Mecca.

Two of the heavy bags swung and twirled from the combinations thrown by two locals. The buzzer rang, interrupting the reggae radio soundtrack. The locals leaned against the cage, catching their breath.

I was taller than both of them. One had black hair that swooped forward on his head, like a melting chocolate ice cream cone. Tribal tattoos snaked around his arms. The other was chubby and round, like a collection of independent spheres arranged into the shape of a body. Even his eyes were almost perfectly round.

The wooden stairs sagged and creaked as I descended to the bare concrete floor. I sat down in a wooden chair; it looked like it was purchased at a garage sale, separated from its dining set family. The two locals worked the heavy bags for a few more rounds while I wrote in my notebook and flipped through my guidebook. When they finished, the rounder one introduced himself as Curt and told me that his friend was Travis. They were firefighters, coming in for a morning workout before their shift. Curt was quick to invite me to their training sessions, even offering to let me borrow a pair of his gloves. I told him that my attendance would depend on my class schedule.

Curt's grin cut a deep swath in his thick cheeks. "School first, you know?" he said.

Apparently, Curt is a joker too.

While Curt and Travis packed their bags, a mother came down the stairs with her two daughters, about ten and eight years old. When she reached the heavy bags, a few feet from where I was sitting, I thought that maybe I was wrong; maybe she was just their older sister. She was trim, fit, and toned. She wore a black sports bra and black yoga pants. A less shy version of myself might have even talked to her, hit on her, but after hearing the little girls call her Mom, I gathered my things and left to change instead. As I rounded the corner near the wooden stairs to find the changing rooms, the two girls settled on the apron of the boxing ring.

The changing room doubled as a single bathroom. My shorts were around my ankles when I noticed a neon-pink sign hanging next to the mirror.

"BE AWARE OF MRSA INFECTIONS!!! WATCH OPEN WOUNDS!!!" the paper read. Angry cartoon germs ran around the page baring their fangs. I read the box at the bottom of the page: "Hawaii has the highest rate of staph infections in the United States."

I looked at the blisters on my feet. Great. I'm doomed.

When I came out of the changing room, a blur of pig tails whizzed past me. The older girl was chasing the younger. They jumped into the boxing ring, rolling underneath the rope. They stood, ran seven choppy steps to the other side, and barrel rolled underneath the far rope. They sprinted between the cage and the ring and, like go carts running an obstacles course, wove through the heavy bags. Their giggles and clapping flip-flops mixed with the chirp of Bob Marley's "Jammin." Their mother focused on the heavy bag, peppering it with jabs, hooks, and crosses.

I waited for an opening in the little girl traffic and stepped through the archway at the back of the gym into the mat room. The plywood walls were covered in a thin white base coat. One-story mirrors lined the front wall. A solid-blue mat covered the floor. Lime green mold frosted the open windows. The room was simple and plain, but this was my heaven. I had seen the videos on BJPenn.com and on You-Tube; I knew that jiu-jitsu magic happened here.

I began stretching half an hour before class was scheduled to begin.

The afternoon sessions were generally smaller than the evening sessions. Since it was Friday, my first class was even smaller than usual, which was perfect for me. I had no idea what to expect as far as training and intensity, so I was nervous (scared out of my mind, actually). This gym was the home to one of the best fighters in the world and the stomping ground for many other professional fighters. I was some white belt from rural Pennsylvania. How could I ever expect to hang with these guys?

My first class included six other people: two college students from the University of Hawaii at Manoa (which is on Oahu) named Ro and Zay, two lab technicians, Rocky and Christian, who came in on their lunch breaks, a fighter from Toronto, Canada, named Frank, and a tattoo artist named Chris. Ro had a shaved head and a dark complexion and looked as if he might be Filipino. Zay looked Chinese and had hair like an anime character, tall and spiky. Rocky and Christian both looked distinctly local. Rocky was older, perhaps in his forties, and was built like a body builder. Christian was smaller with a physique much more typical of a lab technician.

Frank was a squirrely-looking lightweight, and his skin was almost as pale as the snow stacking up by the foot in his hometown. He was in Hilo to prepare for a mixed martial arts bout set for February in Ohio. Chris had his head shaved bald and was covered in tattoos. Ink traced the lines of flowers etched down the side of his head and neck. Japanese designs coated his arms, and his legs were more of the same. While the rest of us stretched in the middle of the mat, Chris kept himself separate, lingering along the wall.

Jay Penn came in at 12:05, sat along the wall beneath the mirror, and instructed Ro to lead the warm-ups. Jay's jaw line and brow line were much more defined than his younger brother, BJ, and he wasn't nearly as tan. He was smaller too, about five foot six and 140 pounds. He looked more like a track star than a fighter. I didn't know it at the time, but Jay has severe asthma. A third of his lung capacity has been rendered useless from the condition, and a crescent-shaped scar traces the length of his shoulder blade, one reminder of his many surgeries.

Jay Penn (photo courtesy of Thomas Kappler)

We jogged in a circle. We did side shuffles, rolling break falls, and shrimping. Jay continued watching, expressionless, as we circled up and did crunches, thirty for each of us there, each person picking a variation until everyone had gone. By the third set, I began to suspect that I was out of shape. By the fifth set, my abs were in a painful knot. The twenty-five push-ups that followed the crunches were fairly easy, but the tension and pain lingered in my abs.

When we finished, Jay said, "Line up on the wall." He counted us and said, "Two people down. Guard pass drills. If the guy on top passes, he stays. If the guy on the bottom sweeps or submits, he stays."

Since I was at the front of the line, I lay down. My guard, fighting from my back, was the strongest part of my grappling game, so I was confident that I would do well starting from there. Jay put thirty minutes on the timer.

Zay came into my guard, smiled, shook my hand, and we started. After some effort, but not much, I was able to sweep him. After beating Zay, I was feeling good about myself. Maybe I could hang with BJ's fighters. Maybe I was a prodigy.

Zay smiled, shook my hand, and returned to the line along the wall. Frank stepped forward into my guard. We shook hands and began.

Frank postured up, and I tried to break him down, but he pressed me flat on my back. Then he shifted his hips to open my guard, raised his knee, and passed. In just a few seconds, with virtually no effort, Frank beat my best position.

I shrugged it off and went to the end of the line. After a few rounds, it was my turn to start in Chris' guard. He seemed annoyed about having to roll with me. He apathetically shook my hand, gripping loosely and rolling his eyes. We started. One moment I was postured up, and the next a triangle choke was cutting off the blood flow to my brain, submerging my world in darkness. Chris sighed, and I returned to the line.

The rest of the half hour was a matter of pure survival. I accepted the fact that I couldn't pass the guards of Frank and Chris, who had been dominating the mat for the majority of the drill. I just tried to keep from having to tap, but it was futile. Triangles. Armbars. Omoplatas. Flower sweeps. Scissor sweeps. Elevator sweeps. Every move I made was a mistake for them to exploit.

By the time the buzzer rang, signaling the end of the guard-passing drill, I was spent. Sweat dripped from my face like a leaky faucet. My heart was trying to punch a hole in my chest. My lungs heaved, fighting to suck oxygen from the humid Hawaii air. I glanced at the other faces in the room.

Zay and Christian seemed almost as tired as I was but not quite. Ro and Rocky looked like they had just taken a light jog, a jog that didn't even wind them. Frank looked the same as he did when class started, and Chris still looked bored.

Jay took off his tennis shoes, motioned for Chris to come forward, and began teaching.

"I noticed that people were having trouble with this guard pass," Jay said as Chris put him into guard.

Jay began to execute a common guard pass that I had seen taught many times before. When he got halfway through the move, he instructed Chris to perform a counter, a counter that Chris had used multiple times on me just a few minutes ago. When Jay described and demonstrated his personal variation on the move, he looked directly at me. It seemed like Jay was basing his instruction on where I struggled during the drill. If I was receiving personalized instruction on my first day, I could only imagine what the teaching over the next five months was going to be like.

He demonstrated the move a few more times, and we broke into pairs. I drilled with Frank, who executed the technique with finesse and pressure. I bumbled through the move. My balance was awkward. My pressure was weak. My finesse was nonexistent. I lurched and stumbled like a drunken toddler. I had a basic understanding of what made the pass effective, but my mind and body were light-years behind the likes of Frank and Chris.

We continued drilling the move, and Jay made his way around the room, correcting and adjusting the techniques of his students as he went. When he came to Frank and me, he critiqued my hand placement and my pressure, instructing me to pinch my elbow tight against my chest when I gripped the hip, so that I had optimal control over my opponent for the pass. As Jay began to step away, Frank called him back to ask a question.

Frank asked Jay how to deal with a common counter to the pass, a counter that caused Frank a visible amount of frustration.

"Oh, that's easy," Jay said with a smile.

Jay motioned for me to put him into my guard, and we went through the move. I countered at the right point. Jay executed a simple but unorthodox re-counter.

Frank's eyes were wide, and his mouth hung open. He looked like he had just seen the cure for cancer. "Oh man, that is nice!" he said, jumping into my guard. With the giddiness of a Christmas morning, he explored the potential of the move.

I too was impressed by the technique, but it wasn't the technique itself that had me excited. Based on that move, I knew that Jay's approach to grappling was much different from anything I had ever seen before. The jiu-jitsu that he taught was his own, a perspective on the art not found anywhere else but inside the walls of the BJ Penn Academy. Whether or not I earned my blue belt before I left, I would return home with an arsenal of moves that no one in Pennsylvania (and perhaps the mainland as a whole) had seen.

Class concluded, and though my body was battered and sore, I was optimistic. I felt like I was on the verge of something special, like I had a treasure map and was just a riddle away from untold wealth. I thanked Jay for the class and hiked back to my room to recover for the evening training session. My walk home was considerably slower, and I was happy to reach my ratty dorm and fall asleep.

I slept straight through until 5 pm, when it was time to walk to the 6 pm session.

When I donned my gi for the evening training session, a white Gameness competition weave that I had purchased just a few weeks before boarding the plane, my body was stiff, my joints like rusted hinges. Pools of blue and purple started to form beneath my skin, some in the shape of hand prints, but most were the circumference of the knee or elbow whose impact inspired them.

Stepping into the mat room, I was immediately aware that I stood out. My gi was white and crisp. The locals that packed the mat were wearing gis that had seen month upon month of training. Their pant legs were frayed, their lapels worn, the extra fabric stitched on to their knees ripped away. The blue gis were faded, and the white gis were a grayish brown. I had often read about how martial artists judge the experience of other fighters by assessing the wear on their equipment, especially their belts. A faded and tattered black belt is expected to be more dangerous than the fresh and stiff black belt. Based upon their gis alone, my neophyte status was glaring. Even the white belts had done more training than I had, way more.

I didn't see any familiar faces. None of the people from the afternoon class came back for the evening session. Was I the only one training twice a day?

We began class with a warm up. We jogged, shuffled, shrimped, did break falls, and circled up for exercises. We did thirty crunches for each person in the room (about fifteen people showed up that night) and ten push-ups for each person in the room. Once the warm-up was finished, Jay put half an hour on the clock, and we did guard-passing drills.

My first attempt at the drill brought with it a startling realization: the evening class was much more serious than the afternoon, and I had no chance of even being competitive. The first time I touched hands to signal the beginning of the drill, a tattooed Hawaiian with a mustache ripped at my lapel, jerking me forward. I scrambled to block the collar choke, but as my arm moved to defend, he pounced, wrapping his legs around my torso and applying an arm lock. I fell forward as he arched his body. The pressure came on hard. I tapped, frantically, pleadingly, but not fast enough. My elbow popped before he let go.

Each time I stepped into someone's guard, no matter what his belt rank, the result was always the same. I tapped quickly to chokes, arm locks, shoulder locks, and leg locks. Every submission came on as hard as the first. The usual philosophy of slowly applying pressure to preserve the health of training partners did not seem to apply. They dominated me. They smashed me. These guys were trying to kill me.

I had read that racial tension was an issue in Hawaii, so my first thought was that maybe they were just enjoying beating up the white kid. When I surveyed the room, however, I knew that couldn't be the case. The mat room population was diverse. Other white guys were training that night. There had to be some reason, though. The other matches didn't seem as aggressive. I couldn't understand why they were so hard on me.

After a few matches, my gi was soggy with sweat, hanging heavily from my shoulders. My limbs were tingling, numb from the lack of oxygen. I breathed so hard I wheezed. This wasn't fun. This was hell.

Then, someone snuck a drink of water without getting permission. Jay saw and instructed the whole class to do air squats while we waited in line for the drill. I tried to count how many squats I did before I knelt into someone's guard (I stopped around fifty), but I ended up focusing on my breathing, trying to ignore the forest fire raging in my quadriceps. Each repetition was harder than the last, like someone was filling my muscles with plaster, plaster that seared like hot grease. Tears leaked from my squinted eyes; I hoped that no one noticed.

When the thirty minutes were up, my vision was blurry with pain and exhaustion. Jay taught his own variation of a standing guard pass, but I didn't care. I wanted class to be over. I wanted to shower. I wanted to eat. I wanted to sleep. I wanted the pain to stop.

My classmates seemed unfazed. Aside from me and a few other white belts, the majority of the class had the same stoic demeanor that Chris had that afternoon: calm, expressionless. Were it not for their sweat dripping into puddles on the mat, I would never have known that they had been working out. At that moment, when I realized that I was the weakest, least-skilled student in the room, I wanted desperately to have that mythical martial arts prowess that nullifies pain and makes fighting nothing more than a chess game. I admired the purple and brown belts, and I envied the blue belts. I despised the white fabric around my waist. I massaged the lactic acid out of my thighs and forced myself to breathe. I had to keep up. I had to keep fighting. I would never be one of them if I quit.

Jay finished teaching and put six minutes on the clock; it was time to free roll.

The aggression and harshness that I experienced during the guard passing drill was only a fraction of the pain that could be inflicted through grappling. During free roll, they could attack my limbs and throat from any position, not just from their back. In the guard-passing drill, it was like they were fighting exclusively with a jab. Now, they could attack with their full arsenal.

Each round felt like a fight for my life. I scrambled, pathetically and feebly, to defend myself, but the result was always the same. I tapped. I thought that at any moment my arm or shoulder would snap. I felt like I was in a knife fight, my guts spilling out of my elbows, shoulders, knees, and neck.

After four rounds, the training session was finally over. I caught my breath, packed my white belt, and walked gingerly home, following the trail of dim orange street lights on Kinoole Street.

That night, I sat at my desk and ate dinner, a 7-Eleven prepackaged sweet and sour chicken. The chicken tasted like marinated plastic and the rice like steamed Styrofoam. I washed each bite down with a swig of water. I scraped the bowl clean, consuming every grain of rice and every drop of sauce. I was still hungry.

After a cold shower (the hot water in the dorms did not seem to be working), I collapsed onto my bed. The bruises I noticed forming earlier were now distinct. The tops of both my thighs were purple. Hand print bruises marked my biceps and forearms like tribal war paint. My neck was rubbed raw from snapping lapel chokes dragging repeatedly back and forth across my throat. Tiny scabs formed in lines, dotting the trail of each individual choke. My whole body ached, like every limb and joint had been slammed in a car door. I took one last look at my white belt hanging next to my gis and turned off the light.

Through the window, I could hear the chirp of coqui frogs and the whisper of palm fronds moving in the wind. My first day of training was over, and tomorrow, Saturday, there was no class. I had barely survived one day of training. I didn't think I could survive five consecutive days, especially if all the classes were as tough as the ones I had just experienced. I was here, on the Big Island, by myself, for five months. No one I knew was watching me. I could quit. I could relax. I could bum around the beaches for the rest of my trip.

No.

AMERICANIZE

The slamming of my dorm room door against the wall jarred me from my sleep. An army green duffel bag as wide and as tall as two dresser drawers entered first, bouncing and scraping off the narrow entryway. Following shortly after was my new roommate, the jump rope length strap on his shoulder, pulled taught by his leaning back to keep the weight off the floor. His white lifeguard hat was on backward, keeping his shaggy, dirty-blond hair out of his eyes. Stubble shaded his jaw line. The frayed ends of his white wife beater hung over the edges of his black-and-white O'Neil board shorts. A surfer.

"Sup dude?" he said, dropping his duffel bag on the floor, its impact kicking up a puff of dust.

I grumbled a hello. For a moment, I didn't know where I was. I was disoriented and confused. I rubbed the sleep from eyes and squinted from the bright light pouring through the screened windows. I sat up.

"I'm Jake," my roommate said, leaning over the bottom of my bed to shake my hand.

"Marshal," I said, pulling my hand out from under my sheets to shake his hand.

Jake went back to his side of the room and started rooting through his bag. I could hear the whiz of zippers and the crinkle of plastic, but my desk blocked my view.

"Meet anyone yet?" he asked.

"No, I landed kind of late Thursday night."

Jake's head peaked over the top of the desk. "I met a few girls on the plane that go here," he said before disappearing back behind the cover of the desk. I looked around my bed for my pants. "Yeah man, they're super cool. We're going to hang out tonight, hit up some bars."

Talking to strangers struck a deep fear in me, and talking to strange girls was completely out of the question. I was already envious of Jake's confidence.

"And the one," he continued, "she's the president of the student body or something like that, and she's all about partying."

I told Jake that I thought that was pretty cool. His head popped back over the desk, his grin stretching his stubble into dimpled lumps.

"Yeah, I know. Right?" he said, laughing.

I heard what sounded like the thin mattress being lifted and dropped repeatedly on the bed frame, thumping like an arm full of laundry landing on the floor; Jake was putting sheets on his bed. After a few minutes, Jake was silent.

With some effort, I put my feet on the floor. My joints were stiff and my muscles sore. Everything ached, like my body was a single, seamless bruise. I pulled on a pair of cargo shorts, grunting and breathing sharply. I looked to Jake's side of the room.

Jake looked like he had fallen face first on to his mattress and had gone to sleep on impact. His green duffel bag was still open. His clothes were packed tightly in vacuum sealed bags. I could see a few personal effects, like his deodorant, razor, and tooth brush tucked in the corner, but with the bag being two feet deep, I had no way of knowing what else he had brought with him. Everything he owned was probably packed into plastic cubes and mashed into that bag.

With my map in hand and tennis shoes on (I didn't want any more life-threatening blisters, and I could feel the gobs of antibiotic ointment soaking into my socks), I quietly left my room.

That morning, like the morning before, I woke up at 6 AM, the sun just beginning to rise (long before Jake arrived). Not wanting to eat from 7-Eleven again, I walked two and a half miles to Walmart. The farther away from downtown Hilo (near Hilo Bay, just beyond the Academy) a street was, the less likely that street was to have a sidewalk, and Walmart was pretty far from downtown Hilo. I initially planned to take main roads to the Prince Kuhio Plaza, but as I got closer, the traffic intensified. I walked a narrow gravel shoulder, the mirrors of pickup trucks nipping my T-shirt sleeve. The pickup trucks riding on oversized monster-truck tires were the worst. They ripped past, growling with the tempo of a chain saw but with a deep bass, like the voice of a demon.

I turned on to Makaala, a side street. A bicycle shop was on the corner. Traffic was sparse on this street. Only one junker Toyota pickup passed me. Warehouses with rusted metal siding, their paint long chipped away by tropical weather, lined the road. They sat in the middle of parking lots, surrounded by cyclone fence and barbed wire, the concrete cracked and uneven, weeds fighting up through the gaps.

Other than the green weeds, the whole street was gray. Rusted buildings. Broken concrete. Beat-up cars. Litter along the road. Mounds of spare parts piled like bones. The scenery reminded me of my home, Washington, Pennsylvania, a town on the outskirts of Pittsburgh. Poverty and decay have wracked Washington, leaving business windows empty and industrial structures abandoned. The whole town is like a drawing crumpled into a ball and flattened back out again, a ghost of what it once was. And it was like that here. Were it not for the snow-capped summit of Mauna Kea looming over my shoulder, I might have forgotten I was in Hawaii.

Walmart, too, was not so different in Hilo from Walmarts on the mainland. The parking lot seethed like an ant hill, everything moving, coming and going. Instead of a predominantly white customer base, the people moving in and out of the sliding glass doors reflected the diversity of the state. Some were Asian. Some were Pacific Islander. Some were white. According to my guidebook, *The Big Island Revealed*, Hawaii has no racial minorities or majorities; the population is that diverse.

The ethnicities revealed by their faces were different from what I used to see at Walmarts near my home, but the troubles on their faces were the same. Single mothers herded groups of three and four children, the smallest with both legs through a baby seat, facing the mother as she pushed the cart toward the door. Two children stood in the front of the shopping cart, and the oldest walked alongside. The children wore hand-me-down shorts and T-shirts, faded by wear and dappled with stains. They looked tired.

Near the door, just under an overhang, near the soda machines and quarter-to-ride ponies and race cars, sat a table. A banner taped to the front read "KAU INOA" (pronounced cow ee-noah) and had Polynesian triangles bordering the top and bottom. The locals at the table passed out fliers. At the time, I knew nothing about Kau Inoa. I only knew that BJ Penn, in his recent fights, walked to the octagon wearing a Kau Inoa T-shirt.

I later learned that Kau Inoa translates as "to register," and their stated goal is to take a census of everyone, regardless of where they live, who is of Hawaiian descent. The implications, however, are far greater than a simple preservation of heritage. Being able to contact every Hawaiian could make a united push possible, and that push could be for independence. I, as I suspect most mainlanders, had no idea that secession was a serious cause for Hawaiians. Kau Inoa is just one of many organizations interested in at least discussing such a possibility.

Why mainstream media does not cover such news is a mystery to me. Perhaps it is the physical isolation of Hawaii. Perhaps it's that the underhanded dealings of the United States government reaching the general public is too scary.

The legality of Hawaii's annexation in 1898 is questionable. A group of Marines, at the encouragement of a group of merchants, invaded the islands and locked up Queen Lili'uokalani without a formal declaration of war or even orders from the United States government. What would have been an international incident had it occurred in Europe or Asia went relatively unnoticed by the rest of the world. Out in the Pacific, the incident seemed insignificant, except to the Hawaiians, of course. Instead of apologizing and withdrawing their forces, the U.S. government kept their military on the islands, and after some political misdirection, declared Hawaii a territory and later a state. The result was a massive destruction of Hawaiian culture on the scale of the American Indians. Hawaiians today are still fighting to recover the heritage and property that they lost in the debacle, and they are acutely aware that they got screwed over (and this isn't even taking into account the thousands of Hawaiians who died from the diseases introduced by Europeans).

At the time, I cared little for the fliers or for the cause. My legs were tired. The steadily increasing temperature soaked my T-shirt with sweat. I ignorantly pushed past the small crowd gathered around the Kau Inoa table, not knowing that understanding the Hawaiian independence movement was the key to understanding Hawaiian culture and the Hawaiian people.

Once inside, I set about filling my basket with groceries. My dorm room didn't have a refrigerator, so non-perishables would have to do. I bought twenty or so servings of ramen noodles: beef, chicken, and seafood flavored (the seafood flavor was for special occasions, like a fancy date). I bought cans of tuna and fruit. I bought a bag of assorted plastic utensils.

While going from aisle to aisle, I saw multiple ethnicities and heard a variety of languages. English was common, but I heard Chinese, Japanese, and Hawaiian. I heard a lot of what sometimes sounded like English but the vocabulary and dialect was so unusual to me that I could only understand a few words at time. This was one of the exchanges I heard:

"Brah, wan' get one bag Doritos?"

"Choke Doritos."

"Choke?"

"Choke, fo' da kine."

I later learned that what I was hearing was called Pidgin. Pidgin, like the Hawaiian Independence Movement, was a puzzle I would spend my entire stay on the Big Island trying to solve.

With half of my groceries in my backpack, and the other half filling plastic bags that sliced like razors into my fingers, I followed the same route home. The temperature was in the eighties now, and the humidity was so high that I felt as if I were swimming home. I was breathing heavily, and my body was already tired from training the day before.

On East Lanikaula Street, about halfway to my dorm, a tanker-truck Samoan whizzed past me on a green scooter, going the same direction as I was walking. The scooter looked like a toy underneath his mass. He wore wraparound sunglasses and had his hair pulled back in a pony tail.

As he drove by, he yelled, "Hey!" in a friendly manner and waved with his left arm.

I thought it was a local just being friendly. Then he swerved right onto the shoulder, and cut back hard to the left, forcing his poor little scooter to do a sharp U-turn. He drove back, slowing down as he neared.

He stopped in front of me.

"Hey brah, you wan' buy weed?" he said. Pock marks textured his face. The skin on his lips peeled like a dried onion.

"Nah, man, I'm good."

He grunted and pulled away, the weed whacker buzz of his scooter fading into the hum of traffic. That green scooter would haunt me for the rest of my trip.

Now, after a few hours of sleep (cut short by Jake's entrance), I was on my way back down Kinoole Street to visit Wailoa River State Park, which was next to Hilo Bay. Though I was growing tired of walking every time I wanted to go somewhere, I began to savor the benefits. Moving from footfall to footfall gave me time to take in the details that I would have missed in the blur of driving.

Zebra pigeons sauntered in groups of three or four or five on the sidewalk, their striped necks bouncing with each step, their round gray bodies wobbling back and forth like metronomes. They didn't squawk or chirp or call. The only noise they made was the beating of their wings when they panicked and flew away. The mynas, on the other hand, were obnoxious. They were almost entirely black, save for a bit of yellow extending from their narrow beaks right beneath their eyes. Their chirp, if you could even call it that, sounded like ripping Velcro.

Mixed in with the mynas and zebra pigeons were an assortment of finches and sparrows. The sparrows looked like the typical brown, skittish ones I was used to in Pennsylvania. Many of the finches were plain, but occasionally I caught sight of a buttercup-colored, palm-sized finch bouncing from tree branch to tree branch. To see something more exotic, like a honey creeper (a red bird with a long curved beak), one has to go outside of town.

The more I walked through Hilo, seeing colorful birds, island architecture, and exotic plants, the more local faces and languages I heard, the more I felt like I was in a foreign country. Seeing a United States flag flying on anything other than government grounds was rare. Instead, locals strung up the Hawaiian flag (a union jack in the upper left corner, thick red white and blue stripes running horizontally along the rest of the flag), a display of the pride they had in their heritage.

When I reached Wailoa River State Park, a commercial jet flew low overhead, taking off from Hilo airport. Part of me, the weak part, wished that I was on that plane.

The park was open and flat and covered by thick, lush grass (since Hilo gets an average of 130 inches of rainfall a year, keeping grass green is not a problem. Keeping the grass cut, on the other hand, is). Most of the trees grew along the river that ran through the middle of the park and eventually connected to Waiakea Pond. They were mostly typical palms, except they towered like Egyptian obelisks, and their trunks were as wide as kitchen tables. There were a few banyan trees, and they fascinated me.

Instead of having a solid trunk that fans into branches, a banyan tree is a network of vine like roots that sprout and wrap at random. The trunk looks like braided rope, each strand a different thickness. Some banyans have a base two or three car lengths wide. Offshoots from the branches sink back into the ground far from the trunk, as if it is dripping thin strands of molasses.

A banyan tree. Notice how large the tree is in comparison to the man in the bottom right hand corner.

Lion King–looking trees were on the outskirts of the park, dwarfing nearby cars and buildings. The bases of those trees started relatively narrow and then fanned out into wide, arching branches, like the whiskers of a frayed broom. The only trees blossoming at the time had trunks as thick as lampposts and branches spreading into a Y. A mass of green leaves filled the Y, and orange flowers coated the leaves like glitter.

Two roads ran through the park, one on either side of the river. One bridge was built to be driven over, while the others looked like inch worms caught at the peak of their stride. On the side of the river farthest from the bay was a Vietnam War memorial, a visitor's center, and a tsunami victims' memorial. It was Saturday, so the visitor's center was closed.

Plaques inscribed with soldiers' names lined both sides of the two walkways leading up to the squat, two tiered, square memorial. An ever burning flame flickered at the top of the structure. At the base of the memorial, a quote read, "For those who have fought for it, life has a special flavor that the protected will never know." When I took a picture of the quote, I couldn't find a way to keep my reflection in the polished marble from showing in the photograph. Hawaii might be isolated and left out of mainland news, but the memorial was a reminder that its people have contributed, in the most serious way possible, to the United States.

The tsunami memorial was about thirty yards across and in the shape of a circle. A rippled blue mosaic ran through the middle of the circle, dividing the memorial in half. At the front of the memorial, the side closest to the river, lava rocks were piled into the shape of a wave about waist high. A larger wave, taller than me, made up the back of the memorial.

The park used to be Hilo's Japanese district, but after tsunamis repeatedly brought tragedy to the people living there (in 1946, 159 people drowned, and in 1960, 38 people drowned), the homes were cleared and replaced by the park.

As I read the inscription on the memorial, I heard clapping flip-flops on gravel. I looked up and saw two local children peaking over the small wave at me, their shaggy black hair dangling over their tanned faces. They smiled and waved. When I waved back, they ran back down the slope of the wave toward the river bank, where two elderly men were reclining in lawn chairs, steering remote-control boats.

Remote control boats at the Wailoa River State Park.

Further downstream, toward Waiakea Pond, a mother was fishing with her three children. She reeled in a fish, and while holding it up for the children to see, she said, "I have caught three! How many have you caught?" She laughed, rocking back and forth on a bench, one arm clutching her stomach.

On the other side of the river, closer to the bay, was a statue of the Great Kamehameha, the first man to unite and rule over the islands. He was depicted in a regal pose, a spear in one hand, the other outstretched, palm up. His Mohawk helmet, sash, and the long rectangular cloth covering his naughty bits were a shining gold. His skin was black.

My favorite piece of Kamehameha lore is the legend of the Naha Stone.

When Kamehameha was fourteen (the exact age is debatable; oral traditions vary), he traveled from Kona, a town on the leeward side of the island, to Hilo. Legend said that anyone who could overturn the Naha stone, which weighs 7,000 pounds and is still in Hilo today, would become the first king of all the islands. Not only was Kamehameha young and the stone absurdly heavy, but he was also not a member of the local Naha bloodline. If he failed, he would be killed. Fortunately, Kamehameha was a stud. He flipped the Naha stone. His jiu-jitsu must have been pretty good.

The Great Kamehameha was a well-respected local icon, and BJ Penn sometimes posed like the Great Kamehameha when he weighed in for his fights.

The Great Kamehameha.

Looking down river from one of the bridges, watching fish navigate the current, I caught site of a bright blue mass. I thought perhaps it was a colorful rock or an exotic plant. I leaned over the railing and squinted. It was a blanket. A bit further downstream was a bucket, half sunken into the mud. Near the bucket, a plastic bag was wrapped in some weeds.

I went across the street to see Hilo Bay, thinking that I would be spending a great deal of my time in Hawaii laying on its beach and swimming in its waters. Just a few minutes from the gym, I could stop by after training and bask in tropical rays. I was wrong. The beach was covered in mulch-like debris, thick piles of it, as if someone were about to begin a massive gardening project. The water was dark and murky, not the pristine, transparent sapphire blue that I had seen in travel brochures for Hawaii. In the distance, toward the opening of the bay, was a manmade concrete wall. A local later told me that the wall was built to help prevent tsunamis, but the trade off of the wall was that it ruined the bay. He said that the bay used to be a great place to swim and surf.

Beyond the wall was Coconut Island, connected to the Big Island by a relatively short bridge. I could see poles propped on the bridge and tiny figures moving below palm trees along the beach. I was tempted to explore the island, but it would have to wait. I was tired and hungry. I trekked back to my dorm.

When I arrived, Jake was awake and mostly done unpacking his bag. Clothes filled his closet and dresser. Hygiene items and a few books (*The Abs Diet* sticks out in my memory) were scattered across his desk.

"Hey, dude. You hungry?" he asked, "I'm starved."

"Yeah, me too," I said, reaching for a pack of ramen noodles with about as much excitement as one can muster when reaching for a pack of ramen noodles.

"I saw a Subway down the street. Want to hit that up?" he asked.

I considered my failing budget. I knew that I would later regret indulging in luxuries. The responsible adult decision was to decline and cook my ramen. "Yeah, let's go," I said.

On our way down Lanikaula Street to the nearest Subway, Jake told me about himself. He was originally from Oakland, but lived most of his life in New Mexico. He attended college on the mainland for a while but was more interested in playing soccer than in studying. After blowing out both knees multiple times, he put away his cleats and started drifting. He moved to California but, perhaps feeling that he had not wandered far enough, moved to Oahu and spent the last year and a half or so bussing tables and surfing. Now twenty-four years old, he was looking to finish his degree (in Biology, maybe).

About halfway to Subway, the conversation shifted to me.

"So, you have a girlfriend back home?" he asked.

"Yeah," I said out of pure habit, not realizing my mistake until the word had left my mouth. I wasn't sure how to correct myself. "Kinda."

"One of those deals?"

I forced a laugh. "Yeah, one of those deals."

"How do you like the islands?" he asked after some silence had passed.

"I'm liking it so far. Feels like a foreign country sometimes."

"Yeah, I know. Right?" Jake replied. He used that expression often, following it with a chuckle. He always said it like it carried an acknowledgment of deep understanding, like a trucker saying "I hear ya, brother."

At Subway, Jake ordered two twelve-inch subs. One to eat there and one to eat later. He apparently was having a food dilemma similar to mine. I ordered a twelve-inch sub and a bottle of water. Subway suddenly being in the "splurging" category as far as finances go struck me as odd. I didn't have the money to spare, but as with most of my problems, I thought that if I just ignored it, I wouldn't have to deal with it.

I made up for the splurge by reusing that water bottle for the rest of the trip. I filled and refilled it every time I went to the gym for the whole five months I was on the Big Island.

"So, why did you come to the Big Island?" Jake asked, his mouth full of chicken teriyaki and Italian herb and cheese bread.

"BJ Penn."

"Who?"

"Ever hear of the UFC?"

Jake wiped his mouth with a napkin. "Yeah. Like Chuck Liddell?" he asked. Chuck Liddell is a very popular UFC fighter. He has a Mohawk and Asian script tattooed on his scalp. His nickname is the "Ice Man." He's known for knocking people out. He also has a bachelor's degree in accounting.

"BJ Penn is in the UFC, and he has a gym in Hilo. So coming here on exchange was a good excuse to get here and train," I said.

"You're a cage fighter?" Jake asked mid-bite, his eyes wide, looking up at me.

I laughed. "No no. Just jiu-jitsu."

Jake looked confused.

"It's just the ground fighting, like wrestling with submissions instead of pins. I'd like to get my blue belt before I leave," I said.

"What are you now?"

"White."

"People better watch out! My roommate is a freaking white belt!" he said. Though he laughed when he said that, I couldn't tell if he was making fun of me or not.

We threw our trash in a bin inscribed with "Mahalo" (which means "thank you," not "garbage") and started walking back. On the way, we bantered back and forth, but mostly I listened to his stories. He told me about how his brother is a professional golfer and was temporarily off the circuit because he broke his ankle stepping off of a basketball court. He told me about the girls he met in Cancun. He told me about a junker truck he had left abandoned on the side of the road in Oahu (the papers were still in the original owner's name). Then Jake asked me a question that took me off guard.

"Had any trouble with the locals yet?"

"No. . ." I said, looking back over my shoulder. "Should I be worried about that?"

Jake shrugged. "It happens. Colonization or some shit," he said.

"That doesn't seem fair."

"Yeah, I know. Right? Like, I didn't take your fucking islands. I didn't choose to be a haole (pronounced howl-ee). Don't hate me," Jake said, shaking his head in disgust.

I didn't know what a haole was. Jake explained that a haole was a white person, a non-Hawaiian. A faculty member at the University of Hawaii at Hilo later told me that haole means "without breath." He said that in traditional Hawaiian culture, Hawaiians greeted each other and showed respect by standing nose to nose and inhaling repeatedly, sharing each other's breath. When the white man landed on the islands, he stuck his arm out for a hearty handshake. Hawaiian's decided that the white men didn't have breath to share, hence the term "without breath."

I was a haole. Jake was a haole. Outside of major tourist hot stops, Jake said, haoles are usually unwelcome. With its frequent rain and rocky beaches, Hilo wasn't much of a tourist hot spot.

A few days later, at an orientation for exchange students, the director of the program informed us that an exchange student was watching the sun set from a bench on Coconut Island. A group of locals jumped him. They beat him with a baseball bat. He was rushed to Oahu to have corrective surgery on his jaw. He had curly blond hair and pink skin. He was a haole.

That guy had been at a popular scenic spot, near houses and hotels. I walked home from the gym in the dark five nights a week. The street lights on Kinoole Street were dim and only lit one side of the road. My walk on West Lanikaula Street, the last quarter mile or so, was hardly lit at all. For a seventy-yard stretch, I used the glow of my cell phone to guide my feet.

Staph infections and bank balances and pollution and local politics were suddenly the least of my concerns.

THE MCDOJO MANIFESTO

After Jake's warning that locals were hard on haoles, I began to walk to and from the gym with trepidation. I kept my head down. I watched for shadows coming up behind me. I avoided eye contact with passing drivers, lest I accidently give the stink eye to a pickup full of locals who were cruising the streets of Hilo, haole hunting. At night, I half-jogged back to my room. I was still wearing tennis shoes to let my blisters heal, but I decided I would keep wearing them even after the wounds closed. If I was attacked, my best bet would be to run, and running in sandals is more comedic than effective.

Jake's warnings combined with the exchange student being attacked on Coconut Island spooked me. My fear was, initially, more of a heightened awareness and sensitivity to my surroundings, rather than terror. Reading Chris McKinney's *The Tattoo* pushed me to terror.

Though I had one more week before classes began, I knew that training twice a day and taking thirteen credits was going to be difficult, so I started my required reading early. Other than sleeping and eating, I didn't have much to do. I was always too tired between training sessions to go exploring, so I sat in bed and read, and *The Tattoo* was one of three books on the syllabus for my fiction writing class.

The Tattoo is fictional, but it won the Ka Palapala Poʻokela Award, a Hawaiian award given for excellence in literature, and the Cades Award, one of Hawaii's most prestigious literary awards, so despite the plot and characters being made up, there's a bit of truth to the setting and culture in which the characters exist.

The book follows a half-Japanese half-Hawaiian named Kenji. While getting a tattoo from his mute cellmate, Kenji tells the story of his life growing up on Oahu. His elementary years were full of schoolyard scraps, a cultural phenomenon that was more of a reality than I anticipated. Kenji eventually befriends a young Hawaiian named Koa. When Kenji and Koa reach young adulthood, fighting on school grounds loses its fun. They start driving around town at night looking for haoles. They don't always go alone; they often bring friends, a raiding party. Most of their victims are marines, but they jump a few tourists as well. They don't just fight them. Kenji and Koa punish them:

Anything [Koa] had was for the giving when it came to those he cared about. But, man, when it came to haoles, he became a fucking blood-thirsty animal. He hated all of them. I never asked him why. It always seemed obvious. They'd taken his land. They killed his culture and therefore they'd taken his humanity. Well, if they wanted an animal, Koa was going to give them one they'd never forget. A fucking Grendel, a Scylla and Charybdis all rolled up in one.

So sometimes we'd drive out to Kailua, the closest place where there was guarantee that some haoles were around.

After reading *The Tattoo*, I felt like every local living on the island was waiting to attack me, peering through the slits of their window blinds, taking note of my habits and my routines, watching, waiting to strike.

I found myself making assumptions based on skin color. If a Hawaiian walked in my direction on the sidewalk, I assumed he hated me, so I hated him back. I pushed past with my head down and a fist clenched. If I was just a haole, then he was just a Hawaiian. Suddenly, I was thinking in terms of teams, in terms of us (haoles) and them (Hawaiians). My fear and ignorance combined to make hate.

I brought my new found hate to the mat.

The training sessions weren't getting easier. I was still being thrown and submitted. Submissions came on hard and fast. Stray elbows and knees connected with my face and ribs. I was a punching bag. Each time a Hawaiian was hard on me, I blamed it on his skin color. He was just beating me up because I was a haole. I fought with anger and frustration instead of the calculated calmness that is the norm for experienced grapplers. I muttered curses under my breath, and I scowled.

As much as I wanted to, I couldn't blame the abuse I received on racism. Just like my first day of training, other haoles came to train, and they seemed to get along with everyone else, the Hawaiians included. They weren't being attacked with relentless and unforgiving submissions. Their matches were relaxed and methodical. There was a distinct difference between the way they were treated and the way I was treated. I couldn't understand it.

Then I met Cole.

Cole was a purple belt. He was six foot two and young, in his twenties. Cole had his head shaved. He was pale to the point of looking gray—pure haole. He reminded me of Dennis the Menace.

When Cole stepped on to the mat, he was greeted with smiles and handshakes. He sat along the wall before and after training, talking jiu-jitsu and exchanging jokes with locals and Hawaiians. Despite being a haole, he was a part of the group. He was accepted. If Cole could be one of the guys, there had to be some hope for me. Blaming racism was a cop out, and when I realized that, I was disgusted with myself for giving in to such beliefs.

To be accepted, Cole must have done something different than Jake or the exchange student that was assaulted on Coconut Island. If I thought and acted like the haoles that locals despised, I was doomed to be treated like them. If I wanted to be accepted by the fighters at the gym, and locals in general, I had to fit in, I had to be like Cole.

I studied Cole. When he came into the room, he shook hands with everyone there. He sat along the wall closest to the door. Each time he rolled with someone, win or lose, he smiled or laughed. At the end of a class, he shook hands with everyone still on the mat before he left. The more I watched Cole, the more I realized that anyone who trained consistently behaved this way, haole or not.

When I came into the room, I always kept to myself. I stretched in the corner farthest from the door. I didn't talk to anyone. I shook hands with anyone that I rolled with, but I didn't smile. I was already mad at them for what they were going to do to me. If I wanted to be accepted, I knew I had to change. I had to overcome my shyness and be more outgoing.

I started sitting closer to the door, but I couldn't bring myself to sit by the door like Cole did. I mustered enough bravery to move to the middle of the room. If there were people on the mat when I came in, I forced myself to shake their hands. Their eye brows perked with confusion, but they forced a smile and shook my hand back. Whenever I left, I walked around the perimeter of the mat, shaking hands with each person leaning against the wall catching their breath. I thanked the ones I rolled or drilled with. I told the others to "take care."

When I rolled with someone, I smiled when we touched hands to start the match. When they submitted me, I laughed. I sat up right away and threw myself back into the match as soon as I could. I didn't want them to see me hesitate. I didn't want them to see me quit. I didn't want them to know that I was afraid.

I reread the chapter in my guidebook on local customs and practices. Pidgin was still a mystery to me, even with a list of vocabulary terms. Here are some Pidgin words and their definitions from *Hawaii: the Big Island Revealed*:

Beef—Fight.

Choke—Plenty; lots.

Da kine—A noun or verb used in place of whatever the speaker wishes. Heard constantly.

Grind—To eat.

Howzit?—How is it going? How are you? Also, Howzit o wot?

Mo' bettah—This is better.

Talk story—Shooting the breeze; to rap.

Reading a language is one thing, but being able to understand someone speaking it is another. The paragraph on the shaka caught my attention and was more useful to me than Pidgin.

The shaka is a hand signal where the thumb and pinky are extended while the other fingers are closed. My guidebook said that the shaka "is a friendly act used as a sign of greeting or just to say *Hey*." The origin of the shaka is debated, but my guidebook asserted that it originated in the 1930s. A guard who had lost his middle fingers in an accident used to patrol the railroad for the Kahuku Sugar Plantation on Oahu. Because of his missing fingers, his way of waving off mischievous children was distinct. To warn each other that the guard was around, kids used the shaka. It stuck.

I didn't entirely trust the guidebook, though. Before I started using the shaka, I wanted to know for sure that I wouldn't offend anyone by doing it. I was already expecting a mauling every time I rounded a corner. I didn't want to accidently throw up a gang sign or violate some ancient taboo. I needed a reliable source. I needed to talk to a local.

One morning, before the afternoon class was about to begin, I was stretching on the mat with a few other locals. Ro and Zay, the two University of Hawaii at Manoa students that were in my first class, were among them. Ro was quiet, but Zay was outgoing. Even when I submitted him—and Zay was one of the few people that I could actually beat—he laughed and shook my hand. On a few occasions, he asked me to teach him some of my techniques. Why he asked me for instruction when every other person on the mat was more experienced, I don't know.

Once, after I used the same sweep on Zay three times in a round, he asked me to explain it to him. That particular sweep, called the "old school," I had learned from a book (*Mastering the Rubber Guard* by Eddie Bravo). I never had someone sit down on the mat and teach me the old school. I read the book and studied the pictures. I analyzed Bravo's competition footage, watching the same ten seconds over and over to see how he used the sweep during a match, to see how he responded to his opponent's defenses and counters. A lot of my jiu-jitsu came from books and videos.

My jiu-jitsu career began with self-instruction. When I first saw the UFC on television, I was a freshman in college. Seeing the UFC rekindled my interest in Jeet Kune Do, Bruce Lee's fighting philosophy that advocated winning by any means possible. In the cage, the fight was free flowing. The referee did not break up the clinch like he would in boxing, nor did he stand fighters up as soon as they went to the ground. Mixed martial arts is as close as one could get to a real fight and still maintain a semblance of safety for both men involved. I wanted to train; I wanted to be a martial artist.

I couldn't, however, find a Jeet Kune Do school near where I lived. I found karate, aikido, and Tang Soo Do, but I knew better than to sign up at one of those schools. In America, where fast food chains and Walmarts have become the norm, even martial arts schools are franchised, and mass production dilutes quality. The quality of a fast food burger can't compare to the quality of a burger hand-packed from fresh ground beef and grilled to a customer's specifications at a small-town diner. A martial art is no different.

The focus on profits has hurt martial arts instruction. Ten-year-olds go to karate class three times a week, memorize a few katas (a set series of punches and kicks and stances that when done all at once looks like a solo dance), and as long as Mom and Dad keep up with the fees, their son or daughter can have a black belt in two years or less. The magic is in the fees.

On top of a monthly fee, most schools have a start-up fee. Each time a student tests for the next belt, he pays a test fee, which, in most schools, increases exponentially with belt rank. And some schools have a lot of belts. The American Tae Kwon Do Association, for example, has eleven. The fourth belt is camouflage. I don't have any research to support this, but I am fairly certain that the camouflage belt is not a tradition passed down from ancient Korea. It seems like an effort to artificially extend the path between a white belt and a black belt.

To signify progression between belts, many schools use stripes, which are pieces of tape wrapped around the end of the belt. Each piece of tape signifies that the student is one step closer to the next belt. Getting a stripe is usually associated with a fee. Schools requiring their students to purchase their uniform and equipment (headgear, gloves, shin pads, foot pads, and focus mitts) through the school supplier, which gives the school a cut of the profits, is also not uncommon. Then the school franchises. In Southwestern Pennsylvania, a single Karate chain has ten branches within thirty square miles.

The result: corporate martial arts, a plague of McDojos. Get your black belt fast and easy. Friendly service. No hassles. Supersize to a second degree black belt for just $200.

The McDojo phenomenon has nearly killed the mystique and respect once associated with a black belt. If little Timmy down the street can earn a black belt before hitting puberty, then a black belt can't be *that* dangerous. An adult with a black belt is just as likely to be dangerous as little Timmy. After all, their instructor was the same. They learned the same curriculum and took the same tests and were judged by the same standards. If a guy was a black belt, it used to mean that he was a bad dude. That's not the case anymore.

The worst part of the McDojo phenomenon is the effect it has on individuals. Little Timmy, with his black belt and signed certificates, thinks that he can defend himself. He thinks that if someone were to attack him, he could use his spinning hook kick (the one that has split dozens upon dozens of boards) to end the fight. He fancies himself a fighter. He's too young to critically evaluate his instruction, to question the techniques he is learning. His instructor speaks with confidence and wears a cool-looking kimono. He has trophies in his window and motivational posters on the wall. He inspires Timmy. He makes Timmy feel good about himself.

Timmy won't feel good about himself the first time he takes a haymaker to the nose.

I didn't want to memorize katas. I didn't want to break boards. I was looking for a school that taught me practical techniques, ones I could use on a fully resisting opponent who fully wanted to kill me. If I earned a black belt, I wanted it to symbolize what a black belt used to symbolize.

The aikido school in town also taught Japanese jiu-jitsu (the father of Brazilian jiu-jitsu), which involves mostly standing grappling techniques and standing joint locks, relying heavily on pain compliance techniques. I was more interested in the Japanese jiu-jitsu classes than the Aikido classes. The instructor, a short balding man with coke-bottle glasses and a belly so round he looked like he was eight months pregnant, told me that the Japanese jiu-jitsu classes were for elite students only. The techniques were simply too dangerous to be taught to just anyone. Students had to take the Aikido classes first, and then he decided if a student was worthy of elite training. I wasn't keen on paying for something I wasn't really interested in, and an instructor not teaching all of his students the most effective techniques he knew bothered me.

The kenpo jiu-jitsu school was in the basement of a hardware store and was taught by a police officer. He was small but athletic and was a seventh dan (or some high-degree number like that). Since he worked in law enforcement, I was open to trusting his instruction. He laughed at me when I asked him about ground techniques. He said if he would never teach a woman to use the guard (a core Brazilian jiu-jitsu position), he would certainly never teach it to a man.

When I asked him why he disliked the guard, he said, "It puts a rapist exactly where he wants to be."

Even then, I knew that he very much misunderstood the guard, but I had neither the knowledge nor the experience to defend it. I know now that he really had no concept of ground fighting at all. I was willing to let it slide, but then I looked over my shoulder and saw one of his students, a college-age bouncer with a shaved head, showing my girlfriend a self-defense technique. He was teaching her how to disarm a gun.

"You just have to be fast," the student said, motioning Hilary to point the pistol at his chest.

Yes, faster than a bullet. It was time to leave.

I visited a kenpo karate school in the mall. The instructor was tall and had Tom Cruise hair. He was in his early thirties. Floor to ceiling mirrors surrounded the mats. Trophies lined the waiting area, a little gold man kicking or punching at the peak of each. Many of the trophies were tiered, like wedding cakes, and were taller than me. He crossed his arms and leaned back when he spoke to me, a sarcastic smirk tugging at the corner of his lips. Behind him, children in blindingly white gis practiced katas, yelling and grunting each time they moved. When I told the instructor that I had read about Jeet Kune Do, he laughed at me. I grew up with assholes laughing at me. I didn't need to pay for it.

I found a Jeet Kune Do school and was hesitant to visit because it was farther away than any other school I had visited, but I was desperate. The instructor greeted me in cutoff jean shorts spattered with white paint, like he had just finished priming a room. He gave me the usual monthly-fee spiel and showed me the curriculum, a big chunk of which was kata. I had no intention of ever learning kata, and I couldn't find a listing for the school in the Jeet Kune Do Federation database. I noticed that they offered a class in Erik Paulson's Combat Submission Wrestling. Paulson is well known in the fighting community as being a leg-lock wizard, and he is also one of the few famous Jeet Kune Do instructors. I wasn't desperate enough to start training there, yet.

Even though I couldn't find a school, I was still determined to train. I had been diligently watching the UFC, and the importance of ground fighting was becoming more and more obvious to me. Any fighter not trained on the ground was quickly controlled, beaten up, and submitted. The positioning and technique and strategy of Brazilian jiu-jitsu fascinated me. A knock out could be attributed to luck, but a submission is an obvious display of dominance. Tapping out is an admission of defeat. There is no question as to who is the better fighter when a fight ends by submission.

I decided I could teach myself. I bought a set of Cesar Gracie DVDs and a set of Tae Kwon Do–style sparring pads (a Tron-looking padded helmet, a set of gloves with about as much padding as an oven mitt, and goofy-looking booties). I convinced a friend of mine, Charlie, to buy some pads as well. We started to teach ourselves how to fight.

Words like teach and learn might not be the most appropriate way to describe our sessions.

We would pop in a Cesar Gracie DVD, watch a few moves, and run out to the backyard. We tried the moves without resistance once or twice. Then, we suited up and beat the piss out of each other.

We always started standing. Charlie was six foot three. I am five foot ten. Charlie had the reach advantage. If I wanted to hit him, I had to go inside his punching range and aim up. Charlie was not particularly athletic, but that reach was killer. Though our gloves were thin and our headgear had no face protection and though we were doing takedowns on ground padded only by grass, we never got hurt (a minor miracle). The closest to disaster we came was nearly landing in a pile of dog poop. That was a scary moment.

After a summer of digging dirt out of the nether corners of my body and scrubbing grass stains off of my elbows and my knees, I caved. I needed an instructor. I signed up for the Combat Submission Wrestling classes at the Jeet Kune Do school. Since I could only afford to go once a week, I continued to supplement my training with all the DVDs, books, and YouTube videos I could find. Eddie Bravo's *Mastering the Rubber Guard* was one of those books, and of any approach to grappling I had seen, Bravo's explanations and strategies were the easiest to understand and apply. The old school sweep became my go-to move.

When Zay asked me to teach it to him, I obliged him, even though I felt awkward doing it. I was a white belt. Zay was a white belt. It was the blind leading the blind. I showed Zay how the sweep is dependent on the lockdown, a version of the half-guard where the bottom fighter has both legs woven around one of the top fighter's legs. I showed him how the bottom fighter uses the control of the lockdown to maneuver the top fighter's weight off to the side, allowing the bottom fighter to sit up. I showed him how to use a palm-up grip to grab the top fighter's foot. I showed him how to time the unlocking of his legs with his pressure to get the sweep and avoid landing in the top fighter's guard.

Jay Penn sat at the edge of the mat and watched me teach Zay. His eyes squinted, like he was studying my instruction, analyzing every piece of the move, every piece of me. Jay never said anything. He just watched.

When I asked Zay about the shaka, Jay wasn't around. Ro and Zay were in the middle of the mat. Ro was doing a butterfly stretch. Zay had one leg straight, stretching his hamstring. I gave myself a pep talk, walked over, and sat down next to Ro and Zay.

"Can I ask you guys something?"

Ro and Zay looked at me, suspicious.

"I've been seeing a lot of people do this," I said, extending my pinky and thumb to make the shaka. "What does it mean?"

Zay laughed. Ro chuckled and shook his head, putting his head on the mat to continue his stretch. "It's like 'aloha.' You can use it for 'thank you' or 'hello' or 'goodbye.'"

"Would it be offensive if I used it? Like, would it get me beat up?"

Zay laughed. "No, no, no. If you do it right, you're cool."

"What do you mean?"

Zay showed me the shaka palm facing out, palm facing toward the chest, extended in the air like a wave, and extended out down by the hip. "Whatever you do, don't shake it," Zay said.

"Don't shake it?"

"Don't shake it," Zay said, smiling and nodding. I saw Ro nodding in agreement. He was stretching his quads. "Anything else you want to know?" Zay asked. He seemed genuinely happy to answer my questions.

I thought for a moment. "What about food?" I asked.

Zay raised an eyebrow.

"Is there some local food that I should make sure I try?"

Zay leaned back, supporting himself with his hands. "As far as local food goes, you have to try loco moco. Yeah, try loco moco for sure. And for Hawaiian, you have to try some traditional pork, good stuff," he said.

"What's loco moco?"

"It's rice with chicken and egg and brown gravy."

Loco moco is also delicious.

First, white rice is heaped on a plate (rice is served with everything in Hawaii—breakfast, lunch, or dinner). One or two or three pieces of meat are set on top of the rice. The meat is a fried chicken patty, a hamburger patty, or spam. I liked chicken the best and found one patty to be more than filling, but I saw a few hefty locals down a three-patty loco moco without any trouble. A fried egg is put on top of the patty. The egg can be scrambled or sunny-side up. I preferred sunny-side up. Then a generous serving of brown gravy is poured over everything. The gravy is often so plentiful that the plate must be carried carefully, like a bowl of soup filled to the brim.

I ate a lot of loco moco. Now, each time I visit a restaurant on the mainland, I pray to see loco moco on the menu. My prayers have yet to be answered.

After that conversation with Zay, I resolved to live as much like a local as possible. I wanted to blend in and become a part of the culture. If I blended in, I might not get the snot beat out of me. I wanted to eat their food, use their gestures, and use their expressions. When in Hawaii, do everything possible not to get jumped by locals.

Unfortunately, I was still getting smashed in training. Shaking hands and using the shaka seemed to earn me a bit more acceptance and a few more smiles, but I was nothing more than a Hacky Sack for almost everyone in the jiu-jitsu classes. The more I became a gym rat, the more I began to notice the differences between the two classes, and the harshness of my beatings was one of those differences.

As far as I could tell, no one else but me trained in both the afternoon and in the evening. The afternoon sessions were typically less competitive and more relaxed. Most of the students in the afternoon class were on their lunch breaks, and while they were passionate about jiu-jitsu, they didn't have the die-hard mentality of the students in the evening class. The afternoon students tended to joke more during drills and during free roll while the evening students remained serious and approached every match like it was the pivotal moment of a championship bout. Mouths stayed tense and quiet and eyes stayed narrowed.

Then I began to see a difference between the gi and no-gi classes. I already knew that the style of training varied from gi to no-gi. What I saw at the BJ Penn Academy was a difference in the people.

In jiu-jitsu, and grappling in general, students train with or without the gi. When training in a gi, a student can grab any part of the uniform—the sleeves, the lapels, the pants, and the belt. Almost any grip is fair game, with the exception of hooking inside the cuffs of the sleeves and pants—getting entangled inside a cuff is much too easy, which can quickly lead to broken fingers. The gi essentially becomes a tool, a weapon. Being able to grab a fistful of cloth anywhere on the body makes controlling an opponent much easier and sets up a variety of sweeps and submissions not possible without a gi. Choking someone with their own collar is one of the most common attacks with the gi, but gi work can become incredibly complex. Some grapplers specialize in untucking the tail of the gi and wrapping it around their opponent's throat. One of the setups for this particular submission requires a well-timed somersault to cinch the fabric around the windpipe. Fancy stuff.

Without the friction of the uniform and the easy-access grips, no-gi training tends to have a faster pace. In no-gi, fighters are really only required to wear a pair of shorts, normally board shorts or some sort of spandex, though most opt to wear a T-shirt or rash guard to avoid the many communicable diseases associated with grappling. In the gi, controlling an opponent is as easy as grabbing his lapel, but in no-gi, fighters often battle for the underhook, which is basically having an arm under the opponent's arm, threaded through the arm pit and around the back like a hug. This change in control changes setups for attacks. Without the aid of the lapel and the pants, the number of attacks available for each position decreases significantly, so getting an opponent to move and react becomes more challenging. On top of that, the longer a match goes, the more each fighter sweats. A gi absorbs moisture and the fabric sticks to itself like Velcro. But in no-gi, grips perpetually slip, so fighters are constantly scrambling for a reliable position from which to control their opponent.

Typically, jiu-jitsu purists train more with the gi than without, arguing that the extra grips and variety of attacks sharpen defenses and force fighters to be technical and methodical rather than strong and explosive. As MMA increases in popularity, however, many grapplers are abandoning the gi (which is illegal to wear under United MMA Rules) and training no-gi exclusively. Since they won't be wearing a gi in the cage, they see learning to use and defend collar chokes and sleeve grips as a waste and even counterproductive to becoming well-trained mixed martial artists.

Since BJ Penn's game is built around jiu-jitsu, the debate between gi and no-gi training wasn't as heated in the Academy, and
many of the higher-ranking belts competed in MMA. Consequently,
the gi class was a blend of mixed martial artists and sport grapplers.
Though their overall grappling career paths varied, every person in
the gi class had one thing in common: they loved training jiu-jitsu.
They loved the technique, the strategy, and the finesse.

Most of the students in the no-gi class seemed focused on MMA.
Some were talented grapplers, making the transition from sport jiu-
jitsu to MMA, but many were brawlers anxious to get off the mat and
into the cage. What they lacked in technique they made up for with
spastic explosiveness. Rather than execute a technical escape, they
herked and jerked their way free, relying on the slipperiness of sweat
and their own strength (think of a perfect-form foul shot compared
to a haphazard lob). I was getting beat in both classes, but at least in
the gi I was getting beat by moves. During no-gi, I ate just as many
stray elbows to the jaw and fingers to the eye as I did submissions.
The no-gi students weren't as controlled as the gi students, so they
were more dangerous, more likely to give me a serious injury. I knew
that if I was forced to scale back my training by a few sessions once
classes started, the evening no-gi sessions would be the first to go. If I
wanted to earn my blue belt, I had to stay healthy. I had to think long
term.

And thinking long term, for the most part, depressed me.

With my shaka and my handshakes, I felt like I was moving toward acceptance at the gym, but I was still losing, and losing badly.
In Pennsylvania, I could beat most white belts and even the occasional blue belt. I knew that losing was the key to learning, but I became more frustrated and disheartened with each tap. I was far from
my backyard roots, but my blue belt was still out of reach. Though I
smiled before and after each match, I wasn't being sincere. I wasn't
having fun. I kept training because I didn't know what else to do. Jiu-
jitsu was my life boat, and I was going to stick with it no matter how
much water came aboard.

My twenty-first birthday was the end of that week, and Jake promised me a night on the town, haole-style. Good, I thought. I could use some companionship.

BARE WINTER SUDDENLY CHANGED TO SPRING

or the first time in my life, I spent my birthday alone.

I woke up at 8 AM that Saturday, the time zone change still making me an early bird by default. The sun was a brilliant white, and the wet tropical warmth had not yet settled on the day. Jake was still asleep, his comforter pulled up over his head, his bare feet protruding off the end of his mattress. Fed up with the stiffness of his mattress, Jake had gone to Walmart a few days earlier and bought two thick foam pads. He sank so deep into the foam that the horizon of his bed was almost completely flat. He snored.

Jake had promised to take me out that night for my birthday, but I had the day to myself. I walked down Kinoole Street to downtown Hilo, which is right on the bay. I moved slowly, partially because I was in no hurry and partially because my body hadn't recovered from the week's worth of brutal training. My back was stiff, and my quadriceps grated and strained. With every painful step, I checked and rechecked my map.

In every guidebook I read, Hilo was described as being in a time warp. They said that visiting the town was like stepping back into the 1950s. I never understood that description because on my walks through town I saw wrappers from 7-Eleven, Starbucks, Burger King, Pizza Hut, Subway, and occasionally Taco Bell moving like tumbleweeds down the street (I had yet to discover the sources of the wrappers, but I was searching diligently).

When I got downtown, I found the business district did, in fact, appear to be right out of the 1950s. The storefronts and architecture all had that vintage feel, so much so that the town could have been the set for the first *Back to the Future*. A gas station had a rotating globe on the street corner. Old theaters and playhouses displayed signs with large painted letters lined with fist-sized light bulbs. The movie theater even had a jut-out marquee and a glass ticket-taker's box. The age of the buildings was apparent, but this part of Hilo was quaint, and though it was bustling with tourists in long white tube socks and khaki shorts, the atmosphere was relaxed. Each store and restaurant seemed to be family owned; McDonalds and Hot Topic had yet to invade.

I ate dinner in a small restaurant called Ocean Sushi. The decorations were plain, a few Japanese prints on a stark white wall and a white porcelain Japanese cat on the counter. The tables wobbled and many of the old diner chairs had been replaced by folding chairs; granted, they were nicely padded and expensive-looking, but they were folding chairs nonetheless. Had I simply walked past the window, I probably wouldn't have gone in, but my guidebook recommended it based on the quality (reported as high) and the price (reported as cheap). I sat down by the window, ordered a Sunset Roll and four pieces of tuna nigiri (pieces of tuna over rice).

While I waited for the chefs to prepare my sushi, I watched a middle-aged couple park their car across the street and enter a stairway to an apartment above a loan office. She looked to be of Polynesian descent: black hair hanging to the middle of her back, about five foot four, a round face and crescent moon eyes. He was tall and lanky, pale, bald, unfit, and naked save for a piece of green fabric tied carefully around his waist that covered only a third of his thighs and not enough of his pale, freckled ass.

The sushi was excellent. I savored each piece, the subtle tang of the rice vinegar, the texture of the nori (dried seaweed), and the way the fish melted in my mouth. Eight days of ramen noodles and canned tuna made me appreciate any bite of food that wasn't ramen noodles and canned tuna.

While I nibbled on the last piece of nigiri, trying to make the experience last as long as possible, Frank, the Canadian training at the Academy, walked by the window with his friend Papo. Papo was from the Dominican Republic, six feet tall and built like a gladiator. His profile was like the silhouette of a cartoon Christmas tree—forehead, nose, and chin sloping out at the same angle. If he wasn't always smiling, he would have looked menacing.

I had passed Papo in the gym many times, but never actually met him. Nevertheless, he gave me a big smile and a shaka as he passed the window. I didn't know it then, but in a few weeks Papo would change my jiu-jitsu and my life.

I paid thirteen dollars for my filling meal and walked along the bay toward Lili'uokalani Gardens. As I left downtown Hilo, I passed the farmers' market, a collection of vendors squashed into stalls sheltered by a kaleidoscope of colorful tarps. A cruise ship was in town, so I could hardly see the baskets of pineapples and guavas and bananas for the mob of people packed into the narrow aisles of the market. Not interested in fighting crowds, I put off visiting the market.

About five minutes out of downtown Hilo, I crossed the street to get a better look at a canoeing club unloading their gear in the bay. A driver in a black Ford pickup truck slowed and waved me across. I extended my hand and gave him the shaka as I hustled across the street.

When I reached the other side, an elderly couple stopped me. They each wore white floppy-brimmed hats, sunglasses with strings tied to the stems, floral button-ups, and khaki shorts. An expensive camera that looked like an antiaircraft weapon hung from the man's neck. He sported loafers, she spotless white New Balance sneakers. They were haoles.

"Excuse me," the woman said. "Which way is the farmers' market?"

"Just keep following this road along the bay," I said, pointing back the way I had come. "It'll be on the left side of the road. Look for the tarps and the tents."

"How will we know if we've gone too far?"

"You'll see a bunch of restaurants and storefronts, but really, it's pretty big. It's like half a block. You'll see it."

The man smiled and looked at his watch, "We have two hours before the boat leaves. We should be able to make it back in time."

They thanked me and meandered toward the market, the woman pointing out birds and landmarks and oddities, the man rotating and focusing his camera like a fashion photographer. After about ten steps, I thought of something.

They just asked me for directions.

Apparently, I did not look like *that* much of a tourist. They wouldn't have asked me if I had looked out of place or lost. They must have seen me use the shaka as I crossed the street and assumed I was a local. This was a major development. I was making progress.

Elated by this realization, I skipped (in the manliest way possible) along the bay to Liliʻuokalani Gardens, turning off the main street and following my map and the colossal banyans looming on the not-so-distant horizon. The grating hum of passing traffic faded as I moved closer to the gardens. Then I heard it—a weed-whacker buzz fast approaching behind me. I turned, and there he was, riding his little green scooter, the middle of the frame sagging from his disturbingly large weight.

"Brah," he said, stopping next to me, "wan' buy weed?"

"No, I'm still not interested," I said, trying to look angry and assertive.

He squinted and cocked his head to the side, as though he suddenly remembered having talked to me before. Then he shook his head, put his scooter back into gear, and buzzed off. As I watched him pull away, his lard hanging over both sides of his seat, I wondered if the scooter ever got half swallowed up between those behemoth butt cheeks. I pushed the image from my mind and began exploring the gardens.

The gardens were designed with a heavy Japanese influence, dotted with pagodas, bridges, and arches. A shallow pond wound through the grounds, guided by gently curving walls constructed of lava rocks. Most of the bridges were simple slabs with no railings, and like the walls, were made of black stone. The grass was trimmed short like the green of a golf course and covered the small hills of the garden that wove in and out of lava rock formations. The trees here were, for the most part, like the trees at Wailoa River State Park, large and exotic. Mixed in between the palm trees here, however, were conifers and bamboo.

Most of the fish in the ponds were no larger than a minnow, but a few larger fish emerged from the depths, some two feet long. Their noses and tails came to sharp points, and their fins were transparent. I had to find their eyes to tell the front from the back.

Occasionally, a whole school of fish, each about the size of a thumb, jumped from the water in unison. Sometimes only four or five made the leap, but sometimes as many as twenty or thirty left the water and landed two feet away. They didn't always stop after one jump. I saw one school make three leaps, bounding the length of a pond like deer jumping fence after fence. Their small size and speed made them nearly imperceptible. They seemed to teleport from ripple to ripple, looking like handfuls of gravel thrown into the water.

I admired the park from the top of a small hill, beneath the shade of a banyan tree. The park was busy. Locals picnicked in the sun, lying on blankets. Two children, their tan faces hidden almost entirely by oversized bicycle helmets, peddled up and down the gently curving walkways. They peddled down the grassy hillsides, leaning forward, crouching, trying to be aerodynamic.

A dozen yards away from the children riding bicycles, a couple played Frisbee, and past them, closer to the bay, a family erected a tent to picnic beneath. A steady trickle of locals moved slowly along the paved pathways and over the concrete bridges. I seemed to be the only nonlocal.

After half an hour of soaking in the sun, I decided to visit Coconut Island before returning to the dorms to meet Jake. From where I sat, I could see the island out in the bay. Fishing rods leaned against the railing of the bridge leading to the island, looking, from that distance, like jagged spines on a lizard.

As I stood, I noticed a peculiar animal basking on some lava rocks further down the hillside, nearly hidden by clumps of ferns. It looked like a light brown ferret, except it was thicker, more muscular, and as large as a house cat. I moved closer, hoping to take picture. I startled him. He rolled off the rocks and hid in the ferns. A few feet away, another patch of ferns rustled. There must have been more than one.

I was not in a hurry. I sat down and waited. Just as I suspected, after a few minutes, the creatures emerged from the ferns, poking their weasel-looking heads out before stepping timidly into the open. They looked back over their shoulders and up over their rocks like they expected to be jumped by locals at any moment, but they didn't hesitate long. In just a few seconds, two of the creatures were sprawled out on the black rocks.

I later learned that these were mongooses (it's not mongeese; I checked). Mongooses are known for attacking snakes, and they aren't native to Hawaii. No land animals are. The director of the exchange program at the University of Hawaii at Hilo told me that they were brought to the island to kill the rats. Unfortunately, rats are nocturnal, and mongooses are not (based on the mongooses at the garden, they rather enjoy the sunshine), so they coexist peacefully.

Like me, the mongooses were outsiders; they didn't belong. Yet they were relaxing in the sun, enjoying the island just as much as the locals a few yards away. That was the trick. I had to blend in; I had to relax and enjoy the island just as a local would. I was heading in the right direction after all.

The bridge to Coconut Island was only wide enough for two people, so I weaved around the people lingering along the railing watching the surf, taking care not to bump the long, deep sea-style fishing rods. That day, only children were fishing. Two barefoot boys watched the lines of the rods intently while their pug lay in the shade of a folding chair, tied to one of its legs.

He rolled his eyes when I passed, as if to say, "They never catch anything."

The island itself was just a bit smaller than a football field and surrounded by many smaller islands, masses of lava rock with a few trees growing on them (to think that the Big Island started like that, a Cadillac-sized hunk of rock with a single tree growing on it). Coconut Island, like the garden, was well cared for. In the middle was a lush lawn, with a shower, public restrooms, and grills. In some places, walls had been constructed to divert the strong current that normally smashed off the rocks to instead create calm pools where people could swim. A two-story stone tower was at the northeastern corner of the island. Locals raced up the stairs to the peak and jumped into the water below, doing dives, cannonballs, and can-openers.

I sat at the northernmost point of the island and looked out into the bay while I wrote in my notebook. This must be paradise, I thought. The mothers and fathers playing with their kids on the beach, building sandcastles. Kids jumping from the stone tower into the water, laughing and screaming in one big exhale as they splashed into the water. The wafting barbeque smoke mixed with the salty ocean breeze. The fish darting in and out of the rocks. The ocean rolling in the distance. This must be the Hawaii that everyone talks about, the tropical heaven that guidebooks promise.

Even with the idyllic scene before me, I could picture the sun setting, turning a blond-haired exchange student sitting on a bench into a silhouette. I imagined four shadows rising behind him, their bodies wide, their midnight hair pulled back into pony tails. One gripped a baseball bat, loosely, like a sword sheathed at his hip. In my mind's eye, the shadows pulled the blond-haired boy from the bench, throwing him to the ground. He tried to get up, but they struck him down with their fists and their feet. The bat rose and fell like an axe splitting logs.

My phone rang, jarring me from my dream. The shadows receded.

My mom and dad were calling to wish me a happy birthday. Their voices were comforting, but hearing from them reminded me of just how far from home I was, making me miss the Pennsylvania hills even more. They asked me what I thought of paradise. I told them that it was beautiful. They asked me how training was going, and I told them that it was going well. I didn't tell them about the long walks home in the dark or my fears of being jumped. I didn't tell them about the difficult and painful training at the gym. My mom would have just worried.

When I hung up, I took another look at the scene around me and noted that the locals on Coconut Island, like the locals in the gardens, were with family and friends. The phone call had intensified my home sickness, and it lingered like a punch to the stomach. I realized that the people around me were enjoying both the scenery and each other. They would not have had as much fun alone. That realization made me look forward to spending the night celebrating with Jake.

A gang of dark gray clouds gathered over the bay, so I decided I best make it back before it rained.

I got back to the dorms at about 5. Jake wasn't there. I suspected he had popped out for a few minutes and would be back to get me. I made a bowl of ramen noodles and read. When 7 PM came, I showered and shaved. I dressed, putting on my nicest pair of jeans and a fancy T-shirt. I applied extra deodorant. My face was spotted with the shadows of fading bruises, but I thought that might help me meet a girl. Maybe Jake and a few girls could help me adjust to the island and move on with my life. At 8 PM, I sat in my bed, reading. At 10 PM, I grew restless. I checked the parking lot. Jake's truck wasn't there. I thought that perhaps we were just going out late. At midnight, I began to lose hope. At 1 AM, I undressed and turned off the lights.

Jake came in at 4 AM. He smelled like he had bathed in beer. He threw his keys on his desk and collapsed on his bed. I pretended to be asleep.

* * * * *

A week before my birthday, Jake had seen me looking at the entry for Rainbow Falls in my guidebook.

Guidebooks champion Rainbow Falls as one of Hilo's most beautiful attractions. Just a few miles outside of town, the wishbone-shaped torrent of water is said to be a natural wonder, a gem of paradise. *Hawaii: the Big Island Revealed*, my guidebook of choice, says that Rainbow Falls is "not to be missed!" Easily wooed by pictures and description, I put seeing Rainbow Falls at the top of my to-do list. I was willing to make the three-hour walk to see the falls, but Jake, upon seeing the idyllic picture in my guidebook, said that he would drive me, provided I was okay with a couple of girls coming along. I knew what kind of girls Jake kept around—attractive and wild—so I was more than okay with seeing some romantic scenery with a few beautiful women around.

The day after my birthday, without ever mentioning the previous night, Jake drove Shyra, Leandra, and me toward the center of the island, a steady ascent into rain forest. Shyra had a fitness model's body, blond hair, and a lip ring. Leandra's hair was short and curly, like a tanned baby doll. She had recently cut it and donated it to cancer patients. Shyra and Leandra sat in the back and talked about a hiking trip they planned to go on when they got back to the mainland, a forty-mile trek through the mountains. They were tough chicks.

When we took the last turn, I expected the road to wind through the forest, through dense foliage filled with colorful birds and wild flowers. Instead, a short bend brought us to a parking lot. Three tour buses sat idling, their presence ominous, like pirate ships at a merchant port. Slick, clean, rental cars occupied the other spaces. A gift shop was across the street.

A crowd of Chinese tourists filed out of one of the buses, pointing and nodding fervently all the while. White tourists milled around the parking lot, wearing ball caps, khaki shorts, tube socks, and fanny packs. They dragged chains of children and fussed with movie cameras. The whole scene felt like the entrance to an amusement park.

We parked between a minivan and a tour bus, shooting each other worried looks. We followed the sidewalk to the hill overlooking Rainbow falls.

The falls were like an exotic animal in a zoo enclosure, surrounded by concrete walls, tourists blinding it with camera flashes and intruding stares. I wondered if it paced the concrete walls at night, a tiger with its primal instincts flickering in its eyes, wanting to run, to stretch its legs.

Rainbow Falls.

If I focused the falls through my camera's view finder, I could see it just as the guidebooks pictured it. The lens cut out the peripheral intrusions—the railings, the Chinese tourists, the cruise ship beach bums—but their chatter still leaked in, and so did the grumble of passing traffic and the unnatural squawk of cell phones.

The ambient noise reduced the roar of the waterfall to a pathetic whimper. The water seemed to be saying, "Save me."

"This sucks," I said to Jake.

He nodded and ran his fingers through his surfer hair. "Yeah man, this isn't at all what I pictured," he said.

I slumped over the railing. I wondered if all of paradise had become a series of tourist attractions, connected by easy-access paved trails and fenced in by tube socks and fanny packs. I felt like I had traveled to China to experience authentic Chinese food and was served a Lean Cuisine Sweet and Sour Pork.

No matter what the guidebooks said, this was not paradise. The static of modern life polluted this place. I wanted an Eden, a place pristine and wild where I could shed my twenty-first-century self and experience something that that had not been manufactured, packaged, and advertised.

Jake tapped my shoulder. He pointed at a trail that ran up the side of the river, behind the falls. Shyra and Leandra were on their way up, a segment in the worm of single-file tourists gripping the railing as they stepped from one make-shift stair to the next. Shyra and Leandra didn't use the railing.

When Jake and I caught up, Shyra and Leandra were standing at the base of a colossal banyan tree, about to begin climbing the trunk. The base of this particular banyan was two car lengths wide.

We climbed into the tree, its roots and vines making for easy grips and footholds. The fanny packs and tube socks meandered around the tree like lost cattle, admiring the tropical lattice work of branches. A pale chubby boy in a SpongeBob T-shirt ran toward the tree and reached up, ready to ascend into the canopy. His mother grabbed his wrist and jerked him back, angry, as if he had just run out into traffic.

I realized we were the only ones in the tree. The people below kept their distance. They snapped photos and pointed, but they kept themselves behind some unspoken boundary, following the instructions of an imaginary warning sign.

Leandra inch-wormed across a branch, moving farther and farther from the tree's core with every push. She was barefoot now, her sandals lying somewhere in the leaves below. Shyra reclined in the arms of the tree, studying the networks of leaves and branches overhead. I didn't see Jake.

"Where'd Jake go?" I asked Shyra.

She bit her lip ring and scanned the tree. "That's a good question," she said.

"He went that way," Leandra shouted, now facing us, straddling the branch, pointing to a crevice in the hillside farther upstream.

Shyra and I shimmied down the trunk. Leandra let her body slide off the side of the branch, hung for a moment by her finger tips, and dropped two or three body lengths to the ground.

The trail Jake had taken was narrow and muddy. We ducked under branches and stepped over roots. The sound of water rolling over rocks mixed with the hiss of leaves scraping branches in the wind. I didn't see any signs. I didn't see any railings. I didn't see any tube socks or fanny packs.

The trail stopped at the bank of the river, upstream from the falls. A clump of boulders well over a story tall obscured the view upstream. The rocks grew smaller as they neared the mouth of the waterfall. The water was waist deep at the outlet of the trail, and to the left a cove cut back into the hillside. A rope swing hung from a branch. Its frayed, knotted end moved back and forth idly like the pendulum of a broken grandfather clock.

Three men sat on one of the upstream boulders. Two were younger, in their twenties; they wore their hair in dreadlocks, thick and coarse, like the roots of the banyan tree we had just climbed. The one to the left had a rainbow-colored Bob Marley beanie. The younger men sat a step below and on either side of a gray haired guru, his belly round and jovial. They could have been Rastafarian or just hippies. They had joints in their hands.

I stood at the river bank, admiring the view. Shyra and Leandra dangled their feet in the water. Jake turned to the hippie-folk.

"How's it going?" Jake asked.

"What's up, man?" the one wearing the Bob Marley beanie replied.

"Is it always like this?"

"Like what?" the other young man responded.

"Crowded."

They offered a knowing nod, forcing a sad smile, like they were listening to a touching story at a funeral. The oldest crossed his arms and studied us, up and down, as if he were weighing our worth, our worthiness.

"You know, there's a pretty nice swimming hole just over those rocks," he said, tilting his head toward the large boulders up stream. "We just got a good rain, flushed all the debris out. There's a good spot for jumping too."

The other two nodded, the one on the left taking a drag from his joint, exhaling the smoke slowly out of his nose.

Jake turned to me. "What do you think?" he asked.

Before I could reply, I heard a splash behind me. Shyra and Leandra were down to their bikinis, wading across the stream to the boulders, holding their clothes and sandals over their heads. Jake and I smiled at each other, shrugged, stripped down to our board shorts, and followed.

The water was cold, still carrying the chill from the mountain top that birthed it. The water came up to my ribs, its briskness shocking to my sun-warmed skin. It was refreshing, though, like a strong and deliberate massage on sore muscles.

When we reached the rocks in the middle of the river, Shyra and Leandra were almost to the top. Nooks and crevices riddled the boulders, but centuries of sandpaper water flow had smoothed away the sharp edges. The incline was slight, making the journey to the top no more difficult than climbing a ladder. When we reached the top, Shyra and Leandra were standing, their arms hanging loosely at their sides, their mouths ajar, their eyes fixed up stream.

"Oh, my god," Shyra whispered.

I looked up from brushing the dirt from my hands, and saw what she saw.

We stood at the opening of a horse shoe canyon. At the far end, a water fall emptied over a cliff into an emerald pool. Steep cliffs rose up on either side. The cliffs to the left rose highest, like leaning sky scrapers, dwarfing the world below. On these, brown vines hung over the outcroppings and laced up and down the rocks like dried ivy on an abandoned Victorian mansion.

The cliffs to the right were shorter and also leaned over the water like their left-hand brothers. Since there were no vines on this side, the pattern in the rocks was clearly visible; they looked chiseled, like a collection of sidewalk-gray Lego bricks stuck together at random. Couch-sized rectangular stones cascaded down into the water from a nook immediately to the left of the waterfall. A banyan tree rooted itself in a grass landing and peaked out from under the steep overhang. The ceiling of the nook revealed that this river may have once been a grand lava tube whose roof had collapsed, giving the river a view of the Crayola-blue sky.

We were standing on the border between civilization and nature. Behind us, just a few yards downstream, a crowd of tourists gripped a railing, gawking at the fenced-in thunder of Rainbow Falls. In front of us was the real Hawaii, the unrestrained majesty of nature, a paradise born from fire. There were no signs of civilization here. There were no fences. There were no warning signs. Seeing this canyon, our private Eden, was like finally laying my head on a pillow after a long night of driving.

Jake whooped and scrambled down the rocks. Leaving our clothes on the rocks, we dove into the water. As we swam toward the waterfall, I realized that the canyon was deceptively large. After a few minutes of hard swimming, I was winded but had scarcely made it a fifth of the way across the horse shoe. The bass of the waterfall quivered in the pulse of my heart. The cool of the water opened my lungs.

I rolled to my back and did a lazy whip kick, watching the clouds glide overhead like toy sail boats lolling in a pond. The time it took to cross the canyon didn't matter. Time didn't exist. Time was a construct of civilization, and we wanted to escape.

When I turned back to breast stroke a few yards to the rocks next to the waterfall, Shyra and Jake were crawling up the rocks to the banyan tree growing out from beneath the outcropping. Leandra was bouldering a narrow crevice in the rock face adjacent to the waterfall, one foot braced in front of her, one foot braced behind, trying to shimmy her way to the top.

In the shade of the overhanging cliff, beneath the banyan tree, a stick had been driven into the ground. Sandals were stacked over the stick in a vertical column like battle souvenirs. Whoever had been here before us, swimming in these waters, climbing on these rocks, soaking in this sun, must have seen this place in the old way. The sandals were an offering. Others had come here to escape tour buses and camera flashes and rental cars and left changed.

While Shyra and Jake climbed the banyan and Leandra tried to climb to the top of the crevice, falling over and over into the water below, I sat on one of the rocks at the edge of the water, tracing rippling figure eights with my toes. I tried to gauge the depth, studying how the jigsaw spikes and valleys of rocks faded into blackness. The more I strained my eyes, the more I convinced myself that I could see another layer of silhouettes. The current shifted the shadows; they moved as though they were breathing, as though the river bed was alive.

Shyra came down from the tree and sat next to me. Neither of us spoke. We didn't need to. We just breathed, inhaling the canyon. We sat there for a while, it may have been hours, it may have been minutes, or it may have been a millennium. The sun still shined; the water still flowed.

Jake jumped over our heads, cannon-balling into the water. He surfaced in a freestyle stroke, swimming hard back the way we had come.

"Where are you going?" Shyra yelled after Jake.

Jake paused, whip kicking for a moment. "I'm going to jump," he said, looking back over his shoulder before resuming his stroke.

"From where?" Shyra asked.

Jake turned, smiled, and pointed at a boulder near the rocks we had climbed to reach the canyon. It was over two stories tall.

"Wait! Wait!" Shyra yelled, jumping into the water, replacing the trail of Jake's subsiding wake with her own.

Leandra floated in my direction, cradled and carried by the slow moving current, her chin submerged. She surfaced for a moment, a playful grin on her face.

"Aren't you coming?" she asked.

I shrugged.

Leandra splashed me, laughed, and swam away. I dove in after her, chasing the froth of her kicking feet. When we reached the base of the rock face, Shyra had one arm wrapped around a rock, resting. Jake lingered in the open water. He took a deep breath, dove, and, after a few seconds, surfaced, gasping. He repeated this process five times.

"What are you doing?" I asked Jake.

He smoothed his wet hair from his eyes with both hands in one sweeping motion. "Trying to decide if this water is deep enough for jumping," he said, panting.

"Is it?"

"I think so," Jake said. Then he began to chuckle. "I guess we'll find out for sure," he added as he turned to swim for a gentler incline.

In moments, Jake was at the top, spreading his arms. We watched from below as he surveyed his landing zone, bouncing and rubbing his hands. He took a deep breath and bent his knees. He launched into the air, sailing out over the water. He waved his arms in tight circles, as though he might be trying to fly. He landed feet first and disap-peared.

I tensed, hoping that the water was deep enough to cushion his fall.

Jake surfaced a second later, spraying water from his mouth, splashing and whooping. While Shyra raced him to the top, I ambled up a different path and reclined in the sun at the peak of a rock forma-tion a few yards from where Jake and Shyra were jumping. Leandra found a spot farther downstream.

I watched Jake and Shyra jump from the cliff a few more times. Eventually, they settled next to each other at the top of the cliff, their backs to me, facing the waterfall at the far end of the canyon. Shyra rested her head on Jake's shoulder. Shyra's back rose from a tense deep breath, and slowly fell, relaxing as she exhaled. Seeing Jake and Shyra together made me miss Hilary. I wanted her to see this place. I wanted her next to me, sharing in the experience. We had planned this trip together.

I tried to feel bad for myself—as I had for the majority of the trip—but with the scenery around me, I couldn't. The people that I had left behind, an ex-girlfriend and the false friends, were sitting in a college apartment in southwestern Pennsylvania, snowed-in, pass-ing around cans of cheap beer. I was getting along fine by myself.

Sitting on the rocks, bathing in the light of a tropical sun, admir-ing the view, I realized that my spirit was exhaling too, letting out a heavy sigh for the years I'd spent rushing and worrying and ignorant.

I relaxed. The curtains of my eyes slipped to half-shut. I lay there for some time. I savored the air, the fragrance of the water, and the perfume of the rainforest. I watched as the sun shifted the shadows cast by the trees and the rocks. I listened to the waterfall; the distance turned its thunder into the whisper of a lover sharing secrets beneath sheets.

My back was to Rainbow Falls, but I knew that the tour buses and concrete were still there. I knew that I would eventually have to return to civilization, to schedules, to classes, to bills, and to a job.

But I wanted the dirt to stay under my fingernails. I wanted the water to stay in my hair. I wanted the smell of the rocks to stay on my skin. I wanted to become this place.

PART TWO: CONTROLLING POSTURE

"When I was a boy, the Sioux owned the world; the sun rose and set on their land. They sent ten thousand men to battle. Where are the warriors today? Who slew them? Where are our lands? Who owns them?"

—Sitting Bull

REFUGEES

When I left for Hawaii, I didn't get any parties or any phone calls. The only people to wish me off were my parents and my little brother. They walked me to the edge of the security lines, stopping just beyond the warnings listing banned substances in three different languages. My mother had the same look in her eyes that she had when she dropped me off for my first semester of college, except this time she knew that there would be no weekend visits or coming home for holidays. That realization manifested itself in a subtle glaze of tears.

My father was solemn. He's a 1950s sort of man, who minds his family and his work and doesn't cry. He hugged me, his jagged calluses scraping my hoody as he patted my back. His face, weathered from work, was rigid, and he stood so straight that he seemed to be leaning back. He was being strong, as always. It occurred to me that I never told him that I loved him.

My little brother was quiet. He rubbed his eyes. He was going into the second semester of his freshman year and was basically nocturnal. It was 5 AM, and he hadn't gone to sleep yet. He came along mostly because my parents wanted him too. At that point, we weren't very close. We grew up beating each other with sticks and building forts, but us being only two years apart meant that we both dealt with growing up at about the same time, so for the last few years we hadn't gotten along. He hugged me just the same.

They watched me go through security and disappear into the depths of the airport. I never looked back, but I know that they watched as long as they could.

In Arizona, I turned on my cell phone. My phone vibrated. Hilary had sent me a text message sometime in the morning.

It said, "Godspeed." In retrospect, her brevity was condescending.

Once I had Internet access in Hilo, I sent her an e-mail describing the things I had seen and the things I had done. She responded swiftly. She critiqued my metaphors and my similes and said nothing else.

I decided that such e-mails and insights into my life were better suited for the people that still cared about me. From then on, I sent them only to my family. I quickly realized that of the things I missed about the mainland—familiarity, well-stocked kitchen cabinets, roach-free environments—I missed my family the most.

Like air, they had always been there, and I took them for granted because of that. And not until they were gone did I understand what they meant to me.

✳ ✳ ✳ ✳ ✳

I've never been one for school or going to class or doing homework. If I'm not interested in or passionate about something, it's hard to work at it or stay focused. School has always bored me, and my grades tended to reflect that.

So when I was living on a tropical island just down the street from the gym of one of the best fighters in the world, sitting in a lecture hall taking notes on the role of mitochondria in the synthesizing process of cellular energy or wading through enough research on T. S. Eliot's *"The Waste Land"* to fill an Olympic swimming pool was not appealing. If I ever wanted to graduate college, though, I had to pass my classes.

But I had been in Hawaii for over two weeks and had not seen BJ Penn.

He wasn't teaching because he was deep into a strict training regimen, preparing to fight Joe Stevenson for the UFC's lightweight title. I learned through eavesdropping and general inquiry that BJ did most of his training in the mornings and only rarely trained in the afternoon or evening.

I still wanted to be BJ's apprentice. I wanted him to take me under his wing and personally lead me to a blue belt. BJ, however, was elusive. To show that I was a willing student, I had to take the initiative.

BJ Penn was more important than school.

I skipped my morning class on world literature and went to the gym an hour and a half early. My plan was to casually enter the gym, and if anyone confronted me about my sudden shift in schedule, I had a story prepared. I would tell them how I pulled a hamstring (I would even abbreviate it to "hammy" to suggest that I was familiar with this injury. I also rehearsed a slight limp to make my story more believable) and came to the gym to properly stretch the muscle before class. I had debated forging a doctor's excuse, but I decided that no tough guy (and I desperately wanted to be a tough guy) would see a doctor unless it were serious, like maybe a bullet wound or a case of the clap.

I sauntered into the gym, wearing my backpack in the most nonchalant manner possible, hanging on one strap, suggesting that I was responsible enough to pack my valuables into a reliable container but individual enough to not conform to the "proper" two-strap use of a backpack. Claudia, a plump Californian with curly blond hair and an aged face, was working the desk. She was at the computer, glancing back and forth from a ledger book to the screen, typing intermittently.

I swiped my membership card through the scanner.

"Have a nice work out," the automated computer voice chimed sardonically when my card was verified.

Claudia glanced at me. I panicked.

"I pulled a hammy," I said, patting my leg. I had forgotten to limp through the doorway. My cover was blown. I was going to be banned from the gym. I would never get to see BJ, let alone train with him.

"I'm sorry?" Claudia said, a quizzical look on her face.

"I think I'm going to stretch it," I said, sliding the other backpack strap on to my shoulder, deciding that rebellious people aroused suspicion.

"Good luck," she replied, turning back to the screen.

"Thanks," I stammered.

I opened the door at the back of the gym and stepped onto the balcony overlooking the boxing ring and cage. I saw a bald figure in white board shorts amid a crowd of fighters grappling in the boxing ring. Where the other fighters strained and stumbled and sweated, this fighter moved effortlessly, as though he never touched the mat, gliding from position to position like an ethereal being.

It was BJ Penn.

The tightly wound spring swung the door shut with a thunderclap slam. I cringed, visualizing the small army of professional pain-dispensers leaving the ring, climbing the stairs, and giving me a hostile talking-to before vaporizing me with punches and submissions. When I opened my eyes, the fighters, BJ among them, were still training. Some boxed, bouncing off the ropes, covering their faces with faded and worn sixteen-ounce gloves. Others wore four-ounce gloves and fought takedowns, clinching, sprawling. BJ was on the mat, moving from top position to top position on some poor fighter who was bigger but not nearly as talented.

I crept down the stairs. With a distressing moan, each wooden plank lamented the trespass of a star-struck neophyte. The fighters in the ring paid no mind. When I reached the ground floor, I recognized BJ's sparring partner.

The fighter being dominated and controlled and tossed about the ring was Hermes Franca, a former lightweight title contender. Like BJ, Franca was in the upper echelons of the 155-pound division and was also a black belt in Brazilian jiu-jitsu. He was an experienced and talented mixed martial artist.

And BJ made him look silly.

Franca's face was tense, and he hyperventilated, his body marinating in sweat. As if his limbs were coated in cement, he dragged them from position to position with deliberation.

BJ, on the other hand, looked like he might be ready for a nap. His mouth was closed, his face blank. He flowed from position to position at will, moving like a toreador, forever one step ahead of the slower, heavier Franca. He countered each one of Franca's movements, making it look like Franca had never grappled before.

A bald Hawaiian, more sumo wrestler than mixed martial artist, glanced sideways at me. I realized that I was staring, mesmerized, maybe a dribble of drool lulling on the crest of my chin. I nodded and shuffled to the changing room.

I watched the rest of BJ's training like a voyeur, peeking around the mat room's plywood wall. I was in awe. He didn't seem human. If BJ could dismantle a top-level professional fighter and fellow black belt without breaking a sweat, what could he do to me, a low-level white belt?

I wanted to find out. I wanted to grapple BJ Penn.

From that day on, in every jiu-jitsu class, I stared expectantly at the doorway to the mat room, hoping that BJ would step onto the mat and offer to roll with me. But I would have to wait.

Meanwhile, fitting in at the University of Hawaii at Hilo was a challenge on a par with fitting in at the gym. My classes were a mix of mainlanders and locals from various islands. Some of the mainlanders were attending UH Hilo on a four-year program, and others were there on exchange through the NSE program like I was. Almost all of them were haoles.

They were nice enough, but they were focused on beaches and parties. And beaches were a sensitive topic among exchange students. A great many had assumed that the university was within walking distance of the beach, like a resort (and the definition of "within walking distance" depended exclusively on the definer's level of laziness). Finding transportation to and from the beach was a challenge. And the beach that they were getting transportation to was usually 4-Mile or Richardson's, both of which were beyond the airport. They were also the typical kind of beach found on the Big Island: rock and coral with almost no sand. Lava rock is not comfortable for lying on and tanning. Coral is notorious for dicing up haole feet. And a rocky beach makes water sports, like surfing or body boarding, difficult.

When I tell people that I lived in Hawaii, they usually ask me if I learned to surf. I didn't. Surfing on a sandy Oahu beach is difficult enough. But the Big Island does not have the right beaches for learning to surf. With all of the water up in the air in wave form, its cushion becomes pretty thin. Slip off the board and the ocean is slam dunking your ass into the reef. The ocean isn't always unforgiving, however; with the right tide on the right beach, learning to surf can be very pleasant.

That said, of the five months I spent on the Big Island, I only visited a beach six times. I didn't come to Hawaii for the beaches. I came to Hawaii to train. That difference set me apart.

As far as parties go, I was also an outsider. I wasn't a drinker. I didn't like the taste of beer or hard liquor. I didn't like being drunk. The idea of not being able to control my actions had never appealed to me. And (as may be apparent by now) I was socially awkward. The fewer people around to see me bumble and stutter the better. So the crowded, red-Dixie-cup party scene never suited me. With training five days a week, I was even less inclined to stay out late and wake up late in the afternoon with a hangover. Again, I didn't fit the norm.

Dr. Mark Panek, the professor teaching my fiction writing class and author of two books focusing on local Hawaii culture, confirmed that I was indeed an anomaly among exchange students. We were sitting in his office, a cramped cinderblock room typical of a small university professor. The books that couldn't fit in the shelves were relegated to piles on the floor, rising waist high around his desk. He left the overhead lights off, allowing the 8 AM sun to leak in through the window behind his desk. Backlit, long shadows streaked his large ears and pale bald head. He was a haole. He had a cup of coffee in his hand. A handwritten draft of my short story, "Romeo Is Bleeding," lay on his desk.

In a way, Panek already knew a bit about me. I didn't meet the prerequisite requirements to enroll in his fiction writing course, but the NSE coordinator suggested that I send him an e-mail pleading my case. So I did.

Until that point, I kept my writing experience to myself. The university I attended on the mainland was populated mostly by the same types of people I went to high school with. To achieve—to get a good grade on a test or to win an academic award or to excel in some professional way, was a justification for scorn. If I got an A on a test, I turned it face down and acted like I had performed badly. I didn't want to be lumped into the nerd category. I was a nerd in hiding.

I decided I wanted to be a writer when I was a freshman. After excelling in my composition courses, I approached writing with the same intensity that I approached other things that caught my interest, with an obsessive dedication. I wanted to write for video games and didn't see any point in waiting until after graduation to start. I put a resume and a writing sample up on a GameDev.net and after some false starts, landed my first freelance contract. For six months, I wrote character dialogue for Studio Archcraft's Nintendo DS title *The Black Sigil*. I was nineteen.

I pursued video game writing for a few more months after that and even debated moving into writing for table-top role-playing games like Dungeons and Dragons (yes, I played D&D and enjoyed it. Anyone who has a problem with that can meet me at the flagpole when school lets out), but I discovered Brazilian jiu-jitsu. I stopped playing video games and focused all my energy on the art. Thinking that a video game writer who doesn't play video games would be about as weird as a nature writer who doesn't go outside, I shifted my focus and started writing about grappling. The summer of my sopho-more year, I suggested to Charles Pearson, the owner of Lockflow. com, that he hire a columnist to consistently produce content. I also suggested that that columnist be me. After a few sample articles, he agreed and started to send me monthly checks.

My minor credentials were enough to get me into Panek's class.

"You're an NSE student, right?" Panek said, leaning back in his desk chair, rocking back and forth with the tempo of a lazy porch swing.

"Yes, sir," I said groggily. Juggling classes and training left me in a state of permanent exhaustion. Meeting in the morning, sacrificing half an hour of sleep, caused physical pain.

"What brings you to Hilo?" he asked. He laced his fingers to-gether, his elbows on the arm rests of his chair.

"I came here to train, actually."

He cocked his head.

"There's a UFC fighter that has a gym in Hilo," I went on. "BJ Penn. I came to train at his school."

He looked me up and down. My black eye and Gracie Jiu-Jitsu T-shirt must have made more sense. "An NSE student that didn't come for beaches and sunshine, that's a change," he said. "What do you think so far?"

"I didn't expect the culture shock. I mean, it's like a different country," I said. "It gets pretty frustrating sometimes."

"What do you mean?"

"I'm pretty sick of being"—I paused to use air quotes at this point—"'a fucking haole.'"

"You can't take that personally," Panek said, leaning forward. "That anger—anger that comes on *sight*—is rooted in a long history of well-meaning haoles flooding onto this limited land space across generations. For Hawaiians that has meant loss of land, destruction of culture, and near extinction of their language. The typical haole response to the anger is always personal: '*I* didn't take your land!' But the local guy still sees it happening all around him today in one form or another. He sees Native Hawaiians at the bottom of a range of social indicators that spans areas like public education, mortality rates, incarceration rates, addiction rates. He sees Oprah Winfrey telling a national TV audience that the best place to *invest* in real estate in 2004 is East Hawaii, and then property values in what was one of the only affordable areas of the state skyrocket. Who gets displaced? Who winds up having to move to Las Vegas? And who moves in?"

I didn't know what to say. Panek shared a quote with me from an interview in *Big Happiness*, his recent book on the effects colonization has had on the type of local guy who might be quick to call out a young haole for nothing more than looking at him the wrong way. Kevin Chang, a lawyer working for the Office of Hawaiian Affairs who grew up on the rough edge of Oahu's tough windward side, helped Panek contextualize *stink-eye* and *fuckin' haole*: "The big, lifted 4x4 with the tinted windows and the chrome rims, all the tattoos, the mean looks, the pit bulls," Chang said, "these guys are obviously all trying to compensate. They've been castrated on their own home ground. They know on some level their lives have been taken from them and reduced to doing some menial work to make someone else a lot of money. They may know what was taken from them over the course of generations. . . . The trucks and the tattoos, being all bad . . . even turning to drugs, or worse, to dealing—that may be the only way these guys have left to assert some kind of manhood."

I held my head in my hands. I hadn't realized the far-reaching consequences of colonization, especially given Hawaii's relatively recent annexation. I felt guilty for how I viewed Hawaiians and locals. I had judged them without knowing their whole story.

"So imagine being a local. You're on the beach with your family, a beach your family has visited for generations, and here comes a car full of people from the mainland. They're loud. They're obnoxious. Maybe they're outbidding you on property. On top of all that, they're expecting your 'aloha.' The 'fucking haole' thing makes more sense then."

I nodded. Panek was a haole like me. He may not have been a human mop at the BJ Penn Academy like I was, but he had experienced the same confusions and frustrations with Hawaiian culture. His time living on the island and time spent researching his books gave him a perspective on Hawaii not found in my guidebook. I could use Panek's knowledge rather than trial-and-error my way to understanding the people around me.

"You have an edge over most NSE students," Panek said. "You came here for something distinctly local. They love BJ Penn around here. He's a local guy, one of their own, who made it. If you want a good experience here, stick with the locals. It usually doesn't take much to get past that initial anger—just show some respect. And stay away from all those NSE students who spend all their time trading stories about how 'racist' this place is."

Panek also stressed the importance of distinguishing between "locals" and "Hawaiians." A Hawaiian has Hawaiian blood, a direct lineage to the people that populated Hawaii before Captain Cook ever set foot on the islands. Locals aren't necessarily Hawaiian. They may have grown up on the islands and may even feel a strong sense of pride and loyalty to the islands, but they are technically not Hawaiian. Locals can be of any ethnicity, Pacific Islander, Chinese, Japanese, Korean, haole, black, whatever. Hawaiians and locals may overlap in many ways, such as in the way they dress or in the way they speak or in what food they like; they may even share a similar sense of injustice stemming from the effects of colonization, but ultimately, Hawaiians were the ones that suffered from it.

This distinction also means that there is a difference between "Hawaiian" culture and "local" culture. Hawaiian culture is connected to the original inhabitants of the island, while local culture is what has arisen from mixing Hawaiian culture with the diverse collection of cultures championed by the individuals that now call Hawaii home. In this way, Hawaiian culture has influenced—and plays a major role in—local culture, the culture of which nearly every resident on the island is a part, but local culture does not influence Hawaiian culture because Hawaiian culture applies to a very specific set of people.

In short, the term *local* applies to the people living within the geographic boundaries of Hawaii, while *Hawaiian* applies only to those genetically connected to native Hawaiians.

After talking to Panek, I was on the Hawaiians' side. I hated haoles. I felt guilty for being white. I felt the same way when I first read about the Trail of Tears or slavery. I felt responsible for what people of my race had done. I wished that I could somehow undo the tragedy.

I felt like I had a better understanding of my training partners. Colonization had emasculated them, taken away their distinct roles as men that they once knew in their culture. Perhaps jiu-jitsu was a way to prove that they still had the warrior qualities that their grandfathers and great grandfathers championed. Maybe they weren't so different from me: they were using jiu-jitsu to develop a part of themselves that the rest of the world counted out. I was far from a complete understanding of the people on the Big Island, but Panek's insight cleared away some of my ignorance. I still had a lot to learn, and Panek was a valuable guide (and he kind of liked my short story).

Even though I was more familiar with the plight of Hawaiians, being on the receiving end of racism was still hard to stomach.

To make new students feel welcome, the university had a festival. There was food. There were games. There was music. Naturally, the whole celebration was Hawaiian themed. There were lei. There was pork. There was spam.

Though Jake wasn't an NSE student, he was a new student. We went to the festival with some other NSE students. People filled the performance area, an open-air pavilion with about as much seating as one would find at a fairground. A steady drizzle kept us huddled at the edges of shelters, just out of reach from the rain. The majority of the thirty or so NSE students were mixed among tan-skinned, dark-haired locals.

Jake was wearing his usual garb: a pair of flip flops, board shorts, a white wife beater, and a backward baseball cap. I followed him through the crowd. I hadn't talked to him about my conversation with Panek. Jake had obviously had his share of bad experiences with locals, and I didn't want to push the issue. We got some punch and settled at the back of the crowd. I tried, and failed, to avoid the water dripping from the pavilion roof.

Local bands provided the music. Reggae, based on my observations, was the most popular music on the Big Island. Rap and hip hop were a close second. In the gym, no other type of music was played. Once, when I got to the mat room before anyone else, the radio was off. I tuned it to a classic rock station (I never found an alternative rock station. I had to use my iPod or the Internet to get my angry haole music fix). I was in the middle of a full lotus stretch when a local jiu-jitsu student came in. Queen's "Bohemian Rhapsody" was playing. I was enjoying it.

"Brah, who put this rubbish on?" he asked me.

I shrugged. "It was on when I got here," I said.

He shook his head and adjusted the dial. After a few coughs of static, he found his station of choice. Flo Rida's "Low" was halfway through. I held on to the echoing chords of Queen as long as I could, but her apple bottom jeans and the boots with the fur quickly replaced them.

The more popular radio stations seemed to play a mix of reggae, rap, and hip hop. The reggae they played ranged from local talent to reggae legends like Bob Marley. Marley was something of a local hero. His image adorned T-shirts, stickers, flags, and tapestries. While I was on the Big Island, the Bob Marley Festival came to Kona, a touristy city on the dry side of the island. His message of peace and love and cultural loyalty seemed to mesh well with the "no worries" philosophy of Hawaii. Also, Marley is an icon of marijuana culture. I didn't have much experience, but I saw more than a few public instances of ganja smoking in Hawaii. And if the marijuana-by-scooter local is any indication, there's a market for the stuff on the Big Island (or in Hilo at least).

For aspiring local musicians, reggae seemed to be the genre of choice. So, the next band setting up at the festival, like the band before it, played reggae. They started to tune their instruments. Jake and I weren't paying attention. Jake chatted up some girls. I talked to some guys from the NSE program (I had no idea how to talk to girls).

The band started to play. The crowd of locals swayed to the reggae beat and cheered when the singer approached the microphone.

I was explaining why I was on the island and how jiu-jitsu works (I had that conversation a lot) when Jake hit my arm.

"What's up?" I asked.

His usual ear-to-ear mischievous grin was gone. He was pissed. "Listen," he said.

I listened. I hadn't paid much attention to the music. It had drifted into the background. The cheering of the crowd made hearing difficult. I focused. The lead singer was on the chorus.

"Haoles to my left, haoles to my right," he sang, "I think I'm going to get violent tonight." He repeated it. "Haoles to my left, haoles to my right. I think I'm going to get violent tonight."

"Fuck this shit," Jake said. He walked out into the rain, back toward our room.

Even though I knew Hawaiians had their land stolen, even though I knew Hawaiians were struggling to preserve their culture and maintain their identity, even though I knew that haoles had infected the islands, I couldn't handle the racism, especially at a university-sponsored event.

I followed Jake to the dorm.

Until I came to Hawaii, race was never an issue for me. I was raised to be accepting of others' differences, but then again I lived in a predominantly white area and never really had to contend with racial tension firsthand. Now that it was all around me, I wasn't sure how to cope. I frequently found myself switching sides. If I had a bad experience with a Hawaiian, like a particularly rough rolling session or some stink-eye on Kinoole Street, I found myself on the side of the haoles. When I was in the company of haoles who mostly talked about tanning or drinking, I was on the side of the Hawaiians. From a distance, it's easy to say that the right thing to do is to ignore color completely. But being in the midst of it is different. When someone attacks you for your color, reverting to an us-versus-them philosophy is like a reflex. When you're being attacked, you want allies, people that are like you.

Hawaiians felt attacked by haoles, so they teamed up with other Hawaiians.

Haoles felt attacked by Hawaiians, so they teamed up with other haoles.

Logically, I knew that the majority of the people living on the Big Island weren't outwardly aggressive toward outsiders, but a few negative experiences flavor a whole crowd.

How could such a cycle be broken? Maybe throw a wussy haole kid who loves jiu-jitsu into a mat room with Hawaiians who love jiu-jitsu and see what happens. Maybe, just once, the cycle could be broken.

THE ADVENTURES
OF THE RED BARON

unlight—warm, like a heat lamp bulb. White sand—fine and as soft as powder. Water—blue as raspberry Jell-O, pulsing, breathing. Wind, kicking and hissing, twirling dust devil tornadoes up and down the beach. Bodies, like plastic dolls, dressed and posed, picnicking, sunbathing, reading. Trees, lining the hill, shading the rocky footpath down to the shore.

Hapuna Beach.

I had fallen asleep. I sat up and lifted my sunglasses and rubbed my eyes. My board shorts were still damp, and the wind had folded my towel up around my legs. Sand stuck to my toes.

Jacqueline, an NSE student from Minnesota, was lying on her stomach to my right, reading an issue of *Cosmo*, brushing grains of sand from the glossy pages each time the wind blew. Sarah, an NSE student from South Dakota, was lying on her back to my left, tanning. They both had iPods. Generic pop leaked from Sarah's headphones. Jacqueline listened to country.

I met most of the NSE students at dinner in the cafeteria. If I was training, I didn't have time to sit and eat. I would fill a to-go plate, leave it in the community refrigerator of my dorm (Hale Kauanoe), and hustle down Kinoole Street to the Academy. When I came back to my room around 8:30 or 9 that evening, I would shower, eat, finish an article for Lockflow, think about doing some homework, do laundry (a daily battle to keep my training gear clean) and go to sleep by midnight.

After a few weeks of attending class in the morning, training at noon, coming back to campus for class again, filling a to-go plate, and training in the evening, I knew that I couldn't maintain that routine and stay healthy. I was perpetually tired and perpetually sore. I slept through many of my classes (Bio Lab on Tuesday afternoons was especially difficult to survive. My lab partner did not appreciate my routine dozing, especially since we shared a grade). As I neared the end of the first month, I knew that I needed to rest. I was the only student at the Academy training twice a day. I stepped into each class stiff, a month's worth of bruises coating my body, slowing my movements. I grunted and moaned, painfully lifting my gi pants to my waist and tying my belt. Unlike the other students, I was never fresh for a class. With only a few hours separating each training session, I never fully recovered. I began to think I was overtraining. If I stayed exhausted, I decided, I would be prone to injury and to sickness. And I still didn't feel welcome in the class, which added to my frustration and exhaustion. I started taking the Tuesday night no-gi class off.

The first Tuesday night I took off, I went with Jake to the cafeteria. If I wasn't in class or at the gym, I was doing homework or sleeping, so I didn't have much time to meet people. Jake did. Since many NSE students lived on our floor, Jake had already become friends with most of them. We sat down at the end of a long table, populated by a combination of students from the mainland, both NSE and traditional.

I didn't say much. The warm food on my plate had my full attention (I was sick of eating ramen noodles after about a day). Mahimahi. White rice. Loco moco. Fresh pineapple. Yogurt. Cheesecake. Bliss.

The students at the table complained about Hilo's frequent rain. They expected more sunshine. They talked about going to Kona to party. They talked about that night's coming beer run. They talked about what beaches they wanted to see and how tan they wanted to get. They discussed flying to Oahu for the Pro Bowl and how great the parties in Honolulu would be when they did. I was only half-listening, but talk of visiting Honolulu led to talk of Pearl Harbor.

Then Sarah said, "I don't see why everyone wants to visit Pearl Harbor. What's so special about it?"

The table went silent. Jake held a fork full of rice in front of his mouth, frozen, his eyes fixed on Sarah.

"It's Pearl *fucking* Harbor," Jake said.

Sarah looked at him. "So?"

Jake said, "Pearl Harbor is a big deal."

"Why?"

Jake dropped his fork. It tinged off his plate.

I interjected. "Because of what happened there," I said.

"What happened there?"

Jake put his head in his hands. "Holy shit," he said, half-whispering.

"It was bombed," I said. "In World War II."

"They made a movie about it," Jake said, beginning to rub his eyes.

"I still don't see what the big deal is."

"I'm getting dessert," Jake said, standing quickly and walking away from the table.

With heads shaking, the rest of the table resumed eating. I was horrified. To know so little about her own country or the place she was now living—to not even have accidentally heard about Pearl Harbor—how does that happen? I suspected a voluntary ignorance, an intentional, willful desire to be uninformed. Stupid haole, I thought.

Conversation at the table eventually turned to me. They asked where I was from, what I was studying, and why I came to Hilo. My first two responses were pretty generic. The last one inspired a few quizzical looks.

"You came here to what?"

"To train."

"Like, in a cage?"

"Something like that."

"That's crazy."

"I might be, a bit."

Jacqueline asked me if I was going on the Hapuna Beach trip, which was sponsored by the NSE program; they were providing transportation and food, and most of the NSE students were going. Jacqueline batted her eyelashes. At the time, I didn't pick up on what that meant.

The weekend following that dinner, a yellow school bus took me and the majority of the NSE students up the Big Island's east coast. The road traced a near perfect outline of the island, bending and twisting and jackknifing at each inlet and each rocky outcropping. Once we cleared Hilo, the view was consistent: rain forest on the left, ocean on the right. After a few miles, we cut inland to stop in Waimea and pick up food.

Cinder cones—hills as tall as water towers and symmetrical, like they were formed from sandcastle molds—surrounded the town. These steep conical hills form around or downwind of volcanic vents. The trees weren't thick, lush rainforest trees. They were scraggly and weathered.

The air was chilly when we stepped off the bus—shorts and hoody weather.

When I told my lab partner that I visited Waimea, she said, "It's freeze-ass, yeah?" Well, it was not as warm as Hilo, but freeze-ass to me meant a few feet of snow and frozen water pipes (at least).

A few months later, I overheard locals at the gym talking about Waimea. A Filipino police officer said, "You know, we have all the seasons on the Big Island. Up on Mauna Kea, it's winter. Hilo is spring. Kona is summer. And Waimea is fall."

Permanent seasons. What a place.

We got back in the bus and drove to the Kona side, cutting across the upper half of the island. We parked on a hillside overlooking Hapuna beach. And we poured out of the bus. Like children at recess, most of us ran down the hill to the beach, dragging towels, bags, and toys. I didn't realize how much we stood out until I saw the faces of a local family just about to light a barbecue in one of the nearby pavilions.

They looked sad, as if they had just spotted rain clouds. Perhaps they had—a rain cloud of obnoxious haoles, thundering, stealing the sunshine, their trampling eroding a local backyard.

I swam a bit, but I didn't have the energy or coordination to skim board or body board or snorkel with the other NSE students. I went to sleep instead.

When I woke up from my nap, I tried to read a chapter of Tim O'Brien's *The Things They Carried*, but the wind was too strong. I slathered on a new layer of sun screen (a Pennsylvania winter had left me a ghostly pale). I knew that sun burned skin wouldn't go well with a gi top and mat time (I began to realize that I was making decisions based entirely on how they would affect grappling). I got up and walked down the beach, toward the cliffs at the southwest end. Sarah and Jacqueline didn't notice my stirring.

An off-road-equipped jeep with surf boards strapped to the top was parked on the rocks, thirty feet or so above the beach. Three or four locals, college-age men, sat on the rocks, barefoot and shirtless, loosely hugging their knees. They watched two local women and another local man of about the same age jump from the cliff into the water. The jumpers didn't hesitate. They held hands and stepped to the edge and leapt, smiling and laughing as they fell. I envied their courage.

When I came back to my towel, the NSE students were gathering for a group picture. Jacqueline waved for me to join the group. As

I stood on the beach, posing smiling, I wondered what the fighters at the Academy would think if they saw me with a mob of haoles. Would it be another reason for them to reject me? Another reason to grind my face into the canvas?

As we drove through Waimea, back toward Hilo, it began to rain. The sun at our backs sent five rainbows arching through the cold valleys, weaving in and out and over cinder cones. We rounded a bend and dipped into a shallow valley. On the right, Mauna Loa, Mauna Kea's short fat, little sister, spread out across the horizon. To my left, a wide rainbow cascaded into a field. It touched the ground. The other students on the bus remarked about the impossibility of this, yet there it was, the end of a rainbow.

I wanted to see what other wonders the island had to offer.

But the rainbow wasn't good luck. I got a sunburn.

* * * * *

I wanted to see lava, real lava—burning or melting or flowing or oozing or doing whatever lava does. I wanted to throw rocks in it. I wanted to poke it with a stick. I wanted to watch it run into the ocean, throwing steam and water into the air.

JB, Jack, the Red Baron, and I went hiking in Volcanoes National Park to find lava flow.

JB was a geology major. A big chunk of his heritage was Brazilian, and it showed. He had a dark complexion, short black hair, and a matching mustache. He was generally soft spoken, but his voice shifted to a smooth Barry White whisper when he leaned over a girl, his hand outstretched, propped against a wall. He could have any woman he wanted when he talked with that voice. They swooned on command. JB was from a military family, so he moved around a lot, but he had spent the last few years living on Oahu. Now, he was attending class with me at the University of Hawaii at Hilo on the Big Island.

Jack was not Brazilian. Jack was a big white farm boy from Wisconsin whose prized possession was a brown hat with a fish hook on the bill. At first glance, the hat seemed to have a camouflage pattern, but, really, the dark splotches were stains from various adventures: a bit of blood from de-horning cattle, some mud from duck hunting, and some grease from fixing a tractor. His face looked like Dopey from *Snow White and the Seven Dwarves*, except with a bit more chub and a bigger smile. Jack's knowledge of biology was staggering, and he aimed to be a large animal veterinarian.

The Red Baron was the product of one of Jack's schemes. An exchange student like myself, Jack had no way of getting around the island. Quickly growing tired of walking and spending money on taxis, Jack began searching Craigslist for an affordable vehicle. By affordable, I mean cheap, as in "let's count the change in the mason jar" cheap. After multiple false leads, Jack found a 1986 Mazda pickup truck, the Red Baron. Jack and JB split the $550 price tag, which was the owner's counter to their original $650 offer. Yes, the owner insisted on lowering the price.

The Red Baron had manual steering, manual windows, and manual defrost. The radio was on the floor of the velvet cab, and operating the air conditioning was an exercise in deduction: "Did that make it hot or cold?" "Uhh . . . hot. Turn the knob the other way." A strategically positioned piece of plywood replaced the bottom of the original truck bed, which had rusted away some time ago. The red paint was chipping, and the back windows of the cab didn't slide as much they bounced and caught. Jack duct taped a small American flag above the passenger door.

My favorite part of the Red Baron: grass grew at the point where the cab and the bed met. The grass didn't seem to be struggling either. It was about five inches long and a lush green.

The Red Baron, despite its receding bed line and flakey shell, ran like a champ.

At 11 AM on a Sunday morning, we loaded our gear into the Red Baron. Jack, despite JB's recommendation to wear pants, wore shorts. I was slightly more prepared with jeans, but like Jack, I was wearing tennis shoes and had packed only a rain coat, some water, a flashlight, and a first aid kit.

Jack, JB, and the Red Baron.

JB, on the other hand, was wearing heavy-duty hiking boots, the kind with thick tread, heavy brown canvas, and ropelike shoestrings that laced halfway up his shin. JB's belt had a clip for his GPS, a clip for his camera, and a loop for a hammer (for extracting geological samples). He was wearing a gray Columbia all-weather jacket, and he packed his flashlight, water, trail mix, first aid kit, spare batteries, and assortment of maps into his waterproof backpack. JB had been up until 3 AM packing and planning for our trip. I put on jeans ten minutes before we left.

We drove south of Hilo, toward Volcanoes National Park. I road in the cab with JB, and Jack sprawled out in the bed. Shortly after clearing the city limits, on a highway cutting through mountain rainforest, it began to rain. We were driving fast enough that the cab shielded Jack from the rain, but the tread on the Red Baron's tires was nonexistent. After hydroplaning two or three times, JB and I decided that it would be safer if we pulled over and brought Jack into the cab. Being the smallest, I was pushed into the middle, the bitch seat. JB reached awkwardly under my scrunched legs to shift gears.

The drive took about fifty minutes and ended 3,000 feet above sea level. Every 1,000 feet or so, according to JB, the temperature dropped ten degrees. The elevation coupled with the rain made our trip cold and damp.

When I say cold, I don't mean Hawaiian freeze-ass cold. I mean cold like my home in rural Pennsylvania. Anytime a local said that it was "cold," Jack and I rolled our eyes and laughed. Granted, Jack's Wisconsin cold is worse than my Pennsylvania cold by about twenty degrees and a few feet of snow, but the sentiment was the same.

We stopped at the visitor center, finding a spot among tour buses and sparkling rental cars. Wearing rain jackets and carrying backpacks, we seemed out of place amid the sea of tourists in flip flops and floral button-ups. It later occurred to me that other than using the bathrooms and visiting the gift shop, these people would never leave their rental cars. They followed the loop through the park, their rolled-up windows and hard tops sheltering them from the rain and the risk of ever having to actually experience the island they were vacationing on.

The inside of the visitor's center was filled with fancy maps and diagrams and narrated videos. JB studied the wall maps intensely, comparing the trails and estimating distances with the routes listed on his personal maps. Jack and I thumbed at brochures and poked at displays. Bored, I stood next to JB and scanned the map.

"We should take Destruction Trail," I announced, choosing the route based entirely on its name.

"Destruction Trail? Oh tits!" Jack said, appearing next to me. Whenever Jack said "tits," it was meant to mean excitement or approval, kind of like "cool" or "sweet." On the other hand, when he called someone a "tit," which is something Jack did frequently, it meant that person was a jerk or lame or otherwise disagreeable.

JB chuckled and continued looking back and forth from the wall map to the maps in his hands. Jack and I really had no say in what trail we took; JB had the maps and the GPS and the keys. JB could have just told us that we were taking Destruction Trail, and we wouldn't have known the difference.

While we continued to survey the map, a park official approached us.

"Do you gentleman have any questions I can answer for you?" he asked. His name tag said Mike. Mike was pale and had glasses and a Bill Gates sort of look. He was also passionate, helpful, and sincere.

"We were just figuring out the best route to the lava flow," JB said.

Mike frowned and squinted, like a professor trying to decide how to politely tell a student that his answer is wrong, really wrong. "Let me see your maps," he said.

JB handed Mike his maps.

"See," Mike said, "this lava flow isn't there anymore. We got a bunch of earthquakes in July that closed off that lava channel."

JB was visibly embarrassed about having outdated maps. "Where is it now?"

"It's outside of the park now in some pretty thick rainforest," Mike said.

JB had a GPS. Jack and I had our tennis shoes, and the Red Baron was waiting patiently outside. We could find our own way to the lava flow. Our faces must have betrayed our silent scheming.

"Lava burning through rainforest," Mike said with a grave face, "is pretty dangerous. The burning foliage causes a buildup of methane gas, which can lead to unpredictable explosions."

We thought unpredictable explosions were pretty cool, and we were still planning on winging it and hoping for the best. Mike was responsible and perceptive, though, and he headed us off.

"The only way to visit the flow legally is by helicopter. If you're caught hiking remotely near the flow, you get a $2,500 fine," Mike said.

We could afford to die, but we couldn't afford a $2,500 fine.

"Those tits," Jack said, referring to the state officials who decided upon the fine.

Mike recommended a trail off of Chain of Craters road that led to a lookout for Mauna Ulu. I later learned that JB had planned on taking this trail if the lava flow search didn't pan out, so JB was still prepared despite our minor setback.

We hopped in the Red Baron and took the long way around Kilauea Caldera. JB wanted to show Jack and me some of the major craters.

Breaking free of the rainforest into the lava field felt otherworldly. Pure desolation, like the surface of the moon covered in cinders, stretched to the horizon. Piles of black debris covered the landscape. JB parked the Red Baron, and we walked down a collapsed lava tube to the edge of Halema'uma'u Crater, the largest crater in the park. The rotten-egg smell of sulfur hung in the air. The chilly rain and piercing wind drowned out all other sounds in a ghostly howl, whistling off the black and gray rocks piled around us.

To talk to each other, even from a few feet away, we had to yell. We couldn't even hear cars passing on the road a mere ten yards from where we stood.

And where we stood was quite spectacular.

Some 2,500 feet wide and 3,000 feet long, the massive expanse was humbling. We were flies at the edge of a swimming pool, miniscule and inconsequential. The force of nature that blew this hole in the ground was more powerful and more destructive than anything man has been able to manufacture. In the distance, sulfur deposits blanketed the floor of the crater like sheets of yellow snow. Just beyond the deposits, smoke billowed up from a fissure. A rusty sheen tinged the rock around us, which JB said was the result of iron deposits. The spatters of shimmering dark green were from olivine crystals (a mineral crystallized by magma).

Just off the edge of the cliff, about thirty yards below us, mist formed a rainbow, the rust-covered blackness of dried lava flow making a stark backdrop. I admired the poetic symbol of the rainbow while JB smashed up rocks with his hammer and examined samples. There seemed to be plenty of crushed samples just lying around. Perhaps the destruction all around us was the result not of a cataclysmic volcanic eruption but the persistent tapping of geologists' hammers. Jack listened to JB lecture about mineral deposits and lava flow, while I kicked rocks over the edge of the crater, watching them fall 300 feet to the bottom.

At the edge of Halema uma u Crater.

After taking some photos and extracting lots more sample, we drove the Red Baron farther around the rim of the caldera, stopping at Keanakako'i Crater, an unimpressive hole in the ground. If

Halemaʻumaʻu Crater, the crater we just left, was an atomic bomb, Keanakakoʻi Crater was a firecracker. Some shrubs with wirelike stems and small waxy leaves grew around its rim and down its slope. Surviving in the lava field environment was a testament to their hardiness. They looked like trees growing up out of a parking lot.

JB hopped the guardrail and walked toward the edge of the crater. The closer to the crater he got, the smaller the rocks became, shifting from surfboard-size chunks to tiny pieces of gravel. The edge of the crater was like the lip of a sand dune.

"I don't think that's a good idea," I said.

JB prodded the ground with an extended toe before stepping forward. "It's fine," he said. "I do this all the time."

Jack and I sat on the guardrail, cringing each time JB committed to a step.

JB reached the edge and leaned over, looking down a couple of dozen stories to the bottom. He started to yell and flail his arms—losing his balance.

"Shit!" Jack shouted, reaching out as though he were going to snatch JB.

JB spun around and laughed. He bent over, putting his hands on his knees, guffawing.

"You tit!" Jack yelled, giving in to laughter shortly after.

We drove south on Chain of Craters road to the trail that would take us to the lookout for Mauna Ulu Crater. We parked the Red Baron next to a shiny SUV and set out on the trail.

Making a visible trail over dried lava flow is difficult. With little foliage to trample through and no trees to mark with colorful signs, park officials have to be more creative. To keep hikers from losing the path, reflectors lined each trail like bright yellow Post-it notes. Hiking through a volcano park was just a huge game of connect the dots.

Though the hike to Mauna Ulu was only about a mile and a half, it took us over an hour because we kept stopping to admire miniwonders: dried lava swirled like black cotton candy around trees, hardy green plants with little red leaves at their tips growing on nothing but gravel, and U-Haul-sized pillars of rock thrusting out of the ground like massive black corks.

The rock pattern here was different from the caldera. The caldera was rubble-strewn. Around Mauna Ulu, however, the flow had dried in mounds, like overlapping bubbles. Jack described it very appropriately as looking like the surface of a burned hot dog.

The trail up to the lookout zigzagged through dense rainforest. Water cascaded down the trail in a steady stream. Halfway up, I wanted to turn back. The rain had soaked my jeans. The wind chilled my skin. I hugged myself to keep warm. Jack, in his shorts, must have felt it too, but despite the permanent grimace on his face, he denied being cold. JB, in his thick coat and hiking boots, seemed unaffected. He marched ahead of us, his hood up, checking his GPS intermittently.

Finally at the top, we could see the Mauna Ulu Crater smoking in the distance, its rim towering over us. A dried lava lake was just beneath it.

Seeing smoke plumes leaking from the ground was unsettling. Somewhere, far beneath the surface, a fuse was burning. Geologists have been studying volcanoes for decades, but their ability to predict eruptions and shifts in lava flow is still limited. Technically, the volcanoes on the island were still active. They could come back to life at any time. We were standing on a ticking bomb, which I thought was pretty cool.

Closer to us, thick vegetation filled an older, smaller crater. We could see the trail winding into the distance. Most of what I could see was the gray moonscape of dried lava flow. At one time, the entire expanse must have been covered in red and yellow and white magma, a seething, advancing wave of intense heat and destruction. Now, a forest of trees, at the edge of a gray rainy fog, ringed the horizon.

JB wanted to hike to the summit of the Mauna Ulu Crater, despite there being no official trail. He was confident that his GPS could get us in and out safely. The rain started to blow in sideways sheets, whipping our hoods against our faces. I shuddered. Water soaked through my budget rain jacket and dampened my sweatshirt. Water beaded on Jack's bare shins.

Seeing our shivering bodies and our grim expressions, JB said, "Maybe next time."

I wanted to hike through lava tubes and explore steam vents, but if I was ever to see lava, I would have to wait for the flow to shift.

Our hike back went faster than the hike out; we braced against the wind and shuffled. The Red Baron was alone. We crammed inside the cab. Once again, I got stuck in the middle. We fiddled with the air conditioning and after a few minutes, heat billowed from the musty vents. On the way back, JB pushed the Red Baron to 55. The engine grumbled as we wiped the fog from the windshield with our hands.

An eighth of a mile from our dorm, JB swerved onto the shoulder and slammed the Red Baron into park.

"Check the right front tire," he said, looking at Jack.

Jack wheeled the window down and leaned out. "Yep," he said. "It's flat."

The tire jack that came with the Red Baron was too small to lift the Red Baron high enough for us to remove the tire, which didn't matter because the spare tire that came with the Red Baron was flat. JB called a friend, a short blond girl named Laura, and she provided a jack and transportation to and from a mechanic to have the spare tired filled with air. There wasn't enough room for all of us to drive back and forth from the gas station, and I had to pee, so I walked home alone on a stretch of Lanikaula that I took to and from the gym every day.

The trip was a success. We saw the beginning of the island, lava turning to rock, pathetic scraggly plants digging their roots into porous stone. Life birthed from nothing, a modern day Eden.

We didn't see lava flow. The weather was miserable. And the Red Baron got a flat tire. But those were just minor details. The important parts still worked. The engine still ran, and the grass still grew.

PAPO DROPS A
CANADIAN IN A RIVER

ust when Jay Penn was beginning to give me a noticeable amount of individual attention—giving me advice after a roll, correcting my technique more frequently—he went to England. BJ was fighting Joe Stevenson at UFC 80 for the vacant lightweight title (Sean "the Muscle Shark" Sherk, the previous champion, had tested positive for nandrolone metabolite and was stripped of the title), and most of the Penn family accompanied him for support.

Up until that point, Jay had taught all of the classes, afternoon and evening. Renato Verissimo and Tomas "Papo" Soñe took his place.

Verissimo went by "Charuto," his nickname and moniker. It means "cigar" in Portuguese, and it suited his long, narrow frame. He got the nickname while playing water polo in Brazil. When some of Charuto's friends began training jiu-jitsu, he decided to try it as well. Grappling won his heart, and Charuto earned his black belt in his mid-twenties from Andre Pederneiras. He eventually moved to Hawaii and started training MMA. He had three fights in the UFC, one against UFC Hall of Famer Matt Hughes. In that bout, Charuto nearly submitted Hughes with a triangle choke.

I read an interview where Charuto was asked how Hughes was able to escape; the triangle looked tight, perfect. Asking a fighter a question like that is like asking a football player how he could have fumbled what would have been the game winning catch or asking a soccer player how he could have shanked a crucial penalty kick. These things happen in sports, but for athletes, the sting of what could have been lingers.

Hughes went on to fame and fortune. If Charuto had won that bout, perhaps that fame and fortune could have been his. His life could be different. The year before my stay in Hilo, Charuto attempted to stage a comeback into MMA, fighting twice for Icon and then against Jake Shields in EliteXC. He lost to Shields. At the time of my stay, Charuto was teaching jiu-jitsu and working a full-time job. Among grapplers, Charuto was well-known, but to casual MMA fans he had faded to obscurity, exemplifying the tragically unforgiving nature of the sport: fans are quick to turn and promoters are quick to forget. Charuto deserved the same amount of recognition as Hughes, but for different reasons. Charuto's teaching ability and technical knowledge were astounding, and he genuinely cared for his students as much as he loved his art. A champion in different respects, but a champion nonetheless.

When Charuto returned to teaching (a pinched nerve in his neck had sidelined him for a few months), I was there for his first class. The locals jumped to their feet to shake his hand. Some called him Charuto. Most called him Sensei. Even the Penn brothers (when they happened to be in class), called Charuto Sensei. When Charuto taught, even BJ became a student, asking for advice and accepting criticism. The first thing I noticed about Charuto was his belt. Jay's black belt was fairly new. BJ's was worn and somewhat tattered, but the black had only just begun to fade. Charuto's black belt was frayed like an old T-shirt, and the black ink had faded to a light gray. He had been training for a long time.

Renato "Charuto" Verissimo (photo courtesy of Thomas Kappler)

Charuto smiled and greeted everyone, calling most of them "cousi'." He spoke with a distinct Portuguese accent, but his English was pretty good. On rare occasions, he struggled with word choice, but he was always elated when the right phrasing finally came to him.

"Here you try to . . . try to . . . How you say . . . You try to . . . you try to trick him! Yes! You trick him! I love dat word, trick! It's such a good word. You try to trick him!"

One time, he came to class wearing a baseball cap, and not feeling the need to remove it, he put on his gi and taught the class. A gi with a baseball cap—I had never seen such a thing. That was Charuto's demeanor. After all, who is going to tell him, a world-renowned black belt and known badass, that it was wrong or looked comical? Yeah, no one (and if he reads this book, I want him to know that I think baseball caps should be worn regularly with gis).

Charuto was also vocal about his opinion of whatever happened to be playing on the radio. If he disliked the song, he told the class. If he liked the song, he told the class.

Once, when a high-pitched rapper came on the radio, Charuto blurted, "Man if I ever meet da guy who sings dis song, oh man, you know . . . Gah!" The class continued to roll. "Man, what is 'is problem? It's like somebody cut off 'is balls or something! 'Weeaahh! Weeahhh!' I should be singing dis song!" It was hard to keep rolling after that. The whole class was laughing.

Later that class, when Usher's "Yeah," came on, Charuto began to dance, sliding and gliding through the sea of bodies grappling on the floor. "Aw man, I love dis song!" he said.

Charuto would teach intermittently for the rest of my time in Hilo, but Papo was only in Hawaii for a few weeks.

I originally thought that Papo was Brazilian, mistakenly assuming that any tan-skinned grappler speaking with a Spanish sounding accent was Brazilian. Papo was more serious than Charuto, and his English wasn't as good, but it was good enough. And though he only taught for two weeks, he changed the way I grappled forever.

One afternoon class, Papo announced that we were going to focus on the triangle choke. A triangle choke is finished with the legs, typically from the guard position. The fighter on the bottom traps his opponent's head and one of his arms (only one) between his legs. To turn the position into a choke, he locks one ankle in the bend of the opposite knee (sometimes called a figure-four). The finishing pressure pinches the carotid arteries, cutting off blood flow to the brain.

Throughout the week, we had been focusing on more advanced sweeps and counters. To spend ninety minutes on a choke that most white belts learn in their first day seemed wasteful to some students, but once Papo started teaching, I immediately saw the value of his instruction.

Papo and me.

In jiu-jitsu and in martial arts in general, coaches and fighters often say that "basics win fights." A kickboxer may know, in theory, a dozen different kicks—a crescent kick, a hook kick, a spinning hook kick, a side kick, a spinning side kick. In a fight, he'll probably only use a round kick (a simple swinging of the leg, in a baseball bat motion—generally delivered to the legs, sometimes to the body and head) and a front kick (a big step forward—it looks like the fighter is just pushing his opponent away with the flat of his foot). He probably learned those kicks in his first class. They are simple, direct, and effective. He doesn't expend a lot of energy using those kicks because they are simple and because he has practiced them more than the fancier, more advanced kicks. The strategy for baiting an opponent into leaving an opening for a round kick or a front kick may be advanced, but the kick itself is basic.

Fancy techniques have their place, but in reality, most fights are finished with a basic technique. Everyone knows the right hook, yet it has ended countless fights. In jiu-jitsu, a triangle choke is like a right hook, and my triangle choke sucked. In theory, I knew the move, but in application, I struggled. I could get to the triangle position, but my opponent escaped before I could lock in the submission.

Papo fixed my triangle.

He showed the class a strategy for tightening the figure-four without losing the position. Then he showed the class his personal variation for applying finishing pressure. Compared to how I had been taught to apply the pressure, Papo's method was unorthodox, but it made more sense to me and fit my style. When we rolled at the end of that class, I used Papo's techniques to finish three triangles. Christian, one of the lab technicians I had met on my first day, tapped to two of those triangles.

"Somebody's been paying attention in class. Good student, good student," he said, laughing.

After training ended, I lingered, watching some of the other students roll. I didn't have class that afternoon, so I was in no hurry to walk back. Papo sat down next to me.

"Marshal, did you like class today?"

I told him that I did.

"Good. Class was for you."

I didn't understand.

"You always getting the triangle. So close. But trouble finishing."

He had been watching me roll, and his critical eye spotted a problem with my fundamentals. His personal attention had a near-instant effect on my grappling ability. His dedicating an entire class to me shocked me.

"With these moves, you can finish. You train hard and learn fast. You have nasty triangle soon," Papo said.

I thanked him, profusely.

Papo patted my shoulder and smiled. "No worries," he said, standing. "Keep training. Love jiu-jitsu."

I was still getting the shit kicked out of me, but at least I was learning.

* * * * *

The atmosphere in which you watch a fight has a profound effect on the experience. Watching a fight in person with 30,000 screaming fans is much different from watching a pay-per-view at home with family and friends. Watching BJ fight Joe Stevenson from the mat of the BJ Penn Academy was an experience unlike any other. The entire Hilo community was invited to "Come Support Local Hilo Boy BJ Penn." Fliers were hung all over town: in store windows, on community bulletin boards, at the university, and in grocery stores.

I walked to the gym with Britany, a local from Oahu. She was part Hawaiian and part Japanese (among other ethnicities). She was a year younger than me and was studying environmental science. I met her through JB at dinner one night, and because she did judo in high school (in Hawaii, judo is a high school sport just like football or wrestling), she had an interest in jiu-jitsu and in MMA. I was the only person in our circle of friends that knew anything about fighting, so we talked a lot about martial arts and training and BJ. But from the beginning, she took a distinct interest in me. At the time, I had no idea what signals to look for, romantically speaking, and I immediately counted her out because she had a boyfriend on Oahu. Looking back on it, she was practically holding a sign that said "date me."

I, as usual, was oblivious.

We left the dorms at about 7:30 AM that Saturday morning. Since the card was in England, UFC 80 was airing in Hawaii at 10 AM. Britany and I decided that the mat would fill up fast, so we left early. As we walked to the gym, she flooded me with Hawaiian trivia—the names of trees, customs, the meanings of Hawaiian words. I forgot most of the facts shortly after (I was overloaded and frankly quite distracted), but one piece of information stuck.

Kinoole Street.

Britany asked me which route we were taking to the gym.

"We'll just go down Kinoole. It's easiest," I said.

Britany laughed.

"What's so funny?"

She struggled to catch her breath. "What street are we taking again?" she asked, smiling and poised to resume laughing as soon as I responded.

"Kinoole."

She started laughing again. "That's not how you say it."

For all of January, my whole first month in Hilo, I pronounced it as "Kin-ool." Britany informed me that it in Hawaiian, each vowel is pronounced, so Kinoole is pronounced "Keenoh-oh-lay."

Son of a bitch. How many locals thought of me as just another dumb haole when I mispronounced Kinoole? More importantly, why didn't anyone bother correcting me?

Anytime conversation lulled, Britany would mispronounce Kino-ole and resume laughing. When I told her that she was cruel, she said, "Oh, I'm only joking" and hugged my arm, pressing her head against my shoulder as we walked. She was holding up that sign again, but I didn't see it.

We arrived at the gym at about 8:30 AM. Two big-screen televisions were in the mat room, and the windows were covered with black cloth to eliminate glare. Signs beneath the televisions read "Uncle Charuto says !! No !! !! Touch !! Mahalo." Soon after our arrival, students, locals, and fighters began claiming their seats in the mat room of the Academy, leaving their shoes and sandals at the door. Papo and Frank, the Canadian lightweight that I trained with on my first day, arrived as well. Frank was wearing baggy shorts and an oversized basketball jersey. His hat was on sideways. We exchanged shakas. As the start of the live broadcast neared, the mat slowly disappeared beneath a sea of bodies. The audience was full of men and women, young and old. Some bore the marks of fighters—black eyes and cauliflower ear. Others were local fans, wearing fishing hats and polo shirts. A few had beards that reached their stomachs, a few wore tight jeans and converse shoes, and others had board shorts and sunglasses. Some reclined on blankets and towels, while most were content with the padding of the blue canvas. Children ran back and forth across the front of the room and played in the corners. TapouT and BJ Penn garb were common.

As the card progressed, the crowd consistently cheered reversals and applauded knockouts. There seemed to be little preference for one fighter over another. Applause was given for well-executed techniques and hard punches no matter what competitor they came from. Having watched other UFC cards in public places on the mainland, this surprised me. Often times, mainland fans boo as soon as fighters hit the ground. They see the ground game as boring, and if fighters aren't constantly brawling, they see that as boring as well. In Hilo, they appreciated both heart and technique. A smooth guard pass was worthy of just as much praise as an exchange of punches. As the sport grows in popularity and mainland fans learn more about the technique involved in MMA, their demeanor is improving, but they still have a long way to go.

Britany bumped me whenever something exciting happened.

When Penn and Stevenson began their pre-fight banter, the room erupted with cheers. The flow of adulation tripled when Penn said, "This is the wrong time to fight BJ right now."

A middle-aged man behind me told an older man, "B.J. is such a soft spoken guy." He spoke with a reverence, a whispered respect, as though if he spoke too loud BJ might hear him. I agreed that BJ was soft-spoken, but I always wondered why he referred to himself in the third person in interviews.

The bout with Stevenson was especially important for BJ. When he fought Matt Hughes in 2006, a rematch, he lost in devastating fashion. At the end of the second round, BJ had Hughes in a reverse triangle but wasn't able to finish. Going into the third round, BJ looked tired. His mouth hung open. His hands drooped. Soon, Hughes had BJ on his back. He pinned one arm with his legs and the other with his right arm. Then, Hughes dropped hammer fists on the defenseless BJ until the referee stepped in. Ever since that fight, critics accused BJ of not taking training seriously. They said that he had no cardio and relied too much on his natural talents and not enough on proper preparation. A decisive victory over Stevenson would prove the critics wrong. Sitting there in the mat room, I felt as though the people around me felt the same urgency; they wanted BJ to prove everyone wrong. They wanted BJ to show the world that he was still a champion.

The lights of the Metro Arena went down. The mat room went silent. Hawaii's state motto, *Ua mau ke ʻea o ka aina i ka pono* (the life of the land is perpetuated in righteousness) proceeded Israel Kamakawiwolʻoleʻs "Hawaii 78," a song that laments Hawaii being stolen from its people and westernized. When BJ emerged, making his way through the crowd to the cage, the room thundered with clapping, cheering, and hands slapping the mat. He wore a "Kau Inoa" T-shirt. I had heard that Kau Inoa was part of the Hawaiian independence movement, but at the time I knew very little about the organization or of the degree of BJ's involvement. When BJ finally stepped from his corner and touched hands with Stevenson, the room was quiet again, each person on the mat leaning forward in tense anticipation. Even the children that played and romped through the previous fights were quiet, their elbows resting on their knees, their hands holding their faces, like they were listening to a bedtime story.

With each blow Penn landed, the room boomed.

A construction worker to my left said, "That's it, buddy. Come on!"

Anytime Penn took a punch, I could see reflected in the mat room mirror the face of a mother wincing, her hands held up by her face, throwing jerky jabs as if she were willing Penn to block and counter.

At the end of the first round, everyone in the room was on their feet. The energy was tangible. Each person in the room was emotionally invested in the fight. BJ was their local hero. He grew up among them. Now, he was representing them on an international stage. BJ's fight was their fight, and they came to the mat where he bled to support him.

In the opening minutes of the second round, it was clear that Stevenson's will had been broken. He bled profusely. He seemed lost, disoriented. The moments leading up to Stevenson's submission were a steady escalation of cheering, hands rising little by little before they became full-blown victory pumps. BJ sank a rear naked choke. It was deep. When Stevenson finally tapped, the floor quaked from whoops, claps, stomps, and jumps. Hands raised in victory. Hugging. Tears from the motherly.

I had pitched my account of watching the fight from the Academy to *Ultimate Grappling* magazine. I wanted to explain the feelings of the crowd, to verbalize the connection that locals felt with BJ. I asked Britany about it .

"You can see the support; it's undying," Britany said. "We're big time on supporting family. We all kind of have this connectedness. . . . It gave me chicken skin to know that he was out there, from Hawaii." As I scribbled her reply onto a notepad, she leaned over my shoulder, pressing herself against my back and said, "Oh what, you going to make me famous?"

I laughed, again not seeing the sign.

When I returned to my dorm, I told Jake that Britany had accompanied me to the pay-per-view. He said, "She seems pretty into you, man."

"Nah, she has a boyfriend."

Jake laughed. "So?"

"That means she's off the market," I said, packing my dirty gis into my hamper.

Jake lay down on his bed and pulled his laptop on to his stomach. "Maybe she just wants benefits."

I didn't reply right away. I considered what Jake had said. A few moments of silence passed. "Benefits?"

"Sex."

"Ohhhhhhh."

* * * * *

Papo left Hawaii the weekend after UFC 80 to return to the Dominican Republic. Since the Penn family was staying in England to sight-see, Jay wasn't coming back right away, so Papo taught class up until his flight. Papo's friendly personality and relaxed demeanor made him popular in the gym. Nobody had anything bad to say about him, and when word of Papo's impending departure spread, everyone wanted to exchange goodbyes and have their pictures taken with him.

Some of the fighters, Frank among them, wanted to give Papo a proper send-off. So, they took him out for a night of drinking. The next morning, before training, Papo told and retold the highlight of the party (with Frank sitting quietly on the mat next to him):

"Me and Frank were on dis bridge with dis girl, and she was a bit . . . whas the word . . . drunk. She was a bit drunk. So she go to give Frank a hug, and she hit his hat. His hat went 'wheeew' and fell into the river."

Papo often resorted to sound effects and exaggerated hand motions to compensate for his somewhat limited vocabulary.

"So Frank was like 'oh man! I love dat hat!' I guess it makes him look gangsta and he wanted it back and it was down in the water. So he says to me, 'Papo Papo, hold my ankles. I want my hat back!'"

A huge grin spread across Papo's face at this point, and he extended his arms, pretending to hold Frank's ankles.

"So I'm holding Frank over dis river, and is like two in the morning and is cold! And I start thinking, man it would be funny if I drop Frank. I didn't know how deep the water or if dere were rocks, but I thought even if Frank hit his head, even just a little bit, the funny be worth it."

Papo opened his palms.

"So I let go of Frank, and he go 'Whoo . . . Splash!' Frank get all wet! We in the middle of the city and Frank is all wet! Oh it so funny."

Frank agreed that it was funny, and everyone laughed.

"But he got his gangsta hat back. So it all okay."

Going into that training session, I was feeling pretty good. I was tired and sore (I was never not tired and sore), but Papo's instruction was too good to be missed on account of something as trivial as soreness. I was still getting ground into the mat in merciless fashion, and my homesickness was increasing. If my jiu-jitsu was moving forward though, I was getting closer to my blue belt. That was enough to keep me going.

Then I met Kahali'ilani Nali'ipo'aimoku Seiji Suganuma. His friends called him Poai for short (and don't ask me how to pronounce his full name) I actually heard a few Hawaiian names that were even longer than Poai's.

When I first saw Poai, I was walking to the mat room. He stood by the heavy bags, adjusting his hand wraps. He fought at 205 but walked around somewhere near 240. Whenever visitors stepped onto the mat, they marveled at his size and athleticism. He looked like a body builder with Abercrombie Model sensibilities. A Hawaiian Hercules.

Poai threw a jab, a dull thud. The cross and hook that followed crashed like a wave. The chains holding the bag squeaked as the 120 pounds of sand began to swing. He stepped forward, clinching with the bag. He skipped a leg back and drove a knee into the canvas. As the knee came down, he switched his feet and struck with the other. I decided, quite quickly, that I never wanted to be near those hands, and I was really happy that he didn't take the afternoon jiu-jitsu class.

I met Poai forty minutes later when he stepped on to the mat to roll with me.

Poai Suganuma murdering a heavy bag (photo courtesy of Thomas Kappler).

Besides being much larger (I only weighed 160 pounds) and stronger (my girlfriend used to open jars for me), Poai was a professional fighter. His grappling ability was more advanced than mine. A few seconds into our match, Poai had passed my guard and settled into side control. His weight combined with his pressure collapsed my chest, making inhaling difficult. I fought to keep my posture, protecting my arms and defending the mount. Poai shifted his weight. He tried to mount; I blocked it. He tried to submit me with an Americana; I hid my arm. Poai did a quick push-up and planted his knee in my ribs, on my right pectoral. It hurt, but I decided I could survive it.

Poai turned his hips. His knee dug into my chest and twisted. A horrific pain wracked my chest. I was certain that one of my ribs had broken and was now spearing my lung. I yelled in pain and frantically tapped Poai's leg. He hopped to the side and looked down at me. I clutched my chest and writhed on the mat. My eyes watered. I felt like I had been stabbed. Breathing hurt. A rib had to be broken. It had to be.

Papo came over and knelt next to me. He held my shoulders still and prodded at my ribs, checking to see if anything was broken.

"It feel okay," he said.

I stood. I walked to the bathroom. I leaned my head against the closed door and sobbed. It still hurt. I was tired. I was sore. I was homesick. I was frustrated. The pain in my ribs, in my chest, pushed me over the edge. I don't know how long I stood there, my head pressed against the door, crying for myself. Once I caught my breath, and could inhale without pain, I splashed water on my face and returned to the mat room. I shook Papo's hand and wished him a safe flight. Poai apologized. He was sincere. I didn't know it then, but Poai and I would become friends.

I took the evening session off to recover. I slept. After some rest, I decided that my ribs were, at the worst, bruised. I breathed without pain, but the area was tender to the touch. The weekend passed without incident, and I returned to training. I couldn't quit. I couldn't go home defeated. I had four months of training left. I resolved, again, to get my blue belt at all costs.

When Jay resumed teaching, it was class as usual. A warm-up of jogging, push-ups, crunches. Thirty minutes of guard passing. Some instruction and drilling. Lots of rolling. On the Thursday afternoon of Jay's first week back, we did a takedown drill. Two pairs started on their feet and fought for a takedown. Whoever got the takedown stayed. The loser went to the end of the line.

I had very little experience with takedowns. Most jiu-jitsu schools have their students start grappling from the knees (in Hilo, this was also the case, typically). Starting from the knees requires less space and eliminates incidental injuries that occur from having someone your size or larger falling on you. Since a great many jiu-jitsu fighters do not practice takedowns on a regular basis, they tend to not be very good at them, especially in comparison to a wrestler who has done almost nothing but takedown work his entire life. In a street situation, this isn't much of a problem. If an attacker has no experience grappling, tripping him is pretty easy—that's assuming he doesn't charge in and try and put you on the ground first. In the cage, however, jiu-jitsu fighters have consistently struggled with takedowns. Sure, a jiu-jitsu black belt is a submission wizard on the ground, but if he's fighting a wrestler who can defend takedowns, the ground-phenom is stuck boxing, which often ends badly for the jiu-jitsu man.

It should be noted that this is a new development. Before anyone knew jiu-jitsu, bringing a fighter to the ground and submitting him was no problem for a black belt. Now, any serious mixed martial artist trains jiu-jitsu along with wrestling and kickboxing. To win a fight, you have to be able to funnel your opponent into your strength. A kick boxer uses wrestling to keep from being taken by a grappler. He wants to stay on his feet and strike. A good jiu-jitsu fighter, like BJ, uses striking to set up a takedown that eventually brings the fight to the mat.

If I was going to step into the cage, I needed wrestling. But at that point, I sucked at fighting on the ground, and I sucked even more at takedowns. I had no formal instruction on initiating a takedown or how to deal with common counters. I had watched a few instructional videos, but all I really knew to do was to grab a leg (or better yet, two) and drive forward. I fought valiantly, but I was slammed repeatedly. Jay laughed at my flailing. I continued trying to impress him through effort alone.

As we neared the end of the takedown drill, I gasped for air. It was my turn again. A local fighter named Kris (not to be confused with tattoo-artist Chris) shot in. He had wrestled in high school. I managed a sprawl and improvised a reversal. We scrambled, somersaulting across the mat. We came back to our feet. Kris shot a double and authoritatively (forcefully) put me on my back.

I stood up. My left knee felt stiff. Jay taught a takedown. I tried to drill it, but my knee wasn't cooperating. I looked down. My knee was swelling. Fluid. Bulbous. It continued to swell until even walking was a struggle. I called Jake and asked him to pick me up at the gym.

I hobbled into the cab of his truck.

Jake looked down at my leg. "Knee?" he asked.

I nodded.

"Fuck."

Jake had blown out both knees playing soccer. I too had had knee surgery from a soccer injury (on my right). We both knew the potential consequences. Sprain? Rest and anywhere from a week to two months. Cartilage tear? Surgery and six weeks. Tendon or ligament? Surgery and six months. My health insurance wasn't valid in Hawaii. I couldn't afford an MRI. All I could do was wait and hope the swelling went down.

Jake helped me to our room. I showered and collapsed on the bed. I wondered what I would do without jiu-jitsu—my reason for coming to Hawaii, my escape. I couldn't think of anything.

Then the rain came.

10

HILO RAIN

On the windward side of the Big Island, Hilo received almost daily precipitation. Oftentimes the rain only lasted for a few minutes, a quick downpour or a light misting, but Hilo weather bothered a great many of the NSE students. Frequent, unpredictable rain interrupted beach trips and ruined tanning.

On one occasion, I mentioned the frequent rain to JB. He chuckled. "Oh, you haven't seen real rain," he said.

The week I injured my knee, the real rain came, and it stayed.

You hear it first. A whisper in the distance, coming from down the hill, beyond the bay. Some gray clouds edging the horizon. The whisper grows to a hiss, and you see it, a far off static, an advancing line blurring buildings and trees and cars in a rippling haze. The sound grows as those clouds, once so far away, stampede toward you. The hiss grows to a shriek, but the rain still isn't upon you. The wall of water has 100 yards or so to go. Then it overtakes you, like when you were a kid on the beach trying to outrun a wave, failing, a crash of water hitting you, forcing you into a somersault.

The noise.

The rain drops crashing down make a drum of every parking lot, every rooftop, every car, every tree branch. If you are close to a window, you have to yell to be heard. Visibility is no more than twenty yards, everything washed away in seething gray.

The rain stayed for a week and a half, the sky gushing, relenting only for an hour or so each day.

The weekend was the worst. Forty inches of rain fell in three days. To put that into perspective, Pittsburgh, Pennsylvania, which I once considered to be a rainy city, receives an average of thirty-seven inches of rain *each year*. For more perspective, according to the United States Geological Survey, forty inches of rain equates to approximately 1,086,160 gallons of water per acre (I blew your mind. I heard it pop).

For the most part, I witnessed the rain through my dorm room window. With my knee injured, I had no desire to leave my bed. I read, wrote, and only occasionally went to class. I skipped everything but Dr. Panek's fiction writing class, and that was only because he took writing as seriously as I took fighting. If a student missed class or was late, he lost points. If he came to class with an incomplete draft, he got kicked out. If I couldn't grapple, I thought that I should at least try to make progress with my writing.

The editor of *Ultimate Grappling* magazine e-mailed me to say that he wanted the article on watching BJ fight Stevenson among locals at the Academy. Unfortunately, the article hit the front page of Lockflow.com the day before. I had never published an article in a magazine before. I couldn't pass up the opportunity.

"I sold an article to Lockflow on the subject already, but I had a different angle in mind for *Ultimate Grappling*," I replied.

I had no idea what that angle was, but I started scheduling interviews with gym staff and gym goers regardless. I also needed an interview with BJ. I asked Jay the best way to contact BJ, and he said to talk to BJ before his morning workout. Since BJ was already preparing for his fight with Sean Sherk, I could start my interviews early and talk to BJ whenever he arrived.

I talked to Claudia just as the heavy rainfall was beginning. She described herself as the gym's "MMA Contact." She was from California and brought her Valley Girl sensibilities to the Big Island. Late thirties. Bleach blond hair. A bit husky. She bubbled.

When I sat down to do the interview, Claudia said, "I'm a writer too."

"Oh yeah? What sort of writing do you do?"

"I haven't published anything, yet. I feel like I have enough life experience now to start my scripts."

Whether the implication was intentional or not, it was clear: at twenty-one, I didn't have enough life experience to be a writer.

Then she told me that she was a fire dancer and an MMA fighter. She hadn't had any fights, but she was training, she said. I moved away from biographical information and focused on the event. Claudia had organized it.

"It was like a living room experience, and that's what I wanted," she said. "I wanted it to just be Ohana style." Ohana is Hawaiian for family. "Total island style. Completely Hilo. Slippers at the door, just like you're coming into someone's home." Locals called sandals slippers. "What a unique experience to watch BJ's fight from the place he's been training in for months. What a unique and powerful experience."

Claudia explained that the five-dollar entry fee benefited a program called "Fresh Step," which aimed to bring children who were struggling with physical education classes into the Academy (Jay later told me that they dropped the name "Fresh Step" because it sounded too much like kitty litter, but the charitable goal remained the same).

When I asked Claudia why the Hilo community showed so much support for BJ, she said, "He has given our small island town of Hilo something to be proud of."

I tried to discuss Kau Inoa with Claudia, but when I mentioned it her smile faded, and she stammered. After multiple false starts, she said that she didn't feel comfortable talking about it. She said that it wasn't her place. I pressed the question, trying to get some sort of response. Instead, Claudia changed the subject.

She asked me who else I planned on talking to.

"I plan on interviewing some fighters here at the gym and hopefully BJ as well."

"Oh, when are you interviewing BJ?"

"Jay said just to talk to him before his morning workout."

Claudia paused. She stopped bubbling. "I think that Jay is trying to get you killed," she said. "I wouldn't do that if I were you."

At about that time, BJ came into the gym, followed by three fighters. BJ wore headphones. He didn't say anything to the staff. He immediately went to the stair machine and started exercising. His entourage used the treadmills immediately adjacent to the stair machine. None of them smiled. They exuded an air of grim seriousness.

Jay *was* trying to kill me.

Claudia gave me the contact information for BJ's assistant. She said that it would be safer to call BJ's assistant to schedule an interview. I agreed.

I talked to a few students and fighters at the gym.

Kris, the fighter I had been training with when I injured my knee, said, "Hawaii is proud to have a fighter that big in the UFC, from Hawaii, just to represent all the islands together."

The other responses I received were in the same vein. Locals liked that someone from their home state was making it big. Feeling neglected by the rest of the world seemed to be an underlying sentiment for locals, and I could, at least partially, understand the justification for that feeling. Not only are the Hawaiian Islands small and geographically isolated, but they seemed to be politically and socially isolated as well. If Hawaii's controversial annexation and the subsequent fallout were not deemed newsworthy by mainland press, then other minor events weren't going to make the news either. I could think of only one occasion when I had seen Hawaii in the news: a volcano was erupting, and lava flow was advancing on homes.

Other than that, Hawaii was synonymous with vacation. People from the mainland, for the most part, ignored the people actually living on the island, and locals were aware of that fact. Even the way locals said "mainland" seemed to denote this feeling. Rather than say "mainland" as one word, they said "the *main* land," as if they were subconsciously admitting that they were secondary to the rest of the United States and the world in general.

I wondered how BJ felt, if he liked the responsibility of representing the hopes and dreams of a whole people. It's a job he certainly didn't ask for; it was thrust upon him. If I were in his shoes, I could see myself resenting it.

Then again, I couldn't entirely relate to his predicament. Unlike BJ, I have no ethnic majority; I'm a mix of Slovak, Italian, Polish, Irish, German, and a dash of Native American. I also lack the strong geographical tie. Most people from Pittsburgh are loyal to their home only in terms of sports teams, and that depends entirely on how successful a particular team may be doing in a particular season. The fans are quick to turn on individual players, too, if they have a bad game. As soon as the team slips up, they will quickly crucify individual players for their perceived role in the downfall of the team.

As far as I could tell, the support for BJ in Hawaii was consistent. Win or lose, locals loved and supported him. For my article, I needed his view on Kau Inoa and what he thought of his fans in Hawaii. I called his assistant and scheduled an interview. He said I could talk to BJ in two days.

In the meantime, I wallowed in the misery of my injury. Hilary e-mailed me.

She asked me a slew of vague questions, like how Hawaii was, and how I was doing, and if I was having fun. It all seemed sincere until she asked, "And BJ Penn just fought, were you in his corner? Vanguard of Vaseline?"

Vanguard of Vaseline.

I told her that I had been training twice a day, five days a week. I described the workouts and the rolling sessions. I admitted to crying after I thought Poai had broken my rib. I ended the e-mail by saying that I was comfortable telling her this because I knew that the people she could and would tell wouldn't have lasted five minutes at the Academy. I knew that they had never been in a fight and would sooner run than stand their ground. There was nothing they could do to me now.

Who was this talking through me? I didn't behave this way. I didn't pick fights. I didn't speak my mind to anyone. Had a month of training changed me that much? I was ready to fight every single person that had ever wronged me. I was ready to do it with a bum knee. I believed that I was tougher, stronger than anyone who hadn't ever stepped onto a mat or into a cage.

When I hit send, I realized that I wasn't training because it made me happy. I was training to prove them all wrong. I was training to prove that I was going to do what most people never could. Change.

I knew that I was changing, but I didn't know if I was changing for the better.

※ ※ ※ ※ ※

I went to the Academy to interview BJ (it was still raining). My heart pounded. I mentally rehearsed my questions. I wanted the pacing to be perfect, my facial expressions to convey sincerity and interest, and my gestures to emphasize my words without revealing what was going on inside my head; I was like a thirteen-year-old girl about to meet Justin Timberlake.

BJ's assistant said to meet BJ in the mat room at 9 AM. I arrived at 8:30 AM. I paced. I checked the batteries in my digital voice recorder. I tested the audio levels. I reread my questions. I checked the batteries again. I paced some more.

At 9:15 AM, I started to worry. I decided that BJ was simply running on Hawaiian time, the no-worries philosophy of never rushing or being concerned about punctuality. I paced again.

I called BJ's assistant at 9:30 AM.

"Hey, man," he said. "Sorry, but we're not going to be able to make it. We had to change workout times, and everything got screwed up. Call me tomorrow afternoon, and we'll reschedule."

He hung up before I could say anything.

When I got back to my dorm, the editor of *Ultimate Grappling* sent me an e-mail. He wanted the article by Friday. It was Monday. He added that getting an interview with BJ was a must.

As instructed, I called the next afternoon. BJ's assistant answered. In the background, I heard a jumble of noises—talking, yelling, wind, birds. The sound of pounding rain was curiously absent (and it was most definitely still raining in Hilo).

"Hey, man. What do you think of Hilo? You got here just in time for a natural disaster." He was referring to the rain.

I forced a laugh and said that Hilo wasn't bad.

"We still need to schedule that interview, huh? Hang on a second."

I heard BJ speaking in the background. The static of the wind muffled most of what he said.

"Okay, here's the deal," BJ's assistant said, returning his attention to the phone. "We're in Oahu right now. We wanted to get away from the rain. I'll call you when we get back to Hilo. Is that cool?"

I told him that it was. I didn't have any other choice. If I missed my deadline, I might not get another chance to write for *Ultimate Grappling*. If BJ had the means to leave Hilo on a whim, he probably had the means to stay on Oahu indefinitely. The rain showed no signs of easing, and weather forecasts predicated that it would continue for at least another week. I stared at my laptop screen. I couldn't do anything to improve my odds of interviewing BJ before my deadline. It was down to luck.

My cell phone rang.

I looked at the screen. "Incoming call from Gabriel Cash."

I had met Cash in Pennsylvania during my sophomore year of college. He had glasses, a near permanent maniacal grin, and Einstein hair—only brown. He was majoring in chemistry with a concentration in nanotechnology. We both loved jiu-jitsu but there was no place on campus to train. The university had cut its wrestling team and discarded their mats when Title IX was passed. Undeterred, we covered the hardwood floor of the aerobics room with yoga mats, which as soon as we started grappling, slid and exposed the unforgiving hardwood. We had to find real mats.

Cash heard that the dance studio had two wrestling mats, so we started sneaking into the studio just as the dance team finished their biweekly rehearsals. The mats were dusty and smelled like soggy gym shorts. After three training sessions, the campus police told us we needed official approval to use the studio.

We were distraught. Our grappling addiction—and make no mistake about it, jiu-jitsu is an addiction—was not being satisfied. We had the nervous shakes, an emotional hunger for the mat. We couldn't sit still. Our minds were filled with positions and transitions and submissions. We had to train. We took extreme action. Meaning we schmoozed a university administrator.

She heard our plea and dropped the keys to the dance room on the floor next to her desk.

"Oh my. How could I be so clumsy? If someone had those keys, they could, oh, I don't know, *borrow* some mats and take them to a community room in one of the dorms."

Operation Mat Rat was a go.

Four of us donned dark clothing and crept across campus under the cover of midnight. Cash took the lead. As we neared the target building, we put our hoods up, not wanting our faces on security footage. I looked at Cash.

"Put your hood down," I hissed.

"Dude, cameras," Cash said, looking at me over his shoulder.

"Your name is on the back of your hoody."

"Shit. Shit," he said as he planted his back against a wall, removed his hoody, turned it inside out, and put it back on. He pulled the hood down over his glasses. "There. Lock and load."

Each time we approached a corner, Cash would raise his hand, signaling us to stop. He looked left. He looked right. He looked left again. He waved his hand.

We entered the building and shuffled, half-crouched, down the halls. We keyed into the dance room and loaded the cargo onto our backs. We moved toward the door.

"Wait!" Cash said. "One of us should wipe the room down, you know, to get rid of our finger prints."

"Let's just get out of here," I said.

"Fine. Don't whine to me when the SWAT team kicks down your door."

I don't know if the cameras ever picked up a couple of wrestling mats scampering across campus that night. In any case, we stashed them in a dorm community room and had a place to train from then on.

Hearing from Cash made dealing with my knee injury slightly more bearable. He wanted to hear about training at BJ Penn's. I told him about my ribs and about my knee. I told him that I got the feeling that most of the students at the Academy had it out for me. I told him about the rain. I told him about Hilary's e-mail, and I told him about trying to get an interview with BJ Penn.

"Listen, brother," he said. "Things will work out. You're a kick ass writer and a kick ass grappler. You've just pushed yourself to the next level, and the next level is never easier. Just chill, man. Your luck will change."

I spent the rest of the day in bed, watching movies and listening to the rain. Britany visited often. I had decided that we were just friends and that Jake was wrong. Britany wasn't interested in "benefits."

So, I set my sights on a different girl. Her name was Jessica, and she was from Tennessee. On the hotness scale, she was a perfect ten (hate the game, not the player). She spoke with a subtle southern accent, just enough to make it endearing. Her hair was dark, like mahogany, and her figure was long and slim. She was in my fiction writing class, and we exchanged numbers on the pretext of meeting sometime to look over each other's stories.

I couldn't muster the courage to call her.

* * * * *

The rain stopped briefly on Thursday morning. I hadn't heard anything from BJ. My deadline was Friday. I wrote the article anyway. As long as I did everything within my power to get the article published, I was comfortable with failing. I was no longer worried. And the swelling in my knee was beginning to subside, so dwelling on the negative was difficult.

Jake peaked his head over my desk. "Some of us are heading down to Four-Mile," he said. "Want to come?"

Hilo hadn't seen the sun for days, and I agreed with Jake that we shouldn't waste it. Weather forecasts said that the rain would return by the afternoon.

A Hawaiian named Jack (not to be confused with Wisconsin Jack) drove. Jack was short and dark and had a Buddha belly. He kept his black hair short and almost always smiled mischievously. He was from the Kona side of the island. JB rode shotgun while Jake and I sat in the back.

Four-Mile was a stretch of beach just beyond the airport. The section we visited was not so much a beach as it was a rocky coastal pool where it was safe to swim. Hunks of lava rock surrounded the pool, jutting out like boney fingers into the clear water. White sand lined the bottom, dotted occasionally by large black rocks. To the right, a river broke free of a patch of a rain forest and emptied into the pool. The cold of the river mixed with the warm waves.

A metal ladder had been cemented into one of the larger rocks to, I assume, make entering the water easier and safer. Before I set down my belongings, Jack ran to the edge of the rocks and jumped. He curled into a cannonball just before hitting the water. The rest of us followed. JB and Jake jumped. I used the ladder. We stood in the water and tossed a football (it was quickly apparent why I had played soccer in high school). After a few tosses, we noticed a sea turtle among a batch of rocks, his head down in the sand. He surfaced occasionally but quickly returned to digging. His shell was as wide as a hula hoop and colored a mix of seaweed greens and tapioca yellows. His nose came to a point, and his eyes looked like polished black marbles.

Jack said, "They go hella fast, brah."

Since sea turtles are a protected species, touching them is illegal. Jack, apparently, didn't care.

He added, "But they bite really fucking hard."

While everyone else wandered down the beach, I sat on the rocks, an arm's length from the sea turtle. He surfaced and paused to look at me. After a few seconds of remaining perfectly still, he dove again. He didn't seem bothered by my presence.

I opened my cell phone. I called Jessica.

"I'm down at Four-Mile," I said. "I'm sitting next to this sea turtle, and for some reason it made me think of you." It was a lame line, but it was something.

She gasped. "I love sea turtles! I saw this one on Oahu just lying in the sand. He was so cute!"

Maybe it wasn't *that* lame.

She continued, "The Hawaiian word for sea turtle is 'honu.' They're supposed to bring good luck."

I told her that I could use some input for my latest short story. I suggested that we meet up that night and trade. She said that she would love to.

Maybe the honu really did bring me good luck.

JB, Jake, and Jack returned. JB and Jake passed the football back and forth while Jack went snorkeling. After about ten minutes, the honu meandered away from the rocks and glided between JB and Jack, swimming toward the open ocean.

Some time passed, and JB pointed to charcoal clouds lining the horizon.

"We probably have twenty minutes before that rain hits us," JB said. "We should go."

The rain hit in ten minutes. Traffic slowed to a crawl, which annoyed Jack greatly. His windshield wipers couldn't compete with the downpour, but he insisted on swerving around slow-moving vehicles. From the back seat, I couldn't see beyond the hood. Jack seemed to be navigating by instinct alone. I buckled my seatbelt.

That night, I stepped to Jake's side of the room. He was lying on his bed, reading.

"How do I look?" I asked.

"Like you're ready for some pussy!" Jake yelled.

"We're meeting at the library."

"You know what they say about librarians."

"She's not a librarian."

"Maybe she wants to be one when she grows up."

I laughed and turned away. I packed the draft of my short story and a notebook into my backpack and reached for my umbrella (the rain was roaring). My phone rang. It was BJ's assistant.

"Hey, brah," he said. "We're back in Hilo. We'll be at the gym for the next hour if you want that interview."

I had to choose between a perfect ten and BJ Penn. Easy choice.

"Jessica, listen. I just got a call from BJ, and he wants me to go to the gym and interview him now, so I won't be able to meet you at the library. I'm really sorry."

There was a pause. "I totally understand," she said. "Maybe we can meet another time?"

"Tell you what. The interview won't take that long. How about we meet at Starbucks after and go over our drafts then?"

"I would love that!" she said. I could hear her smile.

We agreed to meet in an hour. When I looked up after I closed my phone, Jake was leaning on my desk, staring at me and grinning.

"That was a good move," he said. "You bailed on her, and you still convinced her to upgrade from the library to Starbucks. Beautiful."

I used a move? Sweet.

By the time Jake dropped me off at the door of the Academy, saving me from limping a mile in the torrential rain, I was a mess. My hands shook, and my palms dripped. My stomach fluttered. My legs tingled. My vocal chords quivered; I knew that my voice would crack as soon as I opened my mouth to speak.

I passed by the front desk and through the weight room. I walked down the wooden stairs, my feet stuttering, reality setting in. I was about to interview a UFC champion and one of my heroes. I knew, however, that acting like BJ was just a normal person was the professional thing to do. As I walked by the boxing ring and the cage, toward the mat room where BJ was sitting, I breathed deeply. Be professional. Be professional.

The Thursday night no-gi class was in session. BJ sat against the wall wearing a pair of black board shorts and a white T-shirt. His assistant sat to his right, a well-groomed man built like Jay. Though he had black hair, I couldn't decide if he was local. A member of BJ's posse that I had seen the morning I interviewed Claudia, sat to BJ's left. He had a fighter's face: a chiseled jaw and punch-worn cheekbones. He was significantly larger than BJ and much larger than me. He stared at me, suspiciously. He never smiled.

I shook BJ's hand and sat down on the mat, BJ in front of me. He crossed his legs into a half-lotus and leaned in toward the voice recorder I set on the mat. He looked as though he were about to begin a chore. He didn't smile.

I started with warm-up questions, soft pitches designed to make an interviewee comfortable and receptive. I opened him by asking if Hilo is always this rainy, how often he escapes to Oahu for sun, and how it felt to win the lightweight title.

He replied: "Yes." "Frequently." "It felt good."

The nervous spasms in my hand made taking notes difficult. Some letters took up four lines and half of the words were illegible, even to me. BJ pretended not to notice my nervousness. I pretended not to notice BJ pretending not to notice.

I ran out of soft pitches and went into my serious questions. I asked him what he thought about his fans meeting at the Academy to watch him fight and how he felt about representing Hawaii. He said that it was pretty cool. I wasn't satisfied with that answer, so I let him sit, another interviewing technique. After some silence, he finally opened up.

"Before when I was fighting, I used to be resentful of people being like, 'Oh, you got to win or you got to do this or do that,' but now I love it. Now I feed on that. And I know why I fight; I fight for everybody else. Man if these people are going to put their faith in me and say I'm the best. I'm going to be the best."

I wrote more illegible notes and moved into asking him about his involvement with Kau Inoa. When I mentioned the organization, he tensed. When I formulated my questions, I didn't consider the political implications of Kau Inoa. If BJ said that he wanted Hawaii to return to being a sovereign nation, he would risk offending and alienating his many mainland fans. If he said that he preferred that Hawaii remain a part of the United States, he would risk offending his many Hawaiian fans who believed very strongly in the movement. I inadvertently put BJ in a precarious position.

"Kau Inoa . . ." he said, his voice trailing off. "That's hard to explain."

I waited.

"It's about everybody coming together and doing a census, where everybody can vote on a subject," he said. "'Cause I want to see what all Hawaiians have to say. We get all different types of Hawaiians saying they want sovereignty or a nation within a nation." BJ's passion was building. He became more animated. He chopped his hands as he spoke. "Sit there. Put it to a vote. And see what everybody has to say. I think that's the best way. That's why I like how Kau Inoa is running their thing."

I asked BJ if he had a preference in regards to sovereignty.

"More important than me, I just want to see what all of the Hawaiian people have to say," he said.

Critics have called BJ arrogant, lazy, and selfish. After seeing him in the gym, I decided that his confidence in front of cameras and in interviews was misinterpreted as arrogance. In person, BJ was quiet, mild-mannered, and even a little shy. If talking thirty seconds of trash before a fight upped his marketability, I couldn't fault him for doing it. If he did it to reinforce his own confidence, that's fine too. Every fighter knows that going into a fight doubting yourself is a slippery and painful slope that ends in defeat.

As far as being lazy, BJ himself admitted that he relied too much on his natural talents and underestimated the value of conditioning and strength training. He also said that he had learned his lesson and was changing his ways. Seeing him relentlessly maul Stevenson was proof enough for me that BJ had changed, but seeing him training for his fight against Sean Sherk a week after beating Stevenson (long before the bout was officially announced) made me a devout believer.

And BJ being selfish was baseless, especially after having talked to him. My interviews with locals revealed that BJ was more than just a fighting champion to the people of Hawaii; he was a champion of their culture, of their very way of life. BJ didn't volunteer for that responsibility. It was given to him. When he fought, BJ carried the burden of every local, of every Hawaiian into the octagon. No mainland fighter has to contend with that sort of pressure. To enter to Hawaiian music and proudly display the Hawaiian flag is an act of selflessness, and BJ's life is fighting. He was always fighting for his people.

I thanked BJ for the interview and shook his hand. I also shook hands with his assistant and his friend.

When Jessica picked me up in her white Crown Victoria, it was still raining. The downpour reduced passing high beams to candle flickers. I was riding high on my honu luck, hoping it would carry me through my night with a perfect ten.

11

THE FICKLENESS OF HONU LUCK

The Starbucks in Hilo was just like every other Starbucks I had seen on the mainland. Hipster couches. A checkerboard nobody plays. Bottles of Fiji water. Wicker baskets holding overpriced CDs by artists you've never wanted to hear. Young white people on laptops and iPods and cell phones.

Jessica and I sat in Starbucks for an hour, reading each other's stories. Her story was about a young couple discovering that they were going to have a baby. Mine was about a Mexican kid named Romeo who killed a police officer in self-defense. I drank a Java Chip Frappuccino, and she drank a chai latte. The rain left dark, wet streaks in her hair, and drops of water lingered in the soft valleys of her shoulders. She slowly twirled her hair as she read her story aloud.

And I was still riding my honu luck.

"I couldn't really relate to the characters until halfway through the story. Your descriptions were too abstract, too detached for me to really understand what was going on," I said. "Once they sat down and began talking about their relationship, then I got into it. You didn't explicitly say that they had been together for a long time, but I gathered through their dialogue that they had been together for at least a few years, which was really well done on your part."

Jessica scribbled my critique onto the back of her draft. I continued.

"Pregnancy is a compelling conflict to me because it's not the traditional character versus character conflict or the character versus himself conflict that you see in many stories. A potential child is simultaneously a uniting force and a dividing force, but you cut the story off right when she reveals that she's pregnant. As a reader, I want to see what happens after, how they cope, how they overcome the challenge."

We sat in silence while Jessica finished writing notes. She dropped her pen on the table and picked up her draft.

"Oh my god, you're completely right," she said, flipping to the last page. She paused and looked up at me, her bangs lulling for a moment over her face. She pulled her hair carefully away from her eyes.

That was a signal. I didn't have much experience with that sort of thing—girls and all—but I knew, for sure, that her playing with her hair was a signal.

I read my story aloud, and she gave me some suggestions. My story, like hers, needed a great deal of revision and polishing. I couldn't help but notice the way she leaned in, a starry look in her eyes, when I leaned back.

That was a signal.

Her leg grazing mine, too often too be accidental, that too was a signal.

She put her hand on mine to accentuate a point, and she let it linger—also a signal.

"I have so much homework to do tonight," she said, rolling her eyes and pulling her hair away from her face with both hands. "I have to do this eight-page literary analysis. It's such a waste of time."

"I know what you mean," I replied. "I'm going to be up all night getting this article finished."

She smiled. "You should come over. We can do our work together!"

I knew that Jessica lived in Paradise Park, which was about thirty minutes away from the heart of Hilo. If I went over that night, I'd be staying. I fully expected myself to panic, to begin stuttering, to fumble over myself, to blow the night in one epically embarrassing move. But I didn't. I was calm and confident.

"That sounds great, but you have to let me focus on my work you know," I said, grinning (Jake would have been proud of that line).

We packed our things and ran out into the downpour. We laughed as Jessica twice dropped her keys before unlocking her car. Our clothes were heavy with rain and lust.

Jessica rented half of a house in a secluded corner of Paradise Park. Her driveway was mostly mud, which wasn't much different from the road we used to get there. Jessica's landlord was away, and she told me how she took advantage of that privacy by hanging her laundry in her underwear. She only did that once though; after a few seconds outside uncovered, she had eight new mosquito bites. I liked the idea of Jessica in her underwear.

Inside, Jessica poured some wine and offered to make food. Neither of us was hungry. Jessica didn't have any furniture, only a mattress. She put a pillow against the wall, at the end of her mattress. She told me to sit down and plug in my laptop. While I worked on my article, Jessica changed into sweatpants and a tank top (without leaving the room), grabbed a notebook and a cinderblock-sized literature anthology, and curled up next to me. She draped her leg over mine.

We didn't talk much; we didn't need to. Our proximity replaced dialogue. Her foot glided up and down my calf.

Twenty minutes passed, and Jessica was sinking deeper into the sheets and closer to me. I knew that as soon as I finished my article, the rest of the night could begin.

Knock. Knock.

"Are you expecting someone?" I asked.

"I don't think so. I'll be right back," Jessica said. She set her book down and went to the door. The linoleum creaked as Jessica neared the door. The deadbolt thunked free of its chamber. The door moaned open.

"Hey girl!" a voice cackled, a voice that was most definitely not Jessica's.

The female chatter accelerated to an indecipherable speed.

"Wine!" the strange voice shrieked. A cabinet opened, a glass tinged, and a cork pulled free of a bottle. "What were you doing out so late? I drove home an hour or two ago, and your car still wasn't here."

Jessica explained that she had gone to Starbucks to work on a story with a friend (me).

"Oh, is he here?" the voice asked, almost as an afterthought. A shadow turned the corner before the question was even finished.

I had heard of this creature before but had never seen one in person. This, I was fairly certain, was the beast known as the "cock-block." She was large, two or three times as wide as Jessica, blond, and her face was permanently contorted into a Venus flytrap smile. She swaggered toward me, a full glass of wine in her hand (a bad sign). She introduced herself as Erika.

"What are you doing?" Erika said, landing next to me on the mattress. I almost fell off.

I explained that I had an article due the next day for *Ultimate Grappling* magazine.

"Ultimate what? Grappling? What is that?"

I explained to her, as best as I could, the basic idea of MMA and BJ's importance in the sport.

She frowned. "That doesn't sound very interesting."

Never before have I sincerely wanted to hit a woman. Just one good shot. To the nose.

"Let me read it," she said, snatching my laptop.

She slurped her wine as she scrolled through the article.

"Oh, I don't like this."

"Okay, thanks."

"I think you should move this here."

"I'll keep that in mind."

"Most of it works, but the ending doesn't. I want to be swept off my feet at the end of a story."

"I'll see what I can do."

Erika shoved the laptop into my arms and waddled to the kitchen to refill her now empty glass. For the next hour, I sat on the mattress without a beautiful Tennessean girl inching closer and closer to me, closer and closer to being in my arms. Jessica and Erika stayed in the kitchen, drinking wine and eating grilled cheese. I revised, refined, and polished my article.

For the most part, I ignored the conversation in the other room, focusing as much as possible on the importance of the article I was writing. One piece of dialogue caught my attention:

"He's kind of short isn't he?" Erika asked.

For the record, I'm pushing five-ten. I was shorter than Jessica, but then again, Jessica was supermodel tall.

I didn't hear Jessica's response.

When Erika finally left, she yelled her goodbye as she stomped out of the kitchen and onto the porch. Jessica entered the room.

"I am so tired," she said. "I'll just turn my paper in late. I don't care anymore."

I looked up from my laptop. Jessica was wearing black lace panties and a white bra (given my previous use of adjectives, any further description of her body would be unnecessarily graphic). I told her that I'd sleep on the floor.

"Don't be silly," she said, lifting the comforter to invite me in.

Maybe the cockblock beast hadn't ruined the night after all.

We joked and laughed and poked and tickled. We talked about our lives as our fingers grazed each other's skin.

After some time—judging the passing of time in the growl of Hilo rain is difficult—I leaned in to kiss her.

"What are you doing?" she asked.

"I want to kiss you."

She put her head on my chest.

"I know what that will lead to. It's too fast."

I acquiesced, content to sleep next to a beautiful woman, something I had not done in months. She fell asleep with her head on my chest, and I went to sleep shortly after.

We woke up late the next morning, both deciding to skip our morning classes. As I gathered my things, Jessica, while doing her make-up and hair, yelled from the bathroom, "Do you want to get a shower before you go?"

"No thanks. I'll just get one when I get back to my room."

"Are you sure?"

"Yeah, it's fine."

That afternoon, when I explained to Jake what had happened at Jessica's, he was visibly disappointed in the outcome. When I told him about my attempt to kiss her, he shook his head and leaned back in his desk chair.

"Dude, she has to say that," he said, both hands on the back of his head. "She knows what it will lead to, and she wanted it, man, bad. She took you back to her place. She knows what that means. Girls say that whiney shit because they don't want to feel like sluts. You should have kissed her anyway. Think about what Brad Pitt would have done. He would have kissed the shit out of her. That's what chicks want."

I shrugged.

Then Jake asked about the morning. I told him that she had offered to let me use the shower.

"Oh son of a bitch!" Jake said, throwing his hat against the wall. "You could have showered with her! That was a blatant invitation! She was practically begging!"

"No, I really don't think—"

"She asked if you were sure, right? Why else would she push the issue?"

Oh, fuck.

* * * * *

We decided to go sled riding.

We took Saddle Road to the base of Mauna Kea. Saddle Road is the only route that bisects the Big Island. The only other way to get from the Hilo side to the Kona side is to trace the coast. To reach the base of Mauna Kea, however, Saddle Road is the only option.

Saddle Road was infamous for accidents. Originally built by the military in 1942, not long after the bombing of Pearl Harbor, Saddle Road cut directly through lava flow, the kind of lava flow that looks like an entire valley filled with concrete construction rubble. By the time I had arrived on the Big Island, serious efforts to pave Saddle Road were just beginning and much of the road was still gravel. And that was a significant improvement.

The danger of Saddle Road came from its poorly marked boundaries, its unexpected turns, and its tendency to be obscured by fog and heavy rain. Being riddled with pot holes and covered in loose black gravel was also dangerous. Many local rental car companies explicitly stated their vehicles were not to be driven on Saddle Road or required you to purchase extra insurance if you planned on using the road. The director of the NSE program, during an orientation to island life, urged us to never take Saddle Road for any reason. She said that she couldn't bear the thought of one of us dying on that "strip of hell."

When I saw Saddle Road for myself, in all of its pot-holed-lava-field glory, I was unimpressed. I had seen worse roads cutting through the back hills of rural Pennsylvania, roads without lines or guardrails where a wrong turn took you over a cliff and into a creek bed twenty feet below. The true peril of Saddle Road, however, comes not from its physical state or its geographical location.

Saddle Road was dangerous because the people that use it drove like Jack, who used the left lane to go around blind turns, accelerated down hills, and hardly touched the breaks.

When I asked him about not using his breaks, Jack said, "Brah, you wan' pay for new breaks? Dey fuckin' expensive!"

JB was in the very back of the SUV, where there was no seat or seatbelt. He fiddled with his GPS as he slid from side to side and back to front with each screeching turn. Laura, the girl who helped us when the Red Baron needed a spare tire, sat up front in the passenger seat. She was originally from New Hampshire and had moved to the Big Island to live with her father and go to school. Sitting directly behind her, I could see her reaching for the door handle, gripping her seatbelt, and bracing herself on the dash. Jake sat next to me, and though he showed no visible signs of panic, I did notice him buckle his seatbelt not long after we turned on to Saddle Road.

About halfway between Kona and Hilo, we turned on to an access road, which would take us to the summit of Mauna Kea, 14,000 feet above sea level. The hitch back road was built to access the astronomical observatories at the top. Mauna Kea's height, geographical location, and isolation from air and light pollution made it a prime location for astronomers to conduct research. Despite the scientific advantages of building an observatory at the summit of Mauna Kea, the construction on and use of the mountain has cultural disadvantages. Like most of the interesting places on the Big Island, Mauna Kea is sacred ground. If the idea of sacred ground is alien to you, imagine someone building a laboratory on the battlefields of Gettysburg, and you can almost begin to understand how it might feel to have your land used for science instead of culture, but even that analogy doesn't capture the full scope of the word "sacred."

For Hawaiians, sacred land is a connection to the island, a connection to their ancestors, a connection to their religion, and a connection to their culture. Disgracing sacred ground is like defacing a church, a cemetery, and a historical monument all at once.

While a few people still grumbled about the presence of the observatories, I saw no protests or campaigns against the use of the mountain. I was told that when the observatories were first built, the public outcry was massive, but that was years ago. Now, the presence of observatories was just yet another defeat in a lopsided war, a war that few people were still fighting.

We weren't driving to the top of Mauna Kea to stargaze or to protest; we came for the snow. A storm blanketed the summit the previous night, so Jake stole a trashcan lid from the dorms and Jack dusted off a battered blue boogie board. We were going sled riding. In Hawaii.

Because of the access road and the observatories, Mauna Kea has become a popular tourist attraction. About halfway to the top of the mountain, just before the road turns from a steep but paved road incline to a zigzag nightmare of dirt and gravel, is a rest stop complete with a gift shop and restrooms.

We stopped to stretch our legs and admire the view (Jake immediately removed his shirt). Mauna Kea looked like an overturned snow cone, its steep slope rising without warning from the plains surrounding it. At its base were cinder cones, hills that formed after the majority of the lava from the volcano had dissipated. They too looked like overturned cones and bowls, so much so that they appeared fake, like hills sculpted for a model train set. The grass was tinged with a thirsty brown, and wiry but hardy bushes and trees dotted the landscape. Mauna Loa slouched in the distance.

We didn't bother with the gift shop, but we did find an interesting sign:

"BEWARE OF INVISIBLE COWS."

The fine print of the sign explained that "most of the Mauna Kea access road below Hale Pohaku is open cattle range, and the cows frequently cross the road. Dark colored cows are often invisible in darkness and/or fog. Use extreme caution and drive very slowly in this open range."

When I told Cash, my friend from home, that I didn't ever see a single cow remotely near Mauna Kea, he responded, "Bro, that's because they're invisible."

Right. Right.

The final portion of the road between the rest stop and the summit was treacherous. The unpaved road inclined dramatically. It could fit two cars but not comfortably. Each turn was a hairpin. There were no guard rails. The cars going up fought the terrain with four-wheel drive. The brakes of the cars going down smoldered, a permanent charred smell trailing after them. As we neared the snow at the top, Laura remarked about being thankful for Jack's SUV.

Before she could finish her sentence, a haole driving a sparkling red Mustang with the top rolled down coasted by us, descending the mountain. We stared—surprised, confused, and impressed.

The activity at the top of the mountain was just as surreal as the red Mustang. Parked cars lined both sides of the road. Locals, young and old, played in shorts and skirts, riding boogie boards and skim boards down the hills. They threw snowballs, built forts, and rolled balls for snowmen. Beyond them, closer to the summit, diehard snow boarders and skiers lugged their equipment to lesser peaks and boarded down. The skiing couldn't have been that good, but to be able to say you skied in Hawaii probably made up for it.

My favorite Mauna Kea activity: locals filled the beds of pickup trucks with fresh powder, secured the load with tarps, and then drove back to town as fast as they could. When they reached town, they had snowball fights. Once, while I lounged at Richardson's beach, I witnessed this event, narrowly dodging a stray snowball thrown by a young, barefoot local. His aim was atrocious, but then again, he probably hadn't thrown many snowballs.

We drove to the top and parked next to a colossal white orb that housed one of the many telescopes at the top of the mountain. From the summit, we looked down on the clouds. Other white orbs sat on nearby peaks, and a few Moonraker-style satellites pointed to the sky from small valleys below. We posed for a few pictures and set about being reckless.

At the Summit of Mauna Kea

The slope we chose for sled riding was more of a ladder than an incline; you walked up on the tips of your toes, sometimes using your hands to keep from falling backward. Jake sat on his trash can lid and went absolutely nowhere. Jack hopped on his boogie board and soared down the slope into the valley below, leaving the echo of a steady hiss in his wake. The valley was deeper than I had thought— the white snow reflecting the bright sun left no shadows and there were no buildings or people nearby to serve as reference points. Jack quickly became a spec in the distance below. I watched his spec slow as the slope leveled at the valley, but his momentum carried him up the incline on the opposite side. He slid back down and coasted up the slope from which he had descended. Repeating this process, each repetition he went a shorter distance than the last, until he stopped at the bottom.

That was the best sled ride I had ever seen.

By the time Jack hiked to the top, he was breathing heavily, straining to harvest oxygen from the thin air. He collapsed in a pile of snow nearby and held the board out for whoever wanted to go next. I snatched it and sat down. I dug my heels into the snow, and with a little pull I was on my way.

I felt off-balance; I was sitting too far back on the board, but I couldn't adjust now. I quickly gained speed. The hiss of the board slicing through the snow filled my ears. The cold air stung my face. I hung on.

A shift in the grade rotated the board. I was backward. I looked up at the ever-shrinking silhouettes of my friends. I was still gaining speed, everything to my right and left a white blur.

Then I hit a clump of snow—a small clump, no bigger than a baseball—but it was enough to knock the board out from beneath me, and it was at this point—at this exact moment—that my honu luck ran out. I rolled backward, somersaulting and cart wheeling down the mountainside. I tried to stay relaxed, to keep rolling, to let the momentum dissipate in my rotation rather than end abruptly with a face plant. This was jiu-jitsu thinking.

I kept rolling. Occasionally, my body left the ground, gliding through the air for an eternity before crashing back into the ground. I saw the sky. I saw the snow. Blue. White. Blue. White. Blue. White. I thought to myself, "When am I going to stop?"

JB said that I rolled for a full 8 seconds before coming to rest in a twisted heap at the bottom of the valley. Jack's boogie board slid to a stop next to me. A voice I did not recognize reached my ears.

"Dude! Are you all right?!" it said.

I put my arm in the air and waved and was happy to discover that it was not broken.

It occurred to me that, given my bum knee, I should not have attempted to sled ride in the first place. I staggered to my feet, poking and prodding myself for wounds or injuries, finding none. I looked down and saw where my shoe had scraped the snow from the ground.

There wasn't even a full inch of snow between me and the jagged lava rock of Mauna Kea.

Hiking back to the top to pass off the board felt like finishing a thirty-minute cardio circuit. My chest hurt. I couldn't catch my breath. I felt dizzy. I tasted blood. I tried and I tried, but I couldn't stop wheezing. I lay down in Jack's SUV for a few minutes to catch my breath. Laura crawled into the back seat to check on me. She looked down at me, her strawberry blond hair flowing out from beneath her toboggan.

"Are you going to make it?" she said, laughing at me.

I laughed and pulled her hat down over her eyes.

Like Jack said, riding a honu is a hell of a ride, but when they bite, they bite hard.

✳ ✳ ✳ ✳ ✳

I returned to the gym the Monday after we visited Mauna Kea. The rain had stopped and the sun was shining. The swelling in my knee was gone, and I could move without (significant) pain. The break had been good for me. My body got some much needed rest, and with *Ultimate Grappling* magazine accepting my article, I had started my writing career.

On my way into the gym for the morning jiu-jitsu class, I walked by Ben as he was getting out of his car. Ben was BJ's masseur and assisted in designing and executing strength-training routines.

Larger than Poai, Ben was a goliath with arms and legs like garbage cans. He wasn't Hawaiian, but he was local, falling into a weird limbo where even though he was white, he had just as much, if not more, Hawaiian pride than anyone else on the island. He was older than me, in his late 30s or early 40s. He was a blue belt, and I had rolled with him once before. My legs weren't long enough to wrap around his waist to close my guard, and his strength was such that he just pinned one of my arms to the mat and bent it the wrong way. I couldn't stop him. His grip felt like being trapped in the rubble of a collapsed building.

As I passed him on the sidewalk he said, "Howzit?"

"Not bad. Not bad."

I kept walking toward the door, but Ben called after me. "Hey, I'm sorry, I forget your name."

"I'm Marshal."

"Ben," he replied, shaking my hand (it hurt).

"Sorry, I see you here all the time, but I'm terrible with names." The more Ben talked, the more his speech sped up. It was like a stutter, except he didn't really stumble, he just removed the pauses between his words and sometimes chuckled at random points in his speech. "Are yougoingtothe Beatdown?" he asked.

Beatdown was a local MMA organization, and they were putting on a show in Kona in a few weeks. Even if I had the money to go, I had no way of getting to Kona and back.

"I would, but I don't have a car."

"Hehehe, yeah, I see you always walkin'. You canjust ride with me."

"Really?"

"Yeah. No worries. Andweget there fast."

We exchanged cell phone numbers and went inside to train.

Not long after my conversation with Ben, Chris invited me to train on Saturday and Sunday mornings with some other locals. An invitation that meant more mat time, some one-on-one time with Chris, a talented purple belt (who by all accounts should have been a brown belt), and an excuse to further entrench myself in local culture. The extra rolling would help my preparation for the Kumite Classic, a tournament scheduled a week after I returned to Pittsburgh. I learned later that the decision to invite me was Ethan's idea. Ethan worked for a local airline and was known for his boxing, and he frequently helped local fighters perfect their striking. Ethan always stopped to greet and talk to me at the gym and was a friend of Poai's.

Ben knew me only as a haole kid who came to the gym a lot, yet he was willing to go out of his way to help me. On the mainland, people I had known for years wouldn't have done that for me. And Chris and Ethan felt that I could contribute to their weekend training sessions. The hospitality of Ben, Chris, and Ethan proved that I was finally fitting in at the gym and perhaps with locals in general.

PART THREE: IMPROVING POSITION

"So, we'll go no more a-roving . . ."

—Lord Byron

12

THE KIDS AREN'T ALL RIGHT

I used my credit card to buy my ticket to Beatdown 6. My attempts at budgeting had failed, and my debt was building. My bank was somewhere on the mainland, a place that grew increasingly more alien each passing day. I fantasized that none of my financial problems could cross the Pacific and find me in Hilo.

The problems I had on the island were fading away.

When I returned to training after my knee injury, smiles and handshakes greeted me. The regulars, from white belts to brown belts, asked me where I had been and inquired about my injury. Chris and Poai joked with me.

"Brah, I knew it had to be serious to keep you out of the gym," Chris said.

"Yeah, man. Driving through town wasn't the same. I've gotten used to seeing you walking back and forth from the gym every time I go out," Poai said.

Aside from some soreness, my knee was fully functional, and with a week to rest and recover, I felt sharp, refreshed. I flowed to positions and submissions without thinking, my body naturally sliding into place, reacting to my opponent by unconscious reflex. I was hitting sweeps. I was passing guard. I was taking the back. My body just did jiu-jitsu. The training was beginning to work. For the first time since I had begun training at the BJ Penn MMA Academy, earning a blue belt felt like a real possibility.

But the palpable excitement of an upcoming MMA event in the area drowned out my thoughts of a promotion. Multiple fighters from the academy were on the card, and since the event was being held in Kona, most of the Hilo fighters were matched against Kona fighters, igniting an unofficial rivalry between the towns. The event poster was taped to the rickety wooden door that led to the MMA section of the gym, so everyone that trained knew who was fighting. Before and after every training session, people talked about the upcoming Beatdown and who their friends were fighting.

When Rafaello Oliveira, a visiting black belt from Brazil, filled in for a last-minute dropout, the buzz in the gym turned to discussing Rafaello's fight (focusing mostly on how badly Oliveira was going to hurt his opponent, David Santiago). Rafaello had a brow line like Papo's, and his ears stuck out like mine. I heard (but never confirmed) from various people in the gym that Rafaello came to America to raise money for his family by competing in MMA. He had a wife and a child in Brazil that he wanted to move to America.

Rafaello was a friend and a training partner, so students at the Academy rooted for him, but there was more to it than that. In the fighting world, there's a morbid pleasure in watching someone who has beaten you up beat up someone else. The enjoyment comes partly from knowing that you're not the only person to get your ass handed to you by that particular person. And when you, a white belt, tap to a black belt, you know that the black belt wasn't even trying. You want to see him try, let loose, go 100 percent. This was true of Rafaello: we wanted to see him really fight.

For the week leading up to Beatdown 6, Rafaello taught the afternoon class. His level of technical knowledge was immense, but he struggled with the English language, which sometimes made teaching difficult. I did not fault Rafaello for this. I knew that the English language is idiosyncratic and filled with seemingly contradictory grammatical rules and constructions. I also knew that learning a second language is difficult. I took Spanish from third grade to seventh and only remember how to count to three. In high school, I barely passed French 2 and proceeded to fail French 3 (I took French because I planned on wooing a French girl someday). Rafaello coped with the language barrier admirably and handled it much better than I would have been able to, but sometimes it got him into trouble.

For example, Rafaello often confused the meaning of antagonistic words, like right and left, or up and down, or push and pull. Unfortunately, those sorts of terms frequently come up in grappling instruction.

Once, while I was rolling with another white belt, Rafaello tried to coach me through a sweep. He directed me into the position, telling me where to put my legs and my hands. Then he said in his thick Brazilian accent, "Now pull him with your gwuard, Marshal."

I pulled. Nothing happened.

"Marshal, pull with your gwuard."

I pulled again. The sweep still didn't work.

"Pull!" Rafaello seemed to be getting agitated.

I pulled harder. Nothing.

"Marshal, pull him!" Rafaello was mad now.

I pulled again and still nothing happened.

A voice at the opposite end of the mat coughed, "push."

I pushed, and I swept my opponent, reversing the position with ease.

"Marshal," Rafaello said shaking his head, "I sorry."

Rafaello was happy to help anyone at anytime. I saw him demonstrating a takedown setup on the sidewalk outside of the gym when a student casually inquired about it. He always assisted me when I struggled. If he couldn't describe what I needed to do, he put me into position, bending me like an action figure and then gesturing to explain how I needed to move. He did these things while preparing for what was probably the biggest fight of his career up until that point. Beatdown was a division of Rumble on the Rock, a successful and credible organization based in Hawaii. Many Rumble on the Rock veterans had gone on to fight in the UFC. A win at Beatdown 6 could fast-track his career. With all those possibilities only a victory away, Rafaello dedicated much of his time to helping others.

* * * * *

Watching MMA in person is distinctly different from watching MMA on television. On television, the calm analyses of the commentators, the superimposed round timer in the corner of the screen, and the sleek cuts from camera to camera as the action moves about the cage makes an MMA event seem like any other sporting event. It's clean. It's orderly.

In person, you experience the chaos of the fight. The crowd swells around you, roaring with each punch, jumping to their feet after a takedown, booing when a fighter stalls. You crane your neck to see around the padded poles of the cage. You feel the floor vibrate after a slam. You see sweat fling from a fighter's face when he takes a punch. You hear the dull thuds of fist-rippled flesh when a fighter pins his opponent against the cage and attacks his ribs. Though there's a ref monitoring the action and spotlights illuminating the mat, you feel like you're watching a schoolyard brawl.

Hometown heroes populated the card of Beatdown 6, making the fans in the stands more than that; they were friends and family. Knowing a fighter on a personal level dramatically increases the inherent tension of a fight. Your stomach flutters. Your heart skips. In the hours between when a punch is thrown and when a punch lands, you forget to breathe. I've heard many coaches and corner men say that watching a friend fight is harder than stepping into the cage yourself, and it's true.

As Rafaello paced in his corner, waiting for the referee to start the fight, the true weight of the moment hit me. If Rafaello won, he'd be one step closer to achieving his dreams, to making it to the UFC and making enough money from his talents to provide for his family. He had sacrificed a great deal to come to Hawaii to compete and train, and he was prepared to sacrifice even more.

But if he lost . . .

If he lost, he'd be that much farther from achieving his goals. He might even have to return home, defeated, to his wife and child, with nothing to show for his efforts but cuts, bruises, and debt. That thought, that realization, humbled me. I had wallowed for so long in what now seemed like a trivial despair. I was getting over a girl; Rafaello was going all-in with his life and his career.

Rafaello and his opponent, David Santiago, touched gloves. They circled for a few seconds, jabbing tentatively, trying to gauge the distance. Rafaello shot a takedown, wrapping his arms around Santiago's legs and driving him into the fence. Santiago fought to keep his balance, overhooking Rafaello's arms, struggling to pummel to a better position. Rafaello, maintaining the clinch, spun twice, dragging Santiago to the mat.

Santiago scrambled to full guard. Rafaello postured up and dropped a hammer fist. The shot landed clean. Panicking, Santiago opened his legs. Rafaello passed Santiago's guard and dropped his chest on Santiago, pinning him to the mat. After a few punches, Santiago scrambled to his feet, only to be thrown to the mat again. Rafaello pinned Santiago again and transitioned from control position to control position, dropping punches each time he moved. Santiago was helpless. By the time he thought to escape a position, Rafaello was already in another. Rafaello moved like the ocean, each of his punches a crashing wave that drove Santiago closer and closer to drowning.

Two minutes into the first round, Rafaello secured mount. He sat up and hit Santiago with seven well-placed strikes to the face. Santiago wisely tapped, ending the fight. I finally breathed.

Earlier that day, on our way to Kona, Ben and I discussed Rafaello's potential and his future in the sport. Whenever I rolled with
Rafaello, he maneuvered himself between my legs and snaked his
way to my back, where he promptly choked me. When anyone else
took my back, they went around me. Rafaello went under me. I knew
exactly what he was going to do, but I could never stop it.

Naturally, I was impressed with his technical ability, but I was
just a white belt. I was impressed by pretty much everyone, but Ben
was a blue belt, and he spent nearly every day in the gym, working
with professional fighters. In addition to seeing BJ train each day, he
had the benefit of seeing the many fighters that made the pilgrimage
to Hilo to train. Ben knew fighting.

"Rafael, he's like BJ," Ben said. "His ground game is crazy!
Zoop, and he's on my back, hehehe. He's so fast! His hands need
some work, but he learns quick. He'll be in the UFC, I think."

And Ben was right. A little less than two years later, Rafaello
made his UFC debut at UFC 103: Franklin vs. Belfort.

With the ride from Hilo to Kona taking about two hours, our conversation wandered from topic to topic as the lush Hilo jungle faded
to dry Kona scrub grass.

Ben told me about how, when he was much younger, he divorced
his wife (that bitch) and not long after, in an unrelated incident, was
thrown from the third floor of a parking garage, breaking his ankle
and his back. He spent the next year without work and by himself.
His addiction to aikido and judo kept him fighting; he wanted desperately to return to the mat. Now, he was finishing his massage therapy
certification and planned to stay in the fight world.

He told me BJ's father, Jay Penn (senior), had come to Hawaii
after leaving the Navy and only had fifteen dollars to his name. Ten
years later, Jay Penn was a millionaire. Ben told me about how Jay,
my most consistent instructor, had nearly died on multiple occasions
from severe asthma attacks. He told me that JD, another one of BJ's
older brothers, founded and masterminded the explosive growth of
Rumble on the Rock (of which Beatdown is a part). He also said that

JD could have been a world champion fighter were it not for a shoulder injury. And he told me about Reagan, BJ's youngest brother. He said that Reagan had a genius-level IQ and remarked on the fact that a few visiting black belts had said that Reagan was a more talented grappler than BJ.

When our conversation shifted to Hawaii's history, Ben began to shout, jerking and pounding on his steering wheel, glancing repeatedly to his rear view mirror as though he expected to see a galleon full of missionaries sneaking up behind him.

"Those colonists bastards, theystole everythingfromus," Ben said. "They invaded, lockedupthequeen, and stole everything."

As I mentioned before, the annexation of Hawaii was a sordid affair that was set in motion when Captain Cook first "discovered" the islands in 1778. Once word spread of Hawaii's existence, then known as the Sandwich Islands, it became a hot spot for traders, fishermen, and missionaries. As the haole presence grew, so did their control. They began to infiltrate politics, tweaking government policy to fit their needs. Owners of sugar plantations were especially interested in removing the tariffs on trade between Hawaii and the United States.

By many accounts, American investors had sought to overthrow the Hawaiian government for decades. In 1893, they succeeded. Sanford B. Dole organized the Committee of Safety and summoned American Marines from a nearby cruiser. Dole, accompanied by armed Marines, locked Queen Lili'uokalani in her palace and established himself as president of a new government. None of the parties involved in the coup were acting on orders of the American government, and the president at the time (Benjamin Harrison) was not made aware of the incident until after it was over. Queen Lili'uokalani assumed that the American government would remedy the situation. When Grover Cleveland took office, he refused to annex Hawaii but did little to undo the damage that Dole and his conspirators had done.

When William McKinley took office, he pushed for the annexation of Hawaii and eventually succeeded, making Hawaii a territory in 1900. Dole was the governor. In 1959, Hawaii became a state.

The key fact here is that the annexation of Hawaii began with the invasion of U.S. troops, meaning that Hawaii was ultimately taken by force. Because of this, many Hawaiians argue that the annexation was unconstitutional, and of those with that belief, many argue that the unconstitutionality of Hawaii's annexation is justification for its reversal (in 1993, President Clinton and Congress formally apologized for the overthrow of the Hawaiian kingdom).

It's a story that we've heard before with the American Indians. A people are manipulated and downtrodden because the land on which they live is ripe with resources. To get to the resources, businessmen destroy the culture and the spirit of the people that live near them. The end result? A nation's worth of people left alienated, angry, indignant, and betrayed. For Hawaiians, the wounds are still fresh. Many are less than a generation away from these events. Even the Hawaiian language was almost lost, a tragedy that Ben blamed on the Hawaiian language being made illegal for some time in the 1900s.

Dr. Panek later informed me that this was a common misconception. Speaking Hawaiian was never illegal, but the pressure of Americanization did nearly annihilate the language. While on the island, I met many Hawaiians who actively sought to reconnect with their heritage. Chris, for example, was enrolled in Hawaiian heritage courses at UH Hilo specifically to better understand where he came from and to carry on his culture. He repeatedly encouraged other students at the Academy to speak Hawaiian with him so that they could help each other to learn the language.

Local fighters, time and time again, referenced their sense of injustice. I began to suspect that there was a connection between local fight culture and colonization. It would be some time before I would recognize just how important that connection was.

When Ben and I arrived in Kona, we met up with Iol (pronounced ee-ole) and his girlfriend Sydney, who went by Syd. Iol was a mix of Hawaiian and haole. He had dark Elvis hair, and his tan complexion was tinged with gray. His eyes were narrow, and his jaw was wide. Iol, like me, had recently turned twenty-one.

Syd was a brunette haole, light complected, and looked frail wrapped in Iol's arms. She was nineteen. Iol and Syd greeted Ben with a hug and called him "Uncle Ben," though as far as I knew there was no relation. I learned later that it was common practice for locals to refer to their elders as "Auntie" and "Uncle" regardless of relation, especially if that elder treated them well or looked after them in any way. Iol and Syd clearly appreciated Ben's kindness.

Iol and I became friends almost immediately. Like most Hawaiian (and local) males that I had met, Iol loved to fight. We talked about our training history, our favorite fighters, and the latest MMA news. Though I had never seen him at the Academy, he said that training was his life. As we settled into our seats, Iol said that he was already upset about the fights.

When I asked him why, he said, "Brah, I was s'posed to fight tonight, but he never show," Iol said. "Maybe he hear 'bout da bombs I was gon' strap to his face?" Iol chuckled to himself with a childlike glee.

Before the fights began, Ben took Iol and me down to the staging area. Ben and BJ bro-hugged (a handshake followed by a sort of chest-bump embrace with the handshake remaining intact throughout the entire ritual). Iol and BJ bro-hugged.

I shook BJ's hand, not expecting the same treatment as Ben and Iol, so when BJ pulled me in for a bro-hug, I bumbled awkwardly, tripping over my own feet. Typical Marshal uncool. Since BJ was cornering fighters and doing some promotional work for his brother JD, we returned to our seats.

"I wan' scrap like BJ," Iol said as we sat down. "Back in the day, he ruled Hilo, jus' straight scrappin' all the time. Now look at him, he rulin' the UFC!"

Iol and I talked and joked for the entirety of the fight. He appreciated the fight game in a way that none of my haole friends did. He spoke jiu-jitsu. Our heritage may have been different, but we were of the same breed.

When the fights ended, Iol invited me to the after party and offered to take me back to Hilo in the morning so that Ben could return
that night. Before he left, Ben shook my hand and patted my back,
his colossal hands knocking me forward a few feet. Since Syd was
underage, we dropped her off at Iol's hotel room. On our way to
Lulu's, a club in Kona, we picked up Malga, a childhood friend of
Iol's. Malga appeared to be all Hawaiian—dark hair, dark skin, a
round belly, wiry facial hair, and round eyes that protruded as if they
might fall out of their sockets if he leaned too far forward.

When Iol stopped the car, Malga yanked the door open and yelled,
"Aloha, braddahs! We gon get drunk!"

The car rocked from side to side when he dropped himself into
the backseat.

Iol introduced me and said, "Don't worry Malg', Marshal's one
cool haole."

"Oh mahalo," Malga said. "When I first saw you, I thought you
might be one of dem Cali haoles, all 'duuuuude' and shakin' your
shaka like one retarded haole."

Before we entered Lulu's, Iol offered me advice.

"Don't hit on no local girls," he said. "Da local boys will get
pissed, especially if you be one handsome haole."

"Oh what, you think he's sexy?" Malga said, starting to laugh.

"No. No, I jus' meant—"

"You better no drink tonight, Iol," Malga interrupted, laughing
so hard that he spoke in wheezes. "You be cheatin' on Syd with one
sexy haole!"

Iol, with a smile, pushed Malga.

Malga doubled over, laughing so hard that tears leaked from his
eyes. He slowly caught his breath, and gasped, "Oh, mahalo. Mahalo."

Lulu's was on the second floor of a building otherwise occupied
by what appeared to be cliché tourist beach shops. With the exception of the restrooms, Lulu's was essentially one giant deck, with
two bars and a dance a floor. When we arrived at 11 PM, locals and

tourists were already crowding the club. Malga immediately claimed a spot at the bar, where he intended to stay for the rest of the night.

Iol ordered a beer. I ordered a Red Bull (designated driver). We followed the ripples of the earthquake bass to its epicenter, the dance floor, and lingered at the edge, overwhelmed by the sheer number of bodies writhing and bouncing to the club mix. Flashing colored spots traced bodies and faces like the roaming hands of midnight lovers. In the dry Kona heat, small beads of sweat clung to foreheads and slowly trickled down tense necks. We yelled in each other's ears to talk, and our hearts beat in rhythm to the thundering speakers.

Iol tried to work up the courage to talk to the tan local girls while I focused on the pale tourists. We would each pick a target, repeatedly say that we were going to walk over and talk to her, and when one of us stalled, the other would laugh and push him in the direction of an attractive female. One would watch while the other strode toward the girl, moving confidently at first, but with each approaching step, that confidence waned. What if she had a boyfriend? What if you stuttered? What if you tripped? What if your hair was out of place? What if she laughed in your face, and her friends laughed with her? Her rejection would be humiliating, unlivable.

We'd turn around before ever reaching the girl. We didn't chide each other too much because we both knew how hard it was. We tried for the rest of the night, not once successfully approaching a girl. Before his Beatdown opponent had backed out, Iol had been fully prepared to be locked into a cage with another human being where they would then fight until the other quit. He could have been cut with an elbow, rendered unconscious from a high kick, crippled by a knee-ripping heel hook. He was excited about it, looking forward to it even, unafraid of the potential painful consequences.

And now, he couldn't talk to a girl. A beautiful woman, it seemed, yielded more power than a fighter.

Later, fighters from Beatdown 6 came and went. After eight weeks of dieting, their tolerance for alcohol had weakened. A single drink had them giddy, and soon they were on the dance floor, their drinks raised above the throbbing crowd, smiles on their faces, their cauliflower ears bobbing drunkenly. Rafaello didn't come out, but Charuto did.

His towering stature commanded the room. Many locals, upon seeing his face, called out to him, shouting "Charuto" or "Sensei" before running over to shake his hand and hug him. Charuto always laughed and grinned, and said, "Howzit cousi'?" He moved through the crowd in this manner, never making more than two consecutive steps before a local stopped him. Some I recognized from the gym, but most of them I did not.

The haoles at Lulu's stared at Charuto as though he were an obscure celebrity, someone worthy of their attention but they didn't know why. Though Charuto had fought in the UFC, on the big stage, the people rushing to greet him knew him for more than that. Charuto was kind to them. He shared his jiu-jitsu with them. They looked up to him because of who he was, not because of who he fought.

Charuto didn't stay long. He had a few drinks and slipped out.

Iol and I collected what was left of Malga just before closing. Malga had sat at the bar for three hours, ordering drink after drink, an army of empty bottles and glasses amassing before him. He wrapped me and Iol in his arms, hugging us.

"Aloha, braddahs! Let's cruise. Hella drunk. Mahalo!"

I drove Iol and Malga back to their hotel room. By the time I herded them to their room—past the angry eyes of hotel security unappreciative of Malga's constantly shouting "Aloha!" and "Mahalo!" to every passing person, car, or cat—it was 3 AM. I pushed Iol and Malga into the hotel room, locking the door behind me.

Malga trotted down the short hallway, threw his arms into the air, and yelled, "Aloha!"

A female voice I didn't recognize shouted back, "Shh! The kids are asleep!"

The kids?

I walked into the bedroom. Syd sat on one bed holding an infant. A large blond haole, who, I presumed, was Malga's girlfriend, lay in the other, an infant stirring on the bed next to her. Malga and Iol took their scoldings like children, scoffing and laughing in their girl-friends' faces. While they bickered, I borrowed a blanket from the closet and took a cushion from one of the chairs to use as a pillow. I closed my eyes and pretended not to hear them fighting.

Neither Iol nor Malga had mentioned being a father, not at the fights, not in the car, and certainly not at the bar when we were try-ing (and failing) to hit on girls. Iol told me later that he and Syd had moved to California after high school, Syd for college and Iol to train. Syd got pregnant, so they moved back to Hilo. When I met them, their son was eight months old.

Aside from coaching a local girls water polo team, Syd didn't work. She alternated between staying with her parents and staying with Iol. Iol worked nights at the Hilo Police Station, not as a police officer but as a secretary of sorts. Since Syd normally took the car, Iol went to and from work on a skateboard. Money and time were in short supply, making it difficult for Iol to pay his bills let alone own his own car or train consistently.

How many Iols are there for every Rafaello? For every person that's moving closer to achieving his dreams, how many have al-ready been permanently sidetracked, doomed to never see his dreams made reality?

And more importantly, which one was I?

13

SWIM DA ODDA WAY

Iol saved me a lot of walking. Whenever Syd wasn't using the car, he'd pick me up at my dorm and take me to the gym. He typically missed the evening classes because he had to work, but for about a month, Iol and I trained together every day. We'd roll before class started, and we'd roll when class ended. Though Iol had twenty pounds on me, I kept up. He typically won, but I could fight off losing for ten minutes or more.

He wasn't that much different from me. He loved to fight, talk about fighting, and watch fighting. And like all locals, he spoke Pidgin and loved to cruise. The more time I spent with Iol, the more comfortable he became with speaking Pidgin around me. After hour upon hour in the gym, I had grown accustomed to deciphering Pidgin. I appreciated its rhythm, its reggae bounce.

My guidebook recommended that non-locals avoid attempting to speak Pidgin. I ignored that advice.

At the end of every phone conversation, no matter how long or short, Iol said, "Shoots." This just meant that he agreed or "alright, take care." I liked the brevity of it, and from hearing the word so much, from Iol and from fighters in the gym, it began to linger at the top of my tongue.

One time, Iol called while I was eating dinner. It was a short conversation. We discussed our next training session and what time we wanted to meet.

Without thinking, I said, "Shoots" and closed my phone.

Before I had set my phone on the table, it began to vibrate. I answered it.

"Brah, what did you say?" Iol asked.

"Huh?"

"Just now. What did you say?"

"What are you talking about?"

"Brah," Iol said, speaking slowly. "Did you say 'shoots'?"

"I might have."

"Don't do that."

I paused, embarrassed. "Okay," I said.

"Okay. Shoots, brah," Iol said.

"Farewell, my friend."

"Smart ass."

We both laughed, but the awkwardness lingered long after I hung up. I referred to my guidebook to see what it had to say about my bumble.

It said, "If you do [try speaking Pidgin], the odds are you will simply end up looking foolish."

Iol forgave my minor transgression, and his scolding probably prevented me from getting my ass kicked in the gym or on the street. The language still fascinated me, though. Pidgin is more than just a different accent mixed with slang. It has a unique vocabulary and a unique grammar. Many of the words are derived from English but have distinctly different meanings. An English speaker might be able to pick up bits and pieces of a Pidgin conversation, much in the same way that a Spanish speaker can with Portuguese, but the majority of the conversation will be unintelligible. Though my guidebook provided a list of Pidgin vocabulary, it did not do the language justice. Pidgin is best appreciated in its natural, spoken form.

Pidgin is such an important part of local culture that the Bible has been translated into Pidgin. If you want to pick up your own copy, it's called *Da Jesus Book*. The Old Testament, which was translated directly from Hebrew and was in the process of being proofread when I was living in Hilo, is called *Da Befo Jesus Book*.

From *Da Jesus Book* website, under the "How Come?" section: "Jesus Christ, he fo everybody. He not jus fo da peopo dat talk English. God not one haole, you know." And it continues, "Get plenny peopo dat undastan da local Pidgin mo betta den da English."

And here is John 3:16 in Pidgin:

"God wen get so plenny love an aloha fo da peopo inside da world, dat he wen send me, his one an ony Boy, so dat everybody dat trus me no get cut off from God, but get da real kine life dat stay to da max foeva."

If you read Pidgin out loud, slowly, it's easier to understand (but you'll feel like a dork if your friends are around).

Iol also taught me about another distinctly local practice: diving. Diving is what locals call spear fishing. Typically, they use a "Hawaiian sling" or what's also called a "three-prong" because of the three points at the end. At the opposite end of the spear, about three to four feet (depending on the spear) away from the points, is a rubber sling, which you wrap around your wrist and stretch up the shaft of the spear. When you release, the sling propels the spear.

The only other necessary piece of equipment is a pair of goggles and a snorkel. Divers using flippers, camouflage wet suits, and weights, however, is not uncommon.

When I asked Iol why he went diving instead of fishing with a rod and reel, he said, "Oh wat, you wan' me fo' wait fo' dinna come me? Brah, when fo' dive it no matta if da fish hungry."

Iol and Malga took diving very seriously. They had two freezers full of fish and continued diving for the fun of it. I bumped into Iol at Four-Mile Beach one time, and he invited me to give diving a try. He let me borrow a spear, a pair of flippers, a pair of goggles, and a snorkel. We crawled over the black rocks and swam out to deeper water. We treaded water, passing waves pushing our bodies up and down, the moan of the water muffling the voices of the people on shore.

Iol instructed me to hold my breath, dive as deep as possible, and to approach the fish from behind to keep from spooking them. He even suggested that I avoid having my shadow pass over them.

It turns out that sneaking up on a fish is incredibly difficult. I tried time and time again, but never got within spearing distance. When I managed to inch up on a fish, I'd run out of air, my lungs clawing at my insides for oxygen, my brain pressing against my skull. I'd panic, bumble my shot, and hurry to the surface.

I floated on my back, catching my breath.

"Brah, watch dis," Iol said.

Iol submerged his face in the water and studied the depths. A few moments later, he dove. I watched from the surface, floating on my stomach, breathing through my snorkel. Where I fought my own buoyancy, pawing at the water, trying to pull myself deeper, Iol sank feet first, lifting his hands above his head to force himself down. He calmly turned to his stomach and lightly kicked his feet. He glided through the water. He moved with patience, confident in his lungs, bubbles trickling from the tip of his snorkel like a stream of shimmering marbles. He arced wide and circled to the far side of a mass of lava rock and coral. A school of tiny fish scattered as he approached.

Iol lingered near the rock. It seemed like he held his breathe for whole minutes.

He waited, his gaze fixated on the rocks. His spear arm took aim, its three prongs pointed at the rock. He held the spear in place, calculating his shot like a sniper judging half degrees and timing leaf-shifting breezes.

He released. In a blink, the spear soared into the rocks. Iol lunged after it, gripping it with both hands. He pulled the spear away from the rocks, fighting the struggle of the eel pierced by its points, an eel the length of my arm. Iol pressed the points of his spear into the sand to keep the eel from escaping. The eel's head and tail smacked the ocean floor, obscuring Iol in a golden fog. A few seconds later, Iol kicked to the surface.

"Dis fucka strong," Iol said, laughing. "'Bout broke ma' arm."

"How did you do that?" I asked.

"Brah, diving like jiu-jitsu," Iol replied. "If da fucka see da arm bar, you no get. So you no rush. You a sneaky fucka. You patient. You wait. You trap da fucka, no escape. Den you get da fucka."

I nodded.

"And dose haole lungs no help." Iol laughed.

After a few more dives, I finally speared my first fish. It was blue with a yellow stripe and had pouty lips, and it was as small as a potato chip. Iol wasn't impressed and said that if I kept spearing fish like that I'd starve to death. When I visited a mainland pet store some time later, I saw the same species of fish for sale. My blue potato chip fish was worth $500.

On our way back to my dorm, Iol invited me to go diving with him and Malga that weekend. We wouldn't dive during the day, however; we'd be night diving. Iol said that he knew a good spot north of Hilo. Since it wasn't popular for swimming, the fish were less skittish. Iol also explained that different types of fish came out at night, and they also tended to be bigger.

"Don't sharks come out at night?" I asked.

"Well . . . da kine," Iol said. "Dey just bump you and swim away. No worries."

I disagreed. A shark bumping me in dark water was most certainly, without a doubt, cause for worry. From what I had read about night diving, I knew that technically not much was different. You dive at night instead of during the day (obviously), and you carry a small, waterproof flashlight (since, you know, it's dark). The greatest danger was in losing your flashlight and getting pulled out to sea.

"You'll be there if something happens, right?" I asked.

"We dive far apart," Iol replied. "Too much light too close scare da fish."

I pondered this and asked what I felt to be the most pertinent question. "What do I do if I lose my flashlight?"

"Brah, swim fo' beach."

"What if I can't see the beach because it's too dark?"

"Swim one way. No find land, swim da odda way."

I never went night diving.

* * * * *

I grew increasingly alienated from my haole friends. I didn't go to parties with them, so they stopped inviting me. The more time I spent at the gym and with Iol, the more I began to resent other haoles. I didn't belong with them. At the gym, I fit. I was pale and didn't speak Pidgin, but I fit. The local philosophy made sense to me: respect everyone unless you want to scrap. If you don't want to scrap, just show aloha and no worries.

I met more genuinely nice people on the Big Island than I had met anywhere else in the United States, and of those people, Tiare (tee-are-ay) had the most aloha. Dr. Panek rearranged our writing groups, and Tiare was in mine. Her friends called her Ti, and she was all Hawaiian. At our first group meeting, everyone exchanged short stories. When we finished our critiques, our conversations turned to talking about each other, sharing where we were from and what we were interested in.

When I told Ti about training at the BJ Penn Academy, she said, "Oh BJ, he's such a sweetheart."

"You're friends with BJ?"

"Oh I don't know, I always see him cruisin' at Richardson's when I go beach," Ti said. "He always has lots of aloha and likes to talk story. He's a nice Hilo boy."

She told me that she was from Oahu and that she liked to read romance novels. She read almost one a day. When the conversation shifted back to me, Ti asked about my training schedule.

"I train twice a day on most days," I said.

"That's a lot. Do you diet like BJ?" she asked.

"Not really. I just eat a lot of ramen, a lot of oatmeal, and some whey protein."

"That's no good. You need good food."

I shrugged.

"You're pau eating like that. Come over for dinner tonight." (Pau, pronounced "pow" means "finished" or "done.")

And I did. Ti made baked chicken breaded in frosted corn flakes served over rice, her signature dish. She was friends with Laura, Britany, Hawaiian Jack, and JB, so they came over for dinner too. I saw JB very little in the last few months of my stay in Hilo. When he wasn't locked in his room, studying, he was working his Brazilian charm on local girls. Hawaiian Jack always hung out around the dorms, but he spent most of his time with his ex-girlfriend, having headboard smashing sex that echoed throughout the campus (his ex-girlfriend was crazy). Britany and I were friends. She still wanted to be more than that, but the very thought of a relationship reminded me of Hilary. Laura, who had gone sled riding with us on Mauna Kea, was attracted to me but wasn't interested in a relationship.

As Jake would say, she just wanted "benefits," which I thought was awesome. Our attraction began to build at Ti's, punctuated by playful glances and timid touches. While my relationship with Laura would culminate in a fleeting moment of physical ecstasy, my friendship with Ti would become something lasting.

I ate dinner with Ti at least twice a week, and we spent most weekends together, cruising the farmer's market for fresh fruit, going to Richardson's, or just talking story at her apartment. Ti became one of the best friends I've ever had. She took care of me. She looked out for me. She was always willing to help me (or anyone in need, for that matter).

Ti and Britany

Because of people like Ti and Iol I looked forward to island life, thankful for every sun- and rain-filled moment.

On my way back from Ti's one afternoon, Megan called. Megan and I hadn't spoken, with the exception of a few e-mails, since I had left the mainland three months earlier. I settled beneath a palm tree and listened to her talk. She told me about the snow. She told me about the squabbles occurring in my old group of friends. She told me about her overwhelming course load and the Honors conferences she was attending.

She seemed far away, living in a place that I no longer understood, a memory made in a dream, the details murky and fading. I understood aloha and sunshine and tropical rain. I understood the steady whisper of the ocean and the calls of coqui frogs. Snow. Petty drama. A college apartment filled with drunk haoles, all pretending to be friends but secretly loathing each other, hiding their jealousy and disdain behind Captain Morgan smiles and bleeding mascara. Those things never made sense to me, and I was happy to forget them.

"They still talk about you," Megan said. "Scoot said the other day that you got screwed over, that the way they treated you wasn't fair, but everyone just ignored him."

I didn't respond. I watched a pair of zebra pigeons shuffle down the sidewalk.

"When they do talk about you, it's strange. Sometimes they bring up a 'remember when.' But then they say that you left them, that you treated them badly. The way they talk about you, it's like you're gone forever, like you're not coming back . . . it's like you're dead."

I found no refuge on the mainland. No find land, swim da odda way, and I was swimming as fast as I could.

14

THE COCAINE NOSE JOB

The blur of my routine washed away time. I mechanically followed the rigid structure of my days: breakfast, class, training, lunch, class, training, dinner, homework, sleep. Weeks went by quickly because I never paused to notice their passing. The halfway point of my stay was behind me, and there was still much of the Big Island that I wanted to see, and spring break was an opportunity to explore.

Spring break did not go as planned because we neglected to plan at all. In January, when I was good friends with the other haole exchange students in my vicinity, I proposed a week long road trip where we'd camp at various public parks around the island, seeing all of the beautiful sights that my guidebook recommended. Waterfalls. Lava tubes. Hidden beaches. Isolated sea caves. I wanted to see as many island wonders as possible before my lonely flight back to the mainland.

As UH Hilo's unusually late spring break neared, I pressed Jake and the others to make preparations.

"According to the park website, we need to make reservations in advance if we want to use the campgrounds," I said.

Jake lay on his bed, his white baseball cap turned backwards and pulled down over his eyes. Wisconsin Jack sat at Jake's desk, using his laptop.

"Nah, we'll be okay," Jake said without opening his eyes.

"But it says-"

"Easy, Marsh," Jack said, laughing. "It's not like they have police patrolling the beaches."

Despite their reassurances, I remained concerned. Seeing that there was no convincing them, I moved on to another topic that I thought was important. "Well," I said, "We should at least pick the spots we definitely want to visit, so we can find a campground nearby and budget our time."

"I was thinking we'd just go out, camp a night, come back to Hilo for a day and then go back out," Jack said.

"That seems like we'd lose a lot of time driving."

"Marsh, chill." Jack said. "It's spring break, not Disney World with your mom."

I marked down what I wanted to see and gave up arguing. I prepared as best I could by buying the proper equipment and studying my maps.

Roke (pronounced "Rocky"), a scruffy NSE student from Oregon, agreed that we needed to plan more but didn't say anything to Jack or Jake. JB declined to join us.

We departed Hilo late one morning in the Red Baron (why we didn't take Jake's much newer and more reliable extended cab was never explained to me). We drove south of Hilo, Jack and me in the cab, Jake and Roke in the back. Jake and Roke each opened a beer as soon as the Red Baron began to move.

We followed Highway 11. We passed Volcanoes National Park and continued south. Mauna Loa was on our right, its slopes and peaks lazy, subtle rise after subtle rise that united to become a mountain. According to my guidebook, "Mauna Loa was built from countless thin layers of lava flows, usually less than 15 feet thick," a process that took hundreds of years. On the Big Island, Mauna Kea and Mauna Loa were always in the distance.

Mauna Kea and Mauna Loa were constant reminders that this place, the Big Island, was greater than me. I was insignificant, and the island deserved my respect. Looking up at Mauna Loa on our drive to South Point, I understood, on a very basic level, how Hawaiians could feel a spiritual connection to the island. The island is their world. It gives them beaches and waterfalls, jungles and deserts, fruit and fish. The same volcanic force that gives them land can take that land back without warning. I felt a connection to the island the moment the crisp water of Rainbow Falls washed over me. And I am just a haole. The bond that Hawaiians—born and raised on the island, with a rich cultural history that extends back before the Great Kamehameha united the islands—feel with the island must be a deep one. The island is more than their way of life; it's their constant companion—the mountains, the ocean, always watching, the island itself an ancestor.

We turned our backs to Mauna Loa, and began down the road to South Point, the southernmost point in the United States. Once we broke free of the trees, the ocean was visible at the end of the road, a strip of crumbling asphalt dead-ending in the Pacific. Only one car fit on the road, so if another car came from the opposing direction, someone had to pull off to the side. Locals were quick to pull over and hang a shaka out the window as we passed. The haoles driving sparkling rental cars hesitated, preferring to block the road.

The road to South Point bisected a field, nearly flat, covered in knee high grass. To the right, a small army of windmills faced the window. Some of the blades moved, but many of the windmills were in a state of disrepair. Their white paint flaked off, revealing rust, and their blades stood motionless. I counted more than a dozen seemingly broken windmills, which was unfortunate and perplexing considering the value of energy on islands as isolated as Hawaii.

The same wind that propelled the windmills punished vegetation. Very few trees grew in the field. The few that did were small and wiry, with the exception of one famous tree that has grown almost perfectly horizontal, molded by the winds of South Point. It extends three car lengths, its trunk growing parallel to the ground, its branches barely touching the grass.

The famous windblown tree at South Point

When we arrived, only four tourists lingered near the cliffs, looking over the edge, studying the water thirty feet below. The other fifteen people at South Point were locals. Three sat near deep sea fishing rods, their lines extending into the horizon. One local stood near his open trunk, inspecting his diving equipment. A blue camouflage wetsuit hung at his waist, half-undone. The others sat in lawn chairs arranged around battered coolers. They drank beer and talked story.

Our group scattered. I took photos. Jake wondered to the edge of the cliffs alone, carrying a gallon jug of water and looking pensive. Jack and Roke attempted to catch a mongoose. A few minutes later, the inevitable began: cliff jumping.

South Point is a famous jump spot. It's as safe as jumping from a cliff into an ocean can be. The water is deep, and it's clear, so any rocks that might be dangerous are visible. Most people jumped from one spot, a wooden platform that extended out over the water, a rusty pulley hung from the arch that framed the platform. A rickety ladder extended from the side of the platform down to the water. The ladder, like the pulley, was rusty. It creaked as it swayed in the breeze. To me, climbing the ladder back to the top of the cliff was a scarier prospect than jumping in the first place.

I immediately chose not to jump. Of my top three fears, heights is the first (followed by girls and spiders). I couldn't stand on a coffee table without feeling a dizzying sensation creeping over me, pulling at my consciousness, pushing me to fall. No matter what anyone said, I would not jump.

Jake walked onto the platform first. He peered over the edge. He paused. He stepped back to the safety of the cliff. Roke took off his shirt and with a deliberate stroll walked right off the edge. He landed feet first, the water swallowing him. He surfaced a few seconds later, whooping. He swam away from where he landed and waited for the others to jump.

Jake returned to the platform. He walked to the edge. He paused. He turned away, shaking his head as he stepped back onto land.

Jack imitated Roke, walking briskly onto the platform, maintaining the pace until he stepped over the edge. Like Roke, he landed feet first and bobbed to the surface shortly thereafter.

Jake again stepped onto the platform, stopping at the edge to peer down into the water.

"Don't be such a tit," Jack yelled.

"It won't hurt your pussy too bad," Roke shouted.

Jake stepped backward and then flung himself forward, hitting the end of the platform in a full run. After a few minutes, he made his way up the ladder with some difficulty; Jack gripped the lowest rung and shook it. Jake just laughed.

By this time, a few more tourists had arrived, and they congregated around the platform, watching Jack, Jake, and Roke jump. I retrieved my snorkel from the Red Baron and found a path down the cliff.

Navigating rocks in Hawaii is no easy task. Lava rock tends to be porous, lending itself to developing brittle sharp points. Porous rock is also a haven for sea urchins, which are little spiky spheres from hell. Black sea urchins coated and filled the rocks of South Point, their spines sticking outward, waiting for haole feet (like mine) to spear. I stepped over the rocks as though I were navigating a mine field. I had never been stung by a sea urchin, but I had heard about the misery. Their spines are like needles. Having nine to ten of those in your foot is bad enough, but the spines also release venom, which burns like a wasp sting but worse, and continues to burn and cause swelling for as long as the spines are lodged in your foot.

I successfully entered the water without incident. I spit in my goggles and forced water through my snorkel. Submerging my face, I lightly kicked away from the cliff. The world sprawling beneath me was unlike anything I had ever seen before. The cliff face continued thirty feet below the water ending in a collection of crumbled lava rock frosted with pastel-shaded coral—yellow, green, pink. The mass of rock and coral formed a step, which gave way to a gradually descending mix of rock, sand, and coral below, fading into the darkness of open ocean.

The ocean was alive.

Fish darted in every direction. To my left, a slender yellow fish, like a ballpoint pen wrapped in caution tape, swam against the cliff face, ready to dart into the cracks at the first sign of trouble. A school of chimney-red fish moved in unison, accelerating and pausing like a symphony. A ghostly eel weaved through the rocks on the ocean floor. A stingray the size of a dinner plate rippled over a patch of sand. Farther down the cliffs, away from the jumping point, a pale yellow octopus crawled over the rocks.

I held my breath and sank into the water. I turned my back to the cliffs and stared out into the ocean, the blue sheen that tinted my vision obscured the distance in midnight blue. Warm waves cradled my body, the current rocking me. I savored the feeling of weightlessness and insignificance, 1,100 miles of ocean between me and the closest inhabited island, Kiribati. Could I swim for it? Could my jiu-jitsu take me that far? I had been on the island for almost four months now, which meant I had taken nearly 160 jiu-jitsu classes, roughly 480 hours of training. My body was lean, muscular. I moved with confidence, my back straight, my chin high, my face hard and strong. I was still a white belt, but I felt like a blue belt.

My heart rate slowed. I relaxed completely. I closed my eyes. I thought of drowning.

I remembered being under water in a different time and place. I was seventeen, lifeguarding at Sunset Beach Park. I had jumped from the chair to the sidewalk, my bare feet pounding on the concrete, my arms pumping, my gaze fixed on a sinking five-year-old boy. I dove into the water. He was beneath the surface now, his fingers reaching toward the sun, toward oxygen, toward life.

I dolphin kicked twice. My arms wrapped around his limp body. I carried him from the depths. When our heads broke free, he gasped, the hard panicked inhalation of someone who thought they would never breathe again. I pulled him to the side, out of the water and into the grass. His hand clung to my arm, a white knuckle grip. His lungs coughed water. I noticed that he wore arm floats. They weren't fully inflated.

He put his faith in those floats; he trusted them with his life. And they failed him. He'd be duped again, eventually, by someone or something. The consequences may not be dire, but he would still wade out to where he could no longer touch and discover suddenly that he was alone, with no way back.

Big Island jiu-jitsu saved me when my floats failed, and it taught me how to swim. Were my training partners at the BJ Penn Academy on the mat for a similar reason? What had been taken from them that drove to take sanctuary in violence?

When I rejoined my friends, the sun began to kiss the ocean. Jack sat in a lawn chair, and Jake dangled his legs over the cliff. Roke walked toward the group from the opposite direction; he had been exploring. I tossed my gear in the bed of the Red Baron and grabbed my camera. I discovered that Jack had been playing with it. He had stuck the camera down his pants and taken a picture, leaving it for me to discover.

I was scrolling through my photos when Roke said, "I'm going to do it."

"Yeah, right," Jake said.

"For real, dude," Roke replied.

"Do what?" I asked.

"A mother effin swan dive," Roke said.

"Here?" I asked.

"Yes, sir."

"Tits," Jack said, his head tilted back, his eyes closed.

I sat down on the rocks next to Jake. Roke paced up and down the cliff side, searching for the perfect spot. He stepped down to a lower rock. He gripped land with one hand and leaned over the water, judging the distance and surveying his landing zone.

"Don't even bother pretending," Jake said.

"Shut up," Roke said.

"You're just going to embarrass yourself," Jake said.

"Dude, let me concentrate," Roke said.

"Good thing you stepped down to that rock too," Jake said. "Your fall will be a whole three inches shorter."

"I'm going to kill you."

"Before or after you don't jump?"

Roke turned his back. He bounced, nervously. He breathed deeply. He extended his arms. He closed his eyes, peaking only once at the water below him. He leapt, his body soaring into the air. He arced downward, pointing his face toward the ocean, bringing his hands together above his head. He hit the water.

Roke about to swan dive at South Point

When he came back up, he yelled, "Oh God, that hurt!"

Roke swam slowly to the rusty ladder and climbed back to the top.

"Dude, my head is killing me," Roke said. "It's my ear," he added after a pause.

Roke plugged his nose and blew as though he were trying to pop his ear. His right ear didn't pop; it whistled.

"Oh shit," Jack said, beginning to giggle. "You did it now, Roke!"

The dive ruptured his ear drum. Roke laughed it off, but his eyes betrayed hidden pain and fear.

The sun began to set, and Jake joked that now would be a good time to find a place to stay. I suggested pulling the Red Baron down the beach behind some rocks and camping at South Point. Jack said that he wanted to sleep on a sandy beach, so we thumbed through my guidebook (I was the only person who brought one), and picked the closest isolated beach.

Everyone picked the Road to the Sea, a pair of isolated beaches a few miles from South Point. Everyone but me, that is. The guidebook clearly stated that the road was not two-wheel-drive friendly, and the Red Baron was not four-wheel-drive equipped.

"It'll be fine," Jack reassured me.

Again, I disagreed, but I hopped into the bed of the Red Baron and hoped for the best.

The Road to the Sea cut through a raw lava field. There were no trees, no grass, no flowers. Weeds didn't even grow in the hostile terrain. The road began as a flat gravel stretch, after a mile, it turned to dirt. The dirt road turned treacherous, a collection of canyons masquerading as a path. The Red Baron creaked and clanked as its tires fell into hole after hole and clawed out.

I remembered the Red Baron getting a flat tire driving on well-kept public roads (on our way back from Volcanoes National Park). We didn't have a spare tire. Daylight was fading. We continued driving away from civilization and toward the two black-and-green sand beaches at the end of the Road to the Sea. We stopped twice to unload the gear from the bed to take weight off the tires.

We crested the last hill and coasted to a stop at the beach.

An engine block sat half buried in the black sand like a corpse. Nothing else was left. No doubt the car had made the trek to the beach, where the engine died and was scavenged for parts. I imagined the Red Baron parked next to that engine block, decaying while we hiked back in the dark.

The beach was desolate. The lava flow devastation that began at the beginning of the road extended for six miles and faded into the water where we stood. The olivine crystals mixed with the black sand, giving its green quality, glimmering like a million emeralds. Though the landscape was scarred from the destruction of lava flow, there was a beauty to it. Jake, however, didn't like the idea of a beach without palm trees. We stayed long enough for Jack to take a picture with the green sand in his hands, and we left.

On the way out, the back bumper fell off. Not wanting to be pulled over for not having a license plate (Jack still hadn't bought car insurance), we duct-taped the bumper back on. By the time we were back on main roads, it was dark, and it rained. Roke and I were in the bed of the truck, covered with a tarp. The cab of the Red Baron shielded us from most of the rain, but anytime we stopped, the rain pelted us. The grass in the bed of the Red Baron appreciated the rain, Roke and I didn't.

We found a campground, but it was full. We needed reservations. We debated setting up camp in the parking lot, but some stink eye from locals deterred us.

We found a dorm-room style hotel farther along the Kona coast. An old haole lady worked the desk. When Jake and I inquired about vacancies, she told us that she had two rooms available. Then she looked out the window and saw Jack and Roke gallivanting toward the hotel lobby.

"I'm sorry," she said. "I was mistaken. We don't have any rooms left."

We continued north along the Kona coast, through the rain and the wind. We were still far from the heart of Kona, the center of tourism on the Big Island, so the few hotels that we passed were already closed. We stopped at another beach, hoping to camp, but the access road was blocked by a large, locked gate. Frustrated, we pulled off to a lookout point, which was little more than a roadside parking lot.

Jake leaned against the Red Baron, his head in his hands. Roke turned on his flash light and meandered around the parking lot. Dark circles lingered beneath Jack's eyes. I shivered.

"What are we going to do?" Jack asked.

No one answered. A car rounded the bend, the roar of its engine mixing with the rippling of the rain. It passed, the spray of its tires landing inches from my feet.

"Let's just camp here," Jake said.

"What? For real?" I asked.

Roke yelled from the other side of the parking lot, "Dude! You should see the size of these roaches!"

Jake continued, "For real. We can pull the Red Baron against the wall over there and set up the tarps to stay out of the rain."

"I am not sleeping on the side of the road," I said.

"Don't be such a pussy," Jack added.

Roke shouted, "This one is yellow, and I think it can bench press more than me!'

"We can't stay here," I said. "The cops will drive by eventually."

"Get over it," Jake said, his eyes narrowing.

"No. I am not sleeping here. I'll pay for the god damn hotel room."

Roke's flashlight swept across the parking lot. "There are thousands of them! They're everywhere!" he yelled.

"Why do you have to be such an asshole?"

"Fuck you. Let's drive to Kona and get a hotel."

Jake stepped into the cab and slammed the door. Jack followed while Roke and I took our places in the bed. Two hours later, at about 3 AM, we checked into a Kona hotel room. I slept on the floor while Jake and Jack got drunk.

* * * * *

The next morning, we drove to Place of Refuge.

Place of Refuge was the idyllic paradise advertised in brochures. It was flawless. White sand circled coconut trees. Handmade stone walls bordered clear pools of water. Where the white sand ended, dried lava flow began, smooth mounds of black rock lumped into small islands and peninsulas. Ocean water pulsed through the rocks, flowing in and out with the beating of the waves, leaving pockets of crisp water populated with coral, fish, and sea cucumbers. The sand and the dried lava flow formed a small bay with a grass hat positioned near the middle of the rim.

In traditional times, Place of Refuge was like a get out of jail free card. Since tribal society was strict, many offenses were punishable by death. If a guilty party was able to escape to Place of Refuge, however, a priest would provide a set of atonement rituals, and the crimes would eventually be forgiven. In my mind, this sort of appeal system favored the most athletic and most cunning criminals (precisely the type of criminals you don't want to keep around), and I wondered why the enforcers of tribal law just didn't guard the entrance to Place of Refuge like children guarding home base during a game of hide and go seek (except with spears).

When we arrived at Place of Refuge, we had one extra passenger, a hitchhiker named Tim.

By the time we left the hotel the next morning, the rain had passed and the usual Kona weather returned, a warm sun and a clear sky. On our way to Place of Refuge, a battered Jeep Cherokee pulled up next to us at a stop light. The driver leaned out the window to talk to Jake, who was sitting in the passenger seat of the cab. Since Roke and I were in the bed of the Red Baron, we couldn't hear much of the conversation over the grumble of traffic. What we did hear startled us.

"Sure, just hop in the back," Jake said.

Roke and I looked at each other.

"Did he mean back here, with us?" Roke asked.

I shrugged.

A few minutes later, we pulled over behind the Cherokee. Tim stepped out, threw his bag in the bed of the Red Baron, and climbed in.

Tim was a haole. He said he was originally from Texas but had moved to Hawaii to work as a commercial fisherman. His girlfriend accompanied him, but they had just broken up. Tim had come home early and found her cheating on him with his then best friend. Now, Tim was essentially homeless, living out of his Cherokee until he could get enough money together to move back to Texas. He had left his motorcycle at the Hilo Walmart and needed to retrieve it so that he could sell it. Jake, speaking for all of us, told Tim that we'd take him to Hilo, but since we were on our way to Place of Refuge he would have to accompany us for the day.

Tim sat down next to me. Brown and black stains marred his khaki shorts. His T-shirt was white at one point but, like his shorts, would probably never be clean again. A yellow substance caked and flaked from his scalp, floating away in the wind like dandelion seeds whenever he scratched. A few of his teeth were missing, and he smelled like rotting flesh.

My favorite thing about Tim: his nose leaked at random, with no apparent cause. He'd be in the middle of telling a story—about how he hooked up with a rich housewife on her husband's yacht and wrecked it because he was too drunk to steer, for example—and fluid would spill from his nose like a ruptured water faucet. He'd catch some of it with his hands, wipe the rest away with his sleeve, smile, and continue the story as if nothing happened. Why did Tim's nose leak? Because cocaine had eroded his nasal passages.

Hitchhiking was common on the Big Island. Since many locals drove pickup trucks, allowing a hitchhiker to ride in the bed was relatively low-risk. Jon, a purple belt from Kauai, told me that he frequently hitchhiked to get from one end of the island to the other. He estimated that he had hitchhiked over 300 times in life, without incident. Despite Jon's reassurances about the safety of hitchhiking, I opted not to try it.

When we arrived at Place of Refuge, Tim stayed with us. I had heard that Place of Refuge was the best place on the island for snorkeling, but I didn't trust Tim, and I didn't trust my haole friends to watch my stuff while I was gone, so I didn't wander far, and I didn't swim. I listened to Tim talk about his life (and was skeptical about most of it). He complained about foreign fisherman anchoring wooden rafts in the ocean to attract fish (somehow the growth of plant life in the middle of the ocean attracts smaller fish which in turn attract larger fish). He bragged about the tuna he caught the last time he went fishing. He talked about wanting to buy a boat to sail around South America. He offered to give us weed for taking him to Hilo and asked repeatedly if he could "crash" with us.

At Place of Refuge with Tim the hitchhiker

Jake ignored me. Jack was indifferent. Roke vocalized his frustration to me, but not to Jake or Jack. I wanted spring break to be over. I wanted to escape the haoles. I wanted to be back in the gym. I wanted Charuto, or Jay, or BJ to call me to promote me to blue belt.

On our way back to Hilo, Roke and I were relegated to the bed of the Red Baron again, with Tim. We went back to Hilo the way we came, the landscape we saw the day before rewinding as we neared Hilo. My time on the Big Island was running out. I didn't know if I was over Hilary. I didn't fully understand local culture. Most importantly, I hadn't earned my blue belt and still wasn't a bad ass. Was I going to leave the island a different person?

My mind wandered this way for hours.

About fifteen miles outside of Hilo, Tim turned to me. "You look like you've got a lot on your mind," he said. "Got a girl back home or something?"

"Nah, nothing like that. Just figuring stuff out," I said.

"Dude. Hawaii does that to you. It's some kind of trip. It's like you step outside of your life and can look down on it, on everything you ever were," Tim said.

Maybe I had more in common with Tim than I realized.

15

THE AMISH KID CAN SCRAP

was in the midst of a butterfly stretch when Ilia called my name. I lifted my head. He was a few feet away, lying on the mat. Patrick sat next to him, smiling and tightening the knot on his purple belt. They both drove from Waimea to Hilo three nights a week to train at the BJ Penn Academy. They tapped me out—a lot.

"Marshal," Patrick said. "You from Pennsylvania?"

"Yeah."

"Brah," Patrick said, grinning, "You Amish?" He pronounced it "aim-ish." Patrick and Ilia laughed.

They had connected my haoleness with my chin-strap Abraham Lincoln beard with my home state, Pennsylvania. Before I could respond, warm-ups began, but the workout didn't keep Ilia and Patrick from making the most of their joke.

"Marshal," Ilia said while drilling an armbar, "How you phone home? Morse code?"

Later, during a break in training, I saw movement out of the corner of my eye. Ilia and Patrick held imaginary rods with both hands. They pumped their arms up and down.

"What are you doing?" I asked.

"Brah," Patrick said, "We churnin' buttah!" They collapsed on the mat, laughing.

They were making fun of me but in a friendly manner. I trained on weekends with Ethan, Chris, and Poai and they too subjected me to friendly ribbings. This was it. I had done it. I was no longer an outsider. I was accepted. I was elated, but I still shaved my beard that night. I didn't grow it back.

The Amish joke entertained Jay, thoroughly. When I shaved my beard, he knew why.

"Oh no beard? You can't escape your roots, you know," he said, laughing.

Jay had a unique sense of humor. In the gym, he was generally quiet, except for when he was teaching. He took teaching and training seriously, so he rarely joked in the mat room. When he was rolling or was outside of the gym, however, Jay poked fun at others and gladly talked story.

Once, while we were rolling before an evening class, Jay let me work my guard passing. I opened his guard and fought to clear his legs. He trapped my trailing leg in half guard and tightened his grip on my lapel, cinching the fabric around my neck. I was uncomfortable, but I thought that if I remained calm and continued breathing through my nose, I could work through the pain and pass Jay's half guard. Just a little bit more space and I'd be free. Just a little bit more space.

Then Jay said, "Good morning!"

My peripheral vision was blurry. My tongue tingled. For a moment, I had forgotten what I was doing. I was passing half guard. I gripped Jay's gi and returned to wiggling my leg free. But why did Jay say good morning?

"Did you have a nice nap?" Jay asked.

"What are you talking about?"

"You went to sleep," Jay said.

"No way."

Jay started to laugh, his Hawaiian cheeks rising from his wide arcing grin. "You were sitting upright, your eyes rolled back, snoring," he said. "I pulled your hand off my leg, but when I let go, you went back to grabbing my pants and trying to pass half guard! You were asleep, and you kept fighting!"

Jay tapped me out with an armbar and suggested that I take a break.

After a brief pause, he added, "I feel bad for your girlfriend. You probably armbar her in your sleep!"

From that day on, whenever we rolled, Jay would pause from time to time to ask me if I was tired, adding that he didn't want me falling asleep again.

Jay, apparently, had a similar sense of humor as a child. A white belt visiting from New York invited Jay and I out to lunch one afternoon. Over plates of Chicken Katsu and white rice, Jay told us what growing up in Hawaii was like.

"We would hike up to da kine," Jay said. "Oh what's it called? It's a river outside of Hilo. We used to go there and play all the time. Lots of da kine, waterfalls and rocks for jumping. There was this rope bridge, old style, one bottom rope, one top rope, and you shimmy across. So what do you do? You wait until someone gets to the middle, then you grab the rope and shake."

Jay gripped an imaginary rope and rocked his body back and forth, suggesting that the rope was shaken violently.

"You try to make the guy fall off, but if he don't, at least you gave him a good scare."

After a few forkfuls of Chicken Katsu, Jay began another story.

"This one time, we were climbing the waterfalls, da kine, going back and forth across the river, going as far upstream as we could. It was me, my brother, and one of our friends. We're crossing the top of this waterfall, and the rocks are slippery from the water and the moss, so we're going slow. And da kine, our friend, he slips. He starts to fall. My brother grabs his arm, catches him. This guy's face—he thought he was going to die. In his mind, he knew that he was dead.

So my brother is holding him, and he's still off balance. My brother smiles and lets him go, and he falls twenty feet into the water!"

Jay never said which of his brothers did this, and it was clear that nobody got hurt. His story reminded me of a UH Hilo student that died the previous semester. He was cliff jumping at Boiling Pots, a scenic spot upriver from Rainbow Falls, and he had been sucked into an underwater lava tube. He drowned. I asked Jay what he thought of the dangers of underwater lava tubes.

"The mistake is to try and swim out," he said. "That's how you die. You can't fight the current. You have to relax and let the lava tube shoot you out the other end."

I suspected that there were more variables involved in escaping an underwater lava tube, but Jay spoke with confidence, as though he jumped into lava tubes all the time just for fun. Maybe black belts could do that sort of thing.

After lunch that day, Jay offered to drop me off at my dorm. On the way, I mustered the courage to ask him about earning a blue belt. I knew that inquiring about a promotion in general was disrespectful, but with less than two months left in my stay, I needed to know if my goal was within reach.

"Oh, sure," Jay said. "I'll talk to Charuto and BJ and have them check you out."

Wait, what? I had to prove myself in front of BJ?

* * * * *

I tried to stay close, in tight where he couldn't wiggle free of my lockdown.

He leaned back and pressed his hand into my temple, pinning my head to the mat. His weight crushed my chest. My face scraped back and forth across the blue canvas. I clung to the position.

His hand slipped off my head, his forearm following after, smashing into my face. A flashbulb white haze came over the mat room.

The pain was dull, like I had hit my head on the underside of a table. I tried to focus.

The elbow grinded my cheek, my ear. This time the pain was sharp, like a bee sting. My ear started to ring. Gone were the sounds of fighters hitting heavy bags. Gone was the reggae soundtrack blaring from the radio. Gone was the harsh whisper of the tropical rain falling outside.

All I could hear was ringing, high-pitched, squealing. I felt his weight shift.

I scrambled. I slipped under his arm. I maneuvered behind him. He tried to spin, to face me, but I rolled with him, staying on his back. My legs wrapped around his waist. My arms wrapped around his neck. He rolled face down. I squeezed as hard as I could. He tapped.

I let go and slumped against the wall, trying to catch my breath. Kris sat down next to me and, with a smile, shook my hand. We didn't need to say it. We both knew it had been a good match. I probed my face for cuts, checking the usual areas: the brow line, the cheekbone, the lips. Nothing.

Then I felt my ear. Inside, just above the hole, was a swollen mass the size of a small grape. It was tense, like an overfilled water balloon, and it hurt. Touching it was like sticking a thumbtack in my ear.

I turned to show Kris. He laughed.

"Brah," he said. "You got cauliflower ear!"

Cauliflower ear is common in combat sports like wrestling and boxing. When I returned to the mainland, I spoke to Dr. Philip Pollice (an ear, nose, and throat specialist), about the cause of cauliflower ear.

He said, "Basically, cauliflower ear is the result of repeated trauma to the auricle (or to the ear). It's called auricular trauma, and it usually occurs over a period of time. When you get trauma to the ear, you can develop something that's called an auricular hematoma, or a hematoma under the skin. That's a collection of blood under the skin of the ear. If the blood doesn't get drained, it causes the cartilage of the ear to grow out of control, and that results in this malformed ear."

Once a fighter gets cauliflower ear, there is no way to reverse to it.

For some fighters, the ears look as though the valleys have been filled in, like a clay ear not completely sculpted.

Some are swollen and folded, like fortune cookies.

Some just have cauliflower ear in the upper section of the ear, but it's thick, making the ears look like little flesh-colored hot air balloons.

The worst-looking cauliflower ear is the last kind: the outer ridge of the ear actually collapses into itself in one section, like a balloon animal with a deflated segment.

I wasn't very happy about getting cauliflower ear, and I expressed that to Kris. He just smiled.

"No worries," he said.

No worries?

I have been self-conscious about my ears for a long time, because, well, my ears are huge. Now, most people will assure me that my ears aren't that large at all, but what they don't understand is that my ears have been the same since birth. My ears are just as big now as they were when I came out of the womb. Not only was I not worth showing off to family and friends, but if I was left outside on a windy day, I was liable to be blown away.

Growing up, I hated my ears so much that I once started saving for plastic surgery. Other kids wanted Legos and Super Nintendo, but I wanted Dr. 90210 (I bought some Bruce Lee movies instead).

After twenty-one years, I had finally grown into my ears and was not embarrassed to be out in public. And now, I had cauliflower ear. Drawing more attention to my ears was the last thing that I wanted.

"What should I do?" I asked Kris.

"Keep it. It looks cool."

From wrestling in high school, Kris had gotten the clay kind of cauliflower ear. I decided that he wasn't the best person to go to for advice, so I asked other fighters in the gym.

I talked to Henry, a short and very round Hawaiian. When he trained, he sweated pork grease.

"Keep it, brah. You be one ultimate journalist," he said.

Henry had the deflated balloon animal ear.

I talked to Iol.

"Shoots. If you got cauli' ear, everyone know you tough," he said.

Iol had the clay ear.

I talked to Jesse, a stocky, tattooed local. Jesse carried himself the way a pit bull walks, with a sort of menacing strut and vicious smile. Jesse worked multiple jobs and snuck in the backdoor of the gym to take extra classes.

"Just let it go. It happens to all of us," he said.

Jesse had one deflated balloon animal ear and one fortune cookie ear.

I talked to Jay.

"If you don't like it, drain it, and get used to wearing headgear. That's the only way to keep from getting it," he said.

Jay had normal ears.

Wait, how did he not have cauliflower ear?

"Oh I have it," he said, laughing. "I just drain it to keep from looking like BJ (BJ has serious hot air balloon ear)."

"Isn't draining it expensive?"

"If a doctor does it, yeah," Jay said, adjusting the lapel of his unbleached gi.

"Huh?"

"Just get a needle and a syringe, but make sure you get the thickest needle you can find, and drain it yourself. Oh, and be careful when you pull the needle out. You don't want the ear sucking the fluid back in," Jay said, miming the draining procedure against his ear.

I wanted to ask him how much it would hurt, but this was a place where people came to fight, came to punch and be punched, to twist limbs and have their limbs twisted. Pain was not spoken of. Pain was ignored. Pain was forgotten.

Even the history of pain—written in the scar tissue accumulated on brow lines and cheek bones, noted in the railroad track scares left from knee and elbow surgeries, and etched into cauliflower ears by brutal training sessions—are seen as trophies, rather than regrettable instances of agony and suffering. Fighting makes you ugly.

I didn't want to be ugly, so I set out on a quest to find a syringe and a thick hypodermic needle.

I thought that the rise of drug abuse and the subsequent paranoia of law enforcement agencies and legislators would make purchasing a needle and syringe difficult. After all, some stores won't even sell Wite-Out or cough syrup to minors. If buying simple household items is difficult, buying a needle and syringe must be tough.

No, not really.

All I had to do according to Chris (very slight clay ear) was go across town to a farmer supply store. Sure the needles might be intended for farm animals, but a needle is a needle he said. Chris recommended that I get the needle as soon as possible so that I could drain the ear before it hardened, but I had no way of getting across town. I would have to wait until the following Friday, almost a full week, for Ti to give me a ride.

While I waited for the antidote to my ailment, I went about my daily routine of going to classes at the university and making the trek down Kinoole Street. During that week, I discovered that cauliflower ear set me apart, for better and for worse.

"What happened to your ear?" Jessica asked, her lips curled back around her teeth, her eyes scrunched and wrinkled like she had just witnessed a gruesome car accident.

I explained to her the nature of cauliflower ear.

"That's disgusting. Why would you do that to yourself?"

I shrugged.

The rest of my time on campus was more of the same. People eyed my ear like they would eye a bullet wound, with a mixture of disgust and pity. They were disturbed and astonished that I would willingly put myself in a situation (repeatedly) that could mean permanent disfigurement. At the gym, however, my ear brought smiles to the faces of my training partners and approving nudges to my shoulders.

"Brah, you no be fighter without da ear," Lyle said at the end of a training session, long after the sun had set and the night had become thick with sweat and the chirp of coqui frogs.

One night, I stayed later than usual, talking about an upcoming fight card with Iol. Lyle stepped out of the room and came back some time later with a bucket and mop (he couldn't afford to pay to train three nights a week, so he mopped the mats at night to pay for the third training session). He had discarded his gi top, and for the first time, I got a full view of his tattoos. An assortment of Polynesian bands and triangles wrapped around his arms and ran up his back like vines. The most distinctive tattoo, however, was a uniform group of scales draped over his right pectoral like medieval armor, a Hawaiian warrior tattoo.

As Lyle mopped up and down the mat, I glanced around at the other fighters still leaning against the wall. I could see each of them in the old way, at the prow of a canoe, gripping a spear, ready and excited to be going into battle. They were warriors. They dedicated their lives to fighting. They made personal, financial, emotional, and physical sacrifices so that they could train. I saw in them a sort of strength and dedication—a fighter's strength and dedication—I did not see in normal people.

Until then, I hadn't given it much thought, but nearly every one of my training partners had cauliflower in one form or another. The higher the belt rank, the more fights on their record, the more twisted and mangled their ears.

I started to see cauliflower as a badge or a flag. It was, without a doubt, a means of identifying fellow fighters.

My training partners felt that that fighting set them apart. They had put themselves through a level of pain and sacrifice that most people cannot fathom. These were my people, my brothers. We loved the beauty of combat. We spoke a language of violence that not many understand.

That Friday, I bought my needle and syringe. They sat on my desk like the key to a final exam, tempting yet wrong.

Chris called.

"We drainin' the ear tonight?" he asked.

"No, I think I'm going to let it go," I said.

My left ear was turning to the clay ear, and the little bit of cauliflower shifted that ear so that it angled out more than the other. I liked it.

* * * * *

Scrapping was a part of local culture. I was sure of that much. I wanted to know *why* scrapping was a part of local culture. I suspected that in some way colonization had transmuted the Hawaiian warrior spirit and that transmutation was somehow connected to the local desire to scrap and to the glorification of cauliflower ear.

I pitched an article to *Ultimate Grappling* about local fight culture, and they accepted it, giving me an excuse to research what made local fighters tick.

I scheduled interviews with Chad H'ao, the promoter and matchmaker of Beatdown, and three professional fighters: Poai, Mike Aina, and Ross Ebanez. I scheduled all of the interviews in one day, and set aside time to watch them train.

When I came into the Academy for the interviews, Poai was wrapping his hands, covering his calloused palms and knuckles with yellow fabric.

Poai began to shadowbox. Jab. Cross. Jab. Hook. Uppercut.

Just a few years ago, Poai was working at a restaurant in Japan, not pursuing a career in fighting. A chance encounter brought him into the gym and into a fighter career.

Poai moved to a heavy bag and started hitting the canvas, slowly, as though he were still tagging shadows. After a few combinations, the bag swung like a wind chime during a Big Island thunderstorm. A few feet from the bags, Mike Aina and Ross Ebanez were locked in a clinch, pummeling for underhooks.

Aina was a local with haole roots. His head was shaved and his chin and brow line were hard. Aina started his day at 5 AM, making the drive from Hilo to the summit of Mauna Kea to work on two of the world's largest telescopes. When he finished work at 3 PM, he drove back to Hilo, caught his breath, and started training by 5 PM. That was his routine for every weekday.

Aina started boxing at thirteen, but he graduated high school feeling aimless. He eventually found himself watching a Superbrawl card in Oahu. MMA gave Aina's life direction, and a few years later he entered the cage to fight the heavily favored Nick Diaz. Aina went three rounds with Diaz, losing a controversial split decision.

Ebanez shot a takedown. Aina sprawled. Ebanez escaped the bottom position, and the two resumed clinching. Aina pressed Ebanez against the fence and worked for a single-leg takedown. Ebanez hopped on one leg and strained to drive Aina's head away.

Ebanez had rounded features, and his default facial expression was a grim assassin seriousness, but when he smiled, he looked like a cartoon character. Like Aina, Ebanez started boxing when he was young. When I talked to him, he had fought in so many amateur events that he had lost count. Ebanez started grappling when BJ brought Brazilian jiu-jitsu to Hilo. Under BJ's guidance, he learned the ground game and made the transition to MMA.

Ebanez also began his work day early. By 6 AM, he was on his way to install guardrails somewhere on the Big Island. If he was lucky, he would nap in the truck on the way back to Hilo, giving him some much needed rest before evening training.

Ebanez began to secure a kimura on Aina's far arm. Aina blocked the attempt and reclaimed full guard. He started pivoting for an arm-bar, but the buzzer rang. Aina and Ebanez laughed and followed Poai out of the cage to get water.

Long before the buzzer signaled the start of the next round, they were back in the cage, poised to resume training. They, like most locals, loved to fight. To them, MMA was an extension of the com-petitive spirit and pride that was just as much a part of local culture as scrapping. Aina experienced this growing up on the Big Island.

"You learn to stand up for yourself, for sure," Aina said. "Espe-cially in Hilo, man, it's kind of tough. I'm not sure how it is on the rest of the islands, but out here, we fight for respect. You got to stand your ground."

He paused briefly and continued.

"Out here, you fight one on one. After it's done, it's done. That's the way I experienced it. For me, you fight; you get over it. You don't be a wimp. You don't back down. You get your ass kicked, whatever. You live to fight another day."

Poai said it's all part of Hawaii's world.

"It's just that everyone plays sports in Hawaii," Poai said. "When you play sports, especially contact sports, confrontations are bound to happen. You grew up with that shit, and you learn to either get re-ally fast or learn to tuck your chin. I was really fast by the way."

Sports in Hawaii were treated differently than they were on the mainland. Because Hawaii did not have professional sports teams, high school and collegiate athletics received a great deal of media attention. Schedules and results of local sporting events were aired on television and radio as major news, not as footnotes like on the mainland. The extra attention fueled and intensified competition, sometimes resulting in schoolyard scraps.

This passion for competition, combined with a passion for fight-ing, made MMA a popular sport in Hawaii. Local events were always packed with fighters eager to put on a show.

"Everyone here has a lot of heart," Poai said. "Often more balls than brains, but hey, that's what makes fights in Hawaii awesome."

H'ao was a large Hawaiian with a shaved head. He moved like a lightweight and trained like a professional. According to H'ao, fights in Hawaii used to be all balls and no brains, and he would know. Through his work with Beatdown and previous work with Rumble on the Rock, H'ao watched MMA in Hawaii mature.

"I think the sport has changed in that when it first started in Hawaii, no one really trained to fight," he said. "Everyone was just going there and feeling pretty tough, just going to scrap. Now, more people are making the effort to go ahead and get proper training, learn some technique. We got some more technical fighters, and I would say the way it changed is that everyone, or more people, understand how the sport works now, rather than going in there thinking it's just a fight."

Though the fighters were now more technical, their reasons for fighting had not changed all that much.

"Everyone feels their fighting for pride mostly," H'ao said. "Money and all of that kind of stuff doesn't really matter to most of the boys. It's just pride. Everyone is very proud of where they're from and whom they represent."

Since the geography of Hawaii made it a collection of closely knit communities, fighters often feel like they are representing their town when they fight, as though they are repaying family and friends for giving them a home and giving them support. On a global level, being a fighter from Hawaii is an opportunity to represent a culture and a people that the rest of the world overlooks.

"I think it's because we come from such a small place; that might be the reason why everyone feels the need to fight, to show that we're legitimate coming from such a tiny little, isolated couple of islands away from everyone," H'ao said. "That's what drives everyone. It's to show that, you know, Hawaii is here, [and] we've got tough guys. Don't overlook our little islands."

Ebanez agreed that exposure is a major part of fighting outside of Hawaii.

"There is talent in Hawaii. From the BJ Penn Academy, from Honolulu. There is a lot of good fighters," Ebanez said. "How many fighters out of California are in the UFC? There's a whole bunch. How many fighters have the chance to fight in huge shows from Hawaii? A handful. I think that's what it is. You just want to represent where you come from."

"The Hawaiians are coming out," H'ao said. "We're going to show the world that we got some tough guys coming from these little islands."

The training session was over. The gym was quieter now. The symphony of coqui frogs followed the night breeze through the windows, no longer drowned out by dull thuds of gloves hitting bags and pads.

Aina sat on the stairs at the base of the cage, holding his sweat-soaked T-shirt in his hand. Ebanez stood nearby, taking slow sips from a water bottle. Poai carefully rolled his wraps into tight cylinders, packing them safely into his bag. Aina and Ebanez had another early workday ahead of them, and Poai had a plane to catch, yet they lingered. Their love for fighting had them basking in punches and submissions, and they trained so that their passion would not stay hidden within the gym.

On my way home, I tried to put what Poia, Aina, Ebanez, and H'ao had said into perspective. I had suspected from the beginning of my stay that Hawaiians felt cheated and ignored by the mainland United States and the world in general. Ebanez and H'ao's expression of a strong desire to have Hawaii recognized on a world stage suggested that these feelings had a connection to their hyper-competitiveness and extended beyond Hawaiians to locals in general. Perhaps the cultural phenomenon of scrapping was an indirect result of colonization.

In an article in *Honolulu* magazine entitled "The Destruction of the Hawaiian Male," Keone Nunes and Scott Whitney assert that

"Hawaiian men have been marginalized and disempowered by the loss of their own place in the traditional culture-and by the unrelenting changes brought on by the haole colonizers of the Islands." Nunes and Whitney go on to describe the exceptionally high rate of suicide and juvenile arrests among Hawaiian males, as well as their much shorter life expectancy in comparison to Hawaiian women. These statistics alone may be enough to suggest that local males are struggling to assert themselves and their worth in present-day society, but Nunes and Whitney trace the destruction of the Hawaiian male back to the death of the Great Kamehameha, the legendary Hawaiian that flipped the Naha stone and united the islands.

They state that the heir to the kingdom, Liholiho, was unprepared to shoulder the responsibility of leading the Islands. Two of the Great Kamehameha's wives suggested that Liholiho transfer power to them, and he eventually conceded, sharing a meal with them (a major violation of social norms). By giving royal authority to women and by eating with women, Liholiho permitted the overthrow of *kapu*, a set of traditions and taboos that previously made males an important part of spiritual, economic, and social proceedings in Hawaii. The overthrow of *kapu* created cultural confusion and a "spiritual void" for the Hawaiian people that, according to Nunes and Whitney, missionaries exploited to gain power.

Nunes and Whitney say that "Hawaiian males are still feeling the radiating effects of the initial cultural bomb of 1819." They suggest that Hawaiian males are depicted in modern advertising as buffoons and that Hawaiian women are far outpacing their male counterparts in terms of social worth. They conclude their article by saying, "Because of the loss of cultural status through the overthrow of kapu and the imposition of a foreign culture, contemporary Hawaiian men continue the struggle to find a place for themselves in a late 20th-century Western economy."

The Tattoo, the novel set in Hawaii that I was reading at the beginning of the semester (the one that described two locals hunting haoles), echoes the hypothesis that Nunes and Whitney supported.

Koa, a Hawaiian local, expresses to Kenji, a local with Japanese heritage, a frustration and hate for haoles that stems back to the overthrow of *kapu* and the subsequent loss of Hawaiian sovereignty. The conversation begins when Kenji says that the Japanese are not tough samurais anymore because of the atomic bomb.

Koa retorts, "Fuck dat. Eh, Hawaiians got mo' fucked by da haoles. You know, my grandfadda used to tell me about Kahalui and Kaneohe Bay when he was small kid time." Koa goes on to tell Kenji how fish, taro, and pigs used to be plentiful, how the beaches used to be clean, and how the water in the streams used to be drinkable. Koa blames the loss of culture and the loss of his family's ruling status on haoles. Like the atomic bombs dropped on Japan, the impact of Westernization lingered in Hawaii like radiation, poisoning and infecting the land and its people.

Perhaps this assault on their identity pushed Hawaiians to champion the warrior spirit, expressing their masculinity in the only way they had left: through fighting. Their pride in their history was still strong, and they fought to earn respect, both for themselves as individuals and for their culture as a whole. Local males, like Kenji in *The Tattoo*, grew up alongside Hawaiians and took on their feelings of persecution and alienation. Maybe that's why scrapping was such a large part of local culture. Maybe that's why they kicked my ass when I first came to the gym. They were proving that they were still true men, warriors.

I started up Lanikaula Street, feeling a sense of jubilation over my epiphany.

An ominous shadow skittered at my feet. I looked down. A centipede the size of a hotdog, marched toward me, its army of legs a ghostly blur. A centipede in Pennsylvania was never larger than two inches. The beast before me, however, was a colossus. Pinchers. An exoskeleton. Millions of legs. The aggressive swagger of a trigger-happy gangster.

I screamed, jumped, and galloped up the hill.

A straining green scooter coasted down the hill, a familiar tan pock-marked blimp gripping its handle bars, wearing a Bob Marley T-shirt. He stared at me curiously as he went by.

I hoped that the centipede would beat him up and steal his weed.

16

LOVE IS LIKE A STAPH INFECTION

Memories of Hilary bled into my life, odd triggers leaking rivulets of gut-wrenching nostalgia. A white Honda Accord. Red Converse shoes with mismatched shoelaces. The band Brand New on a car radio. Chuck Palahniuk. Even my white belt. In an instant I'd leave the Hilo sidewalks and be back in Pennsylvania, moving slowly through the West Alexander cemetery, a summer breeze carrying barbeque smoke from the homes across the street, gravel crunching beneath my black Vans shoes. Hilary walked barefoot through the grass. She grew up next to that cemetery. She played in it as a child, hopping from headstone to headstone, using mausoleums for hide-and-seek. I watched her turn to me, the sunlight on her face. She kissed my cheek and handed me a cigarette.

And the memory would end, leaving me 100 yards from where the memory began, 100 yards that I didn't remember walking. That was my first and only cigarette. Three months later, when soccer camp started, I could taste it after my first sprint.

Sometimes I'd go two or three weeks without thinking of her, and then I'd wake up in a cold sweat after a dream.

In one dream, I was back in a familiar college apartment sitting on a worn futon. Icicle Christmas lights dangled from the ceiling, illuminating Sin City posters and a pirate flag that hung over the doorway. Empty beer cans and empty bottles of Bacardi formed a metropolis on the counter. The glow from the lights swam across the swirling room. I couldn't stand up. The beer stains on the couch were like quicksand, sucking me under. Face after face, old friends, flashed before me, cycling out of one of the bedrooms.

"Thanks for being such an asshole."

"Dude, she's the best."

"She's so hot. So, so hot. Mmm!"

I kept sinking. The faces closed in. A moan from the bedroom grew louder. The futon and the lights swallowing me, eating me. The voices louder and more numerous, speaking over top of each other, three or four at a time.

I woke up. The Hilo sun rose over the palm trees. I packed my gi and walked to the gym to train with Ethan and Chris.

When I arrived, Chris told me that one of my nightmares might come true. Chris had been training for his next professional fight, but he had to sit out from training and eventually withdraw from the fight.

"Brah, I got staph," he said, pointing to the gauze wrapped around his arm. "It started out as one pimple, den it broke open, and da fucka no heal. It get bigger. Den one red line start going up my arm, to my heart. Da docta say if I no went when I did, I no go at all."

By "no go at all," Chris meant dead. I envisioned angry cartoon germs, like the ones I had seen on the bathroom flier my first day in the gym, racing toward Chris' heart with spears and machetes and Tommy guns.

Then Chris said, "Marshal, you better scrub fo' days. You train more than all of us."

A week later—despite extra scrubbing and vigilant cut cleansing—I got staph. It started out as a pimple on my knee. When it broke

open, it pussed. I watched it for another day. The wound wasn't closing, and it continued to puss.

My leg was going to rot off.

Chris and me

Since my health insurance wasn't valid in Hawaii, I went to the
University Health Center. I showed the nurse my knee and explained
to her that there had been a staph outbreak at the gym. Admittedly,
the wound on my knee did not look dire (nothing like an infamous
Kevin Randleman photo; his staph was so bad that it looked like
someone had taken fistfuls of flesh out of his side), but given the
combination of symptoms and knowledge that a few of my training
partners had already been diagnosed with the disease, I was sure that
the nurse would immediately hand me a cocktail of super pills.

"Here's some band aids and some antibiotic ointment. Come
back if it doesn't start to heal in a few days," she said.

"See, I'm really concerned that this is staph," I said.

"Don't you think you might be overreacting?"

I looked at her. I imagined a cartoon germ holding a bowie knife in its teeth, crawling up my leg, toward my heart. "No, I am not overreacting," I said.

"Just come back in a few days."

"I'd rather stop the infection now than wait for it to get worse."

She stared down at me. Her eyes narrowed. She said, "Only the doctor can prescribe that medication, and he'll tell you to wait just like I did."

"When will he be here?"

"Not for three hours."

"I'll wait."

The doctor arrived three and a half hours later. When I explained that there had been an outbreak at the gym, he nodded and examined the wound closely.

"It could just be a minor infection, but then again, it could also be the early stages of staph," he said. "In most cases, we just monitor the wound, but since we know there's a high chance you've already been exposed, we'll give you some strong antibiotics now."

He reached into a drawer and handed me a bottle of pills.

The nurse glared at me as I left the health center. I held the bottle out and shook it as I passed her desk.

* * * * *

I trained so much that I became a part of the gym, like a piece of furniture, built-in like the cage and the boxing ring and the mat. I watched dozens of fighters step on to the mat for a week at a time before leaving again when their brief jiu-jitsu vacation came to an end. They came from all over the world, not just the United States. Most were white belts or blue belts that I could submit at will. Occasionally a purple belt came into town, and they would give me a bit of trouble, but eventually, one of Jay's or Charuto's techniques would come through, and I'd get the submission.

One purple belt in particular, though, mopped the mat with me. He was nineteen and about my size, not tan, and had blond hair. His facial expressions reminded me of BJ because he had no expression at all. When we touched hands, he stepped around my guard (despite my best efforts to stop him). I flopped around like a fish for a few seconds, and then he promptly choked me. Every time. Everyone called him Gunny. He was from Iceland. On many occasions, I saw him in the cage with BJ, training with the professional fighters.

When Gunny rolled with me, he seemed bored. No matter what I did, he easily stepped through my guard. It was like magic. I asked him to explain his technique.

"Well, all of your movement comes from your hips," Gunny said. "If I kill your hips, I can defeat everything else, so I just pressure your hips and then pass."

He demonstrated his movement, but it seemed too simplistic. I tried recreating it in other rolling sessions with people that I usually beat, and I couldn't make it work. There was a level of finesse, some imperceptible shift in weight and balance, involved in the technique that he did not explain and that I could not grasp. Gunny was an entirely different beast from anyone else I had ever rolled with. His body and his mind were built for grappling.

Some time after I returned to the mainland, I saw Gunny on the front page of the *Gracie Magazine* home page. His full name was Gunnar Nelson, and he was being applauded for being a phenom. He got his black belt at twenty-one from Renzo Gracie and around that same time won some highly competitive tournaments and difficult matches. I was rolling with a prodigy and didn't even know it.

Gunny wasn't the only visiting grappler to surprise me.

Three brown belts and a white belt from Megaton BJJ (out of Washington State) came in for an afternoon no-gi class. This was a rather tricky move on their part because training no-gi meant that there was no way of knowing that the person I was about to roll with was actually a very talented and experienced brown belt. All I knew was that some guy I had never met was beating me like I owed him money. That night, I saw the same individual in a gi, and I felt much better about myself when he tied a brown belt around his waist. He apologized for not introducing himself that afternoon. He said his name was Evan Dunham (I saw him in the UFC sometime later, arm-barring Ultimate Fighter standout Efrain Escudero, advancing his undefeated record to ten straight wins).

Taking a whooping from Dunham was painful, but acceptable. He was a legitimate brown belt, the real deal. One of his training partners, the white belt, was a problem.

He was nice enough to me but was much larger than me, by about sixty pounds. On top of that, his jiu-jitsu was technical, making him a nightmare to roll with. I fought feebly to counter his strength and weight, but he eventually railroaded me into submission. This white belt was an anomaly, the only white belt left in the gym that could tap me out.

Each time I went to class, I remembered what Jay said about asking BJ and Charuto to "check me out" to see if I was worthy of a blue belt. Where some schools require a test, a demonstration of specific knowledge and techniques, the BJ Penn Academy operated on a gut-feeling evaluation system. When they felt that you were ready, they stopped class and handed you your next belt. After you survived the belt whipping (more on that later), you were officially promoted. The difficulty of this approach (for the student anyway) is not having any clear idea of when you're closing in on your promotion. In my case, I was beating white belts, many blue belts, and the occasional purple belt. I saw white belts that I consistently submitted earn their blue belts, and I saw blue belts that I consistently tapped—or at least put up a good fight against—earn their purple belts. I felt strong. I felt sharp.

I felt like a blue belt.

BJ stepped into the mat room as soon as I touched hands with the Megaton white belt.

My heart froze. This was my shot to prove myself to BJ and earn my promotion.

The Megaton white belt immediately knocked me to my back with his gorilla hands. He pinned my leg to the mat and started to pass my guard. I shrimped, fighting to escape. His weight fell on my chest. I bridged and shrimped again. I got my knee inside. As I closed my guard, I thought I saw—out of the corner of my eye—BJ watching me roll.

I fought to control his posture, but he drove his shoulder into my chin, every ounce of his 230 pounds cranking my neck. The pressure . . . the pressure . . . my dandelion head about to pop from the stem. I couldn't fail, not now, not with BJ watching.

I struggled. I tried to push him away with my legs and with my arms. The weight was too much. His elbow drove into my neck. The blood stopped flowing to my brain. I couldn't breathe. My fingers started to tingle. I wanted to inhale. I needed to inhale. But BJ was watching. I had the superior position. I had my guard. I should have been able to escape. I should have been able to survive. But the blackness, the blackness was closing in . . . My blue belt was slipping away . . .

I tapped.

It took a few seconds for the blood to get to my brain. By the time I could turn my head, I thought that I saw BJ shaking his head through the haze. He got up, and he left the room.

Everything I had worked for in the last four months had fallen apart in twenty seconds of rolling.

I had failed.

When training ended, I hurriedly packed my gear and walked home. I was embarrassed. I was ashamed. I stopped at a 7-Eleven and bought a nine-dollar bottle of red wine. On my way into my dorm, I passed Laura. She was sitting on a picnic table, smoking a cigarette. Her strawberry blond hair floated in the wind, reaching after the embers of her cigarette as the breeze carried them away. She saw the bottle of wine in my hand.

"Celebrating something?" she asked.

"Not quite."

"Any excuse is a good excuse," she said, laughing.

I started to walk away but hesitated. I turned back to face her. "This is a lot of wine," I said. "I won't be able to finish it by myself."

She smiled and nodded.

I showered, changed, and met her at an apartment across campus where she was drinking with friends. The apartment was small, two beds in a room with one bathroom. Two people sat in desk chairs, the rest on the floor or on one of the beds. Laura was on a bed, leaning against the wall, a beer can in her hand.

Laura and I had talked a lot during my downtime between training. She was always smoking near the dorms (promising repeatedly that she would drop the habit, eventually). We talked about her mostly. At the beginning of the semester, she complained about her long-distance boyfriend, who soon became an ex-boyfriend. Her moving from New Hampshire to Hawaii had strained their relationship to the point of breaking. Our conversations were therapeutic for Laura.

I uncorked the bottle of wine, something I had never done before, and poured Laura and myself a glass. Since it was wine, I thought a toast was appropriate.

I called for silence. I raised my glass and said, "To Tyler Durden. The person you want to be is imaginary. The real you just gets the shit kicked out of him."

Everyone looked confused. They glanced at each other. After a brief pause they raised their beers and cheered. "To Tyler Durden!" They chugged.

I stayed until I could see the bottom of the bottle. With each passing glass, Laura inched closer and closer. Soon, her hand was on my leg and her head on my shoulder. She gazed at me with doggy dinner bowl eyes.

She whispered to me, her lips lightly touching my ear. "Let's leave," she said.

We slipped out and wandered drunkenly back to her dorm. The humid Hilo air pressed her white tank top against her skin. Her denim skirt left her legs bare. The orange glow of the dim streetlamps glistened and reflected in her hair like the smoldering remains of a campfire. Her hands moved over my clothes like she was searching for something, carefully, thoroughly.

When we got back to her room, she pushed me on to her bed and climbed on top of me. She started to kiss me. Hard, forceful, almost frantic.

Some time later, we were both naked. Her head lay on my chest, her hair splayed out over my ribs. Her fingers traced lines around my chin, my neck, and my shoulders. She breathed softly. We lingered in silence, not speaking, barely moving.

Laura spoke first. "Who do you think of when you kiss me?" she asked.

I looked at her, surprised and appalled. I forced a laugh. "You," I replied.

I lied.

PART FOUR:
SETTING UP
THE SUBMISSION

"I thank whatever gods may be

For my unconquerable soul."

—William Ernest Henley

17

GRAPPLING A GHOST

didn't mope long. I went to the gym the next day and tapped four blue belts and a purple belt. Whether or not I had the blue fabric tied around my waist, I knew I had the skill of a blue belt, and in many ways, that feeling meant more to me than an actual promotion. I had a competition in Pittsburgh to prepare for, so I had to make the most of my last few weeks on the Big Island.

Besides, I still hadn't rolled with BJ, an experience I had been looking forward to since my first week in the gym, an experience I could have with or without a blue belt, and seeing BJ roll with other students at the gym (and not me), intensified the yearning for the experience.

Once, I watched BJ roll with Jon, the purple belt from Kauai that had told me about his hitchhiking in Hawaii. Whenever I rolled with Jon, he insisted on dismembering me. After each of our sessions, my joints creaked painfully, my ribs swelled from bruises, and my neck burned from the constant brush burn of gi chokes. I did little more than survive against Jon, but even surviving was riddled with agony.

On one occasion, I caught a glimpse of my face in the floor-to-ceiling mirror at the front of the mat room when Jon had me in his clutches. I looked like a squeaky toy, my eyes bugging out of my head and my face turning a cherry red from the lack of oxygen.

Jon was nice enough to me, and I never thought that he was intentionally trying to hurt me, but seeing BJ put the squeaky toy expression on Jon's face was somehow gratifying. Jon collapsed next to me after BJ submitted him with a rear naked choke. Jon's whole body hung limp, like a rag doll propped up against a wall.

"What's it like to roll with BJ?" I asked.

Jon rolled his head toward me. "It's like grappling a ghost," he said.

While I waited (impatiently) for my chance to roll with BJ, I rolled with almost every other fighter in the gym.

Charuto would always let me work, submitting and sweeping me only when I made a major mistake. The first time he offered to grapple with me, I expected him to lunge at me with a flying arm lock, finishing me in a flurry of jiu-jitsu genius.

Instead, he shook my hand and said, "Work cousi', work."

He gripped my lapel and pulled me toward his guard, slow and easy, as if he were rolling with a child. He let me posture up and work to clear his legs. Charuto was calm and composed, the norm for high-level submission artists. He breathed slowly, his mouth closed, his nostrils barely moving. He kept a slow pace, moving only fast enough to counter my attacks. I was running a race, but Charuto was strolling, hands in his pockets, aimlessly kicking a soda can.

Charuto let me win, but he guided me into the positions we had been practicing in class. He let me work through the techniques with some resistance, and he would give me time to counter his counters. Charuto used our rolls to teach me. He could have tapped me out on a whim, but he wanted to see me improve, to grow as a fighter. He wanted me to think about my techniques, so he rolled purely for my benefit, exemplifying his dedication to his students. A black belt letting his students submit him, no matter how good-natured he may be, is very rare.

Reagan, BJ's youngest brother, was just as friendly as Charuto, but he was not as keen on letting students win. His style of grappling was almost entirely cerebral, an elaborate funnel of baits and traps. He planned out dozens of moves in advance, like a grandmaster chess champion. Whenever he submitted me, I was basically submitting myself.

Reagan would dangle an arm or a guard pass or a position, knowing that the temptation to jump on the opportunity would be too strong to resist, especially to a white belt like myself. Each time I committed to exploiting the opening that Reagan purposely offered me, I would invariably find myself twirling through the air, the mat room a whirlwind blur. When I landed, my arm was being hyperextended, or a choke was sliding across my throat.

Grappling with Reagan felt very much like raiding an ancient temple. At the end of the hallway was a priceless treasure, a diamond the size of a basketball or a statue of solid gold. I knew that the hallway was booby trapped, but I could never quite tell how. The floor might give way. One of the tiles might trigger a volley of arrows. An axe might drop from the ceiling. Regardless of the danger though, greed always took over, and soon, I charged headlong down the hallway, hoping for the best.

I never made it to the treasure.

Whenever Reagan finished a match in that fashion, I just tapped and sat up, shaking my head, laughing to myself. Reagan laughed right back, shook my hand, and patted me on the back.

Jay was a fan of playfulness and pressure, despite weighing 135 pounds. He would let me work my game a bit, more so than Reagan did, but not nearly to the extent as Charuto. The first time I grappled Jay, I scooted in, and pulled him back on top of me. I locked in my guard and started to climb my legs up his back, looking to apply an armbar. Jay postured, and with the demeanor of a grocery store clerk stocking the same shelf as yesterday, and the day before, and the day before that, he passed my guard.

I outweighed Jay by forty pounds, and I suspected that I was stronger as well, but despite my straining and squeezing, I could not control him. He would back out of my guard, shuck my legs to the side, and plant his knee in my solar plexus. He would drive his weight into my chest, my body crumpling like a Styrofoam cup. I'd fight to escape the pain, but he was immovable. I would commit too much to fighting off his knee, and he would swivel around, over my head, and lay back for an armbar.

Before my arm reached the breaking point, he would let go, somersaulting over his head, giving me enough time to sit up. As I did, he pounced, spinning around to my back. He would let me escape only to lure me into another submission. Jay would juggle my body, catching me in submission after submission until he got bored and outright tapped me.

Most of my training sessions with Jay went like that (or he choked me unconscious), but after each match, he critiqued my technique, giving me advice on how I might improve.

I endured some world-class ass beatings at the BJ Penn Academy, but no ass beating was more surreal than the ass beating that Urijah Faber gave me.

At the time, Faber was the unstoppable conqueror of the 145-pound division. Known as "the California Kid," Faber forged his legacy with a twelve-fight winning streak filled with explosive, spontaneous action. He slammed opponents, again and again. He knocked them out. He choked them out. He fought without fear and with total confidence. Once, when he was defending a single-leg takedown, his opponent had him pressed against the cage. Faber bounced on one foot, struggling to keep his balance.

Then he jumped into the air, throwing a knee with his free leg while his opponent held the other off the mat. Bad ass.

Faber came to the BJ Penn Academy to prepare for his fight with Jens Pulver, an MMA legend attempting to make a comeback in the

145-pound division. BJ had fought Pulver twice, and one of BJ's students, Joe Lauzon, had fought Pulver as well. Coming to Hilo gave Faber a chance to train with fighters who had already beaten his next opponent, giving him a unique insight into his upcoming fight.

When I came down the stairs to the cages and the boxing ring, I immediately recognized Faber. He was unshaven, and his surfer hair was pulled back in a pony tail. He was muscular, built like a barrel with abs. Fifteen minutes later, Faber joined the guard passing drill. He stepped into my guard.

"Hi, I'm Urijah," he said.

I knew who he was, so I was startled by the introduction. I stuttered, "Hi, I'm Marshal. Nice to meet you."

He let me close my guard, and we started the roll. He buried one elbow in my hip and pried my legs with the other. My guard opened, and he drove his knee over my thigh to begin his pass. I transitioned to half guard, securing my lockdown. I swung my legs, testing his base. His base seemed weak. I felt like I had full control over his body. I whipped my legs and turned to my side, reaching for his far foot. I pulled the foot toward me and drove my weight forward, beginning my favorite sweep, the old school.

Faber's base collapsed. The sweep was working. I started to take the top position.

I was ecstatic. I swept the featherweight champion of the world, one of the pound-for-pound best fighters alive. If I could sweep Faber, maybe I could be the featherweight champion some day. Maybe I was a prodigy. The possibilities were endless. A belt. Sponsors. Girls. Television appearances.

This was huge. Out-grappling Faber meant that I had a successful future ahead of me. I could start training MMA. I could go to the Pan Ams. I could compete in the Mundials, like BJ. I could go to the Abu Dhabi Combat Club. Obviously, the first thing to do would be to cruise my way to a featherweight title shot in the WEC (World Extreme Cage Fighting), so I could dismantle Faber publically, reproducing what I had accomplished in the mat room. He seemed like a nice guy, and I didn't really want to see him lose the belt, but business is business.

I started to pass to side control. Faber swiveled and locked his arms around my throat, his arms a crushing vice. My eyes felt like they were going to explode. I couldn't breathe. My neck popped. I tapped. He had baited me into that choke from the moment I had secured my lockdown.

Served me right.

＊ ＊ ＊ ＊ ＊

Charuto stopped class and told us to line up against the wall. I had seen this ritual many times before; someone was getting promoted.

Charuto reached into a side closet and removed a blue belt. He snapped the belt and paced up and down the line. He looked at each face and at each belt. He reached the end of the line, turned, and walked back. He snapped the belt, over and over, timing his steps with the cracking of the fabric. Snap. Snap. Snap.

"Marshal!" he yelled, turning to face me, smiling. "Get up here before you pass out from all of that training!"

A grin overtook my face. My fingers tingled. My heart thumped. This was joy. Pure, uninhibited joy.

Charuto untied my white belt, tossed it aside, and wrapped the blue belt around my waist.

"Good work, cousi'. Keep training hard," he said.

He tightened the knot.

"Take off that gi," Charuto said. "You know what happens next."

I did. The BJ Penn Academy followed an old Brazilian tradition: belt whipping. Whenever a student was promoted, the other students formed two parallel lines down the length of the mat room, creating a narrow corridor. Every student in line removed their belts and folded them in half. The newly promoted student, with their gi top removed, started at one end of the gauntlet, and walked to the other end and then walked back—taking two whips from every student in line.

Whenever I explain the belt whipping ritual to non-grapplers, they stare at me quizzically, moderately disturbed.

It's a rite of passage. You've already endured a level of pain that is unfathomable to those that don't train. Every time you roll, you are suffering, but you fight through it. You fight through the pressure on your throat, the weight on your chest, the elbow grinding into your cheek, the exhaustion in your muscles. But you survive. You have the mettle to keep going, to push yourself harder and farther. Knowing that you leave the mat room a stronger person than when you came in is a beautiful feeling. It fills you with pride and confidence.

Charuto promoting me to blue belt

The belt whipping christens your commitment to pushing yourself to the next level, and you share that commitment with your training partners. If you haven't already whipped them at some point, you eventually will. The ritual proves to everyone and to yourself that you are willing to suffer to better yourself, that you are loyal to yourself and to your art.

I put my hands above my head and started down the gauntlet. I smiled the whole way, moving slowly, savoring every belt cracking off of my stomach, my ribs, and my back. My training partners cocked their arms back like they were about to pitch a fastball. The snap of fabric against skin echoed through the room. Each step was another sting. I continued to smile.

When the whipping was over, my skin burned. Bruises formed in belt-shaped rectangles, but the ecstasy of the moment overshadowed the pain. Every student in the room shook my hand and congratulated me.

＊ ＊ ＊ ＊ ＊

One night, when I stepped through the teal door, the gym felt more like a crowded bar than a training center. People clustered around the cage and the newly installed mats that replaced the old boxing ring. Fighters coated the mats, both in and out of the cage. With scarcely room to move, pairs of sweaty bodies tussled. BJ was among them.

When I reached the bottom of the stairs, I noticed that the clusters of onlookers weren't fighters. Their ears were normal. Their bodies were soft. They wore TapouT shirts and Cage Fighter hats and Affliction jeans. They took pictures with disposable cameras and cell phones. I didn't recognize their faces, and I had spent enough time in the gym to know anyone who trained with any sort of consistency.

They were gawkers.

These sorts came to the gym from time to time, but usually in small numbers. I had never seen a crowd this large. For some reason, they made me uncomfortable, as if they were in my home without an invitation, watching me shower. I quickly changed and escaped to the mat room, which was empty, save for the five people who had shown up to train in the gi.

We did our usual warm ups: jogging, side stepping, somersault-ing, break falling, crunches, pushups, and stretching. We were begin-ning to drill armbars when BJ jogged into the mat room, putting on his gi as he went. The cloverleaf embroidery on his white gi was still crisp, a contrast to the faded and frayed black belt he tied around his waist.

His eyes pressed into a slant. He shook his head back and forth as if he were trying to wipe away a bad memory.

"Felt like I was a zoo animal," he said, more to vent his own frustration than to justify his unexpected presence to the few of us training.

I could understand why he was upset. To me, the gym was a sanc-tuary. I used training to escape, to surround myself with like-minded people. Since the mat room was isolated, surrounded by walls instead of chain link fence, the gawkers could not easily invade.

BJ took over class and demonstrated a sweep into a shoulder lock. I paired up with a new white belt, and we bumbled through the move. After half an hour of drilling, BJ announced that it was time to free roll. He set the clock to six minutes, and motioned for the white belt I had been working with to grapple with him.

I had a startling realization.

With only five people in the class, BJ would almost have to roll with me. My heart beat faster. My palms began to sweat. A nervous anticipation frothed in my stomach. The buzzer rang, signaling the end of the first round. Rather than seek out a new partner, I stayed in place. I thought that maybe when the next round started, I would be without a partner, and BJ would have to step in. BJ started to make his way toward my end of the mat room when a white belt suddenly plopped down in front of me and reached to shake my hand.

I didn't move. I let his hand hang in mid air. The smile on his face began to quiver, the awkwardness of the moment wearing on him, but I didn't care. He ruined one of my last remaining opportunities to grapple with my idol. He looked at his outstretched arm. He looked at my arm, hanging at my side. He looked up at me.

He closed the gap, grabbed the limp hand dangling at my hip, and shook it. Good for him, I thought. When the match started, I hunted for his arm, unrelentingly. In six minutes, I submitted him nine times. He deserved it. He was screwing with my hopes and dreams.

The buzzer rang again.

I decided to stick to the same strategy. As I retied the knot on my belt, I noticed a green and white blur moving toward the door. BJ was leaving. I had been foiled again. My life was a failure. I couldn't come to the BJ Penn Academy and not roll with BJ Penn.

He turned around. He tucked the tails of his gi into his belt. He straightened his lapels and brushed dirt off his sleeves and looked at me.

He looked at me!

"Come on, Marshal," he said, waving. "Let's roll."

My legs went numb. My body stuttered. I tried to tell my legs to shuffle across the mat, but a flash flood of excitement, nervousness, and pure, primal fear clouded the connection between my brain and my body.

This is my one chance, I thought, don't blow it.

My mind cleared. I wanted to show him what I was made of, what I learned training under his coaches and with his students.

I scooted forward and shook his hand.

I had no delusions that I would submit him or even put up an admirable struggle. I knew that any bit of offense that I was able to muster would be by the grace of the good lord BJ Penn. But still, I wanted to show BJ my game. So I went into the match serious, bent on fighting until I could fight no more.

BJ kneeled on both knees and lowered his head. He reached forward with both hands, tentatively, slowly. He was moving like Charuto, letting me work what I knew instead of clobbering me.

I secured my half guard. If brown belts had trouble escaping my half guard, I thought that I could at least slow BJ down. He let me get the position completely set. I was locked in. I had the position as tight as possible. When my half guard was sunk this deep, no one escaped it without a struggle.

BJ took both of his feet, and methodically peeled my legs off of his. He moved his legs as though they were arms, and he maneuvered his feet like hands. Joe Rogan, a commentator for the UFC, said that BJ's coordination and flexibility were freakish, but I didn't understand it until I felt his toes grip and peel at my calves. I clung to the position like an action hero gripping the steel beam of a bridge, but BJ, having loosened my half guard, lifted his knees, and baseball-slid through my legs.

I laughed, and BJ laughed right back, his big Hawaiian smile scrunching his cheeks into his eyes. I had the presence of mind to brace my arms on my body as BJ settled into side control, a typical chest on chest control like one sees in high school wrestling.

I tried to escape, to hip away and bring my legs between me and BJ, but his pressure increased. BJ, who fought at 155 pounds, turned into a three-car garage. His pressure was more painful than Jay's. When I exhaled, my ribs didn't have the space to expand and refill. I couldn't breathe. I couldn't move. I had never felt more helpless.

BJ untucked the tail of his gi and draped it over my face. With BJ's gi blindfolding me, I couldn't see what he was doing. I could only feel his weight shift, ominous, like listening from inside a closet as a burglar stalked my home. I knew that if I kept my arms tight against my chest, I was safe. No matter how much pressure he put on my chest, no matter how little I could see, if I maintained my posture, he couldn't do anything. This was one of the principles that Charuto, Reagan, and Jay stressed: if I kept a good posture, every limb and muscle positioned in the strongest manner, my opponent couldn't attack my neck, my arms, or my legs.

I felt BJ prod at my arms, checking my strength, gauging my commitment to posture. He pushed my right elbow. He pushed my left elbow. I still couldn't move. I still couldn't see anything but the shadows of a double weave white gi. I still couldn't fully inhale; I could manage only quick, short gasps. I wasn't winning, but I felt like I was surviving. As long as I maintained my posture, I was safe. The gi over my eyes shifted. A hand slid across my mouth, securing a kidnapper's grip. My mouth and nose were sealed. I couldn't breathe. BJ was choking me out with his hand. I had to abandon my defensive position if I wanted to stay conscious. I knew what moving my arms the slightest bit would mean, but I had no choice. He was playing with me the way that Reagan played with me. He knew exactly how to get me to move where he needed me to go.

I reached up and peeled his hand off of my mouth.

As soon as my arm moved, BJ began wrapping it up. He cinched in tighter, moving like an anaconda, slow and with a devastating purpose. He exploited what little space I gave him, and with my arm moving farther and farther from where it was strongest, BJ continued to creep, tighter and tighter. Not only was breathing difficult, but the tension on my ribs grew. Somehow, he was getting heavier. I felt as though my chest cavity was on the verge of collapse from the steadily increasing trash compactor pressure.

I fought to drive my arm back, pushing, struggling, every fiber and sinew flexed and firing.

BJ swung his leg over, straddling my hips, establishing the mount position. He had distracted me by attacking my arm. I forgot to defend the mount. Now I was well into the quicksand. Survive. Survive.

He was still gripping my arm. He slid his knees up my ribs, pinching my shoulders. He leaned down, pressing his chest into my face. The pressure was unbearable. I had to escape. I had to get out. I writhed and squirmed and bucked and kicked. BJ surfed the wave of my desperation, his pressure steady, his face calm.

Then his weight was gone. I breathed.

Suddenly, the mat room was spinning, a blur of colors and shapes and bright lights. When the spinning stopped, BJ was on my back. I don't know what he did to get there. For all I know, he teleported.

He hooked my thighs with his feet. He snaked his arms underneath mine. I covered my neck, knowing full well that he wanted the choke. He covered my mouth again. At that point, I knew that the fight was over. I didn't know exactly how he was going to finish me, but I knew that I was doomed.

BJ and me.

With a bit of disdain, like a child forced to reveal the broken vase he was hiding behind his back, I pushed his hand off my face. BJ immediately gripped my wrist and trapped it with his legs. Now, I had only one free arm to defend my neck.

BJ covered my mouth, yet again.

I pushed it off.

An arm slid around my throat, and I tapped to a choke tighter than Faber's, a drop to the end of a noose squeeze.

Grappling with BJ was painful. It was futile. It was glorious.

BJ sat back and smiled.

"Good roll," he said. "Your half guard is really strong. You've really improved."

I couldn't speak. The lightweight champion of the world had just complimented me. I wanted to play it off, to be cool, but my grin was gargantuan. BJ stood up, patted me on the back, and went back to the cage.

That night, Ethan threw me a going-away party. He barbecued and broke out the karaoke machine. Chris brought liquor. A small group of fighters joined us, Poai and Jay among them. Chris convinced me to drink sake, and soon, we were all singing karaoke. I performed a stunning rendition of "Jesse's Girl" while Chris and Poai sang a duet of Aerosmith's "Don't Want to Miss a Thing" (which I filmed and have yet to upload out of fear that Poai and Chris will hunt me down).

With Chris's arm around me, halfway through butchering "YMCA," I realized that I was among better friends than I ever had in Pennsylvania. Hilo had become more of a home than Pittsburgh. And I was getting ready to leave.

18

WAKING FROM A DREAM

Before I checked out of my dorm at UH Hilo, I opened my wallet and took out the last two pictures of Hilary that I owned, wallet-sized senior-year portraits hidden behind a health insurance card and an expired Mac card. I lifted a fold in the fabric covered by a few wrinkled dollar bills and removed the necklace she had given me when we were juniors in high school. A metal chain with a Capricorn charm, the silver paint long worn to a copper hue.

Her face was soft in those photographs, but the edges were battered and the body wrinkled. She—we—had changed a lot in three years. I knew that I was harder now and showing wear, some cauliflower ear, some calluses, some scars. I liked that my corners were torn and that my young face was rougher and beginning to wrinkle. Each crease—a souvenir—reminded me that I had survived battles and conquered demons.

While I studied the photographs and rolled the charm through my fingers (the necklace was heavier than I remembered), my phone rang.

"Yeah?"

"How's my little haole boy?" It was Ti. She was here to pick me up.

I laughed. "I'll be out in a minute," I said.

"Well, you better hurry. Me and Brit want to go beach with you before you're pau with Hilo!"

I closed my phone. The 7 AM sun was bright. The air was warm. My suitcases were packed. My blue belt was tucked safely into my carry-on (I debated wearing it on to the plane but decided that attracting a mob of swooning girls might make me late for my flight). I opened the door and realized I still had the necklace and photographs in my hand. I walked to my bed, lifted the ratty blue mattress, and put them underneath. The mattress kicked up a cloud of dust when it fell back on to the frame. I shouldered my bags and shut the door.

Ti leaned against her silver Nissan pick-up. Britany sat on the tailgate.

"Good thing BJ got you in shape," Britany said, smiling, "'cause those bags look heavy."

They were.

"Hey Marsh!" Ti said running forward and hugging me. The impact jolted the three over-stuffed suitcases in my hands and rocked the bag on my back. I lost my balance and almost fell over.

"Brah, you drinkin' already? It's so early!" Britany said, laughing.

As we packed my bags into the truck, Jake pulled up; he leaned his head out the window of his truck. He had been running his belongings back and forth from our dorm to his new apartment all morning. We were on good terms again, both having admitted to being assholes during spring break.

"You leaving, man?"

I told him that I was. He stepped out of his truck and gave me a bro hug.

"Take care of yourself," he said. I told him to do the same.

Britany and Ti helped me pack my bags into the pickup, and we drove to the farmer's market. Ti planned on making lunch after we were done at the beach, and she wanted to have fresh ingredients.

I followed Britany and Ti from stall to stall. They surveyed the bananas, oranges, guavas, pineapples, and coconuts. Ti talked with each vendor like they were long-lost family. She called them auntie and uncle and hugged them. Her tote bag steadily filled with food. When Ti was satisfied that she had everything she needed, we crossed the street and meandered through the vendors. I needed a pair of board shorts (mine were buried deep in a suitcase, and I didn't know which), and Britany and Ti wanted to browse.

I quickly found a cheap pair of board shorts, for ten dollars, and started browsing the other vendors. I happened upon a table of hand-made jewelry, wooden charms hung on braided string, decorated with beads. Each charm had a Hawaiian petroglyph etched into wood. I picked up one that was shaped like a small sword.

"What does this one mean?" I asked the elderly Hawaiian woman sitting behind the table. Her gray hair was curled into wisps and her dress swayed in the breeze.

"Oh oh, that one mean 'Feminine Beauty.'"

That wasn't what I had in mind.

I picked up another charm. The wood was cut into a semi-circle and the etching reminded me of Dr. Eckleburg's eyes from the *Great Gatsby*. "How about this one?" I asked.

"That one mean 'Happiness.'"

"I'll take it."

I found Britany and Ti browsing through a collection of hand-made dresses. Ti was picking out four or five different styles and sizes to give to friends and family on Oahu. A hippy-looking couple from New Zealand ran the booth. They had thick dreadlocks. Ti must have been at the booth for a while, because they were all smiling and laughing. They discounted four of the dresses and gave her the last one for free. I never met anyone who didn't love Ti.

Britany looked at the paper bag in my hand. "What'd you get?"

I showed her the necklace.

"Do you know what the means?" She asked with a serious face.

"Uhh . . . yeah . . . it means—"

"It means 'ugly haole boy.'"

I was distraught. "What? No. It can't. She said . . ."

Britany started to laugh. "I'm kidding! How would I know what it means?"

I playfully pushed her, and soon we started to tussle, laughing as we wrestled and threatened to throw each other.

"Children! Children!" Ti yelled, jokingly.

We stopped.

"That's better. Let's go my house and then beach."

So we did. Twenty minutes later, carrying blankets and chairs, we were walking down a wooded path to Richardson's Beach. We found a spot in the grass overlooking the rocky shoreline. Local kids were climbing a metal ladder cemented on a jetty and doing back flips from the railing. Out in the water, a local man on a kickboard towed a raft. Two Chihuahuas wearing life preservers balanced awkwardly on the inflated ridges, stutter-stepping each time the water swelled.

Since I was up late packing the night before. I napped on a towel while the girls went swimming. I woke up some time later to Britany pulling one arm, and Ti pulling the other.

"Marsh. You can't sleep away your last day in Hilo," Ti said.

"Yeah!" Britany said. "Come swim with us!"

They led me down the rocks to a pool hidden in an inlet. I tried to tiptoe into the water, giving my body time to adjust. Britany scowled and poked and prodded and pushed me until I was in up to my shoulders. I tried to explain to her the challenge of submerging the bits just below the waistline, but she wouldn't listen.

The water in the inlet was brackish, channels of mountain-chilled freshwater slicing through the tolerably warm saltwater. With my arms folded and my shoulders permanently shrugged, I anchored myself in a warm pocket. I wanted nothing to do with the cold water.

"Come on, Marsh! Swim! The water's nice!" Ti yelled, her back stroke sending her gliding through the water.

"The water's fine right here. I don't trust the rest."

Ti clucked her tongue.

"Hey . . ." I said, trying to get Ti's attention. "Where'd Britany go?" I looked over my shoulder, and saw a silhouette moving toward my legs, but it was too late. Two hands gripped me ankles and pulled. I splashed and staggered and fell into a pocket of cold water. I slipped and hopped back and forth, trying to find the warm water again. I felt it for a moment, but I went too far and fell back into cold water. I jumped again, fighting desperately to find warmth.

All the time I did this dance, I made a noise that was somewhere between a shrieking chimpanzee and a cartoon character circling his arms frantically to keep from falling off the edge of a building.

"Haoles aren't built for this!" I yelled in the midst of a flurry of curses. "Water is either warm, or it's cold!"

Britany and Ti began splashing me. Some drops were cold. Some were warm. Some just hit my face. Some hit my eyes. They were laughing and having fun, so I didn't mind.

After twenty minutes of romping, they were tired and hungry. As we climbed the rocks to get out of the water, I saw Ethan throwing a football with his son a few yards down the beach. I had thanked him a dozen times already for throwing me a going-away party, but another couldn't hurt.

Ethan was supposed to be working that weekend, but some last-minute changes freed up his time. We talked about my flight plans and how much I missed home. Then he asked the question that I had heard from each of my friends in Hilo:

"When are you coming back?"

"As soon as I can, but it's going to be tough. I have to finish school first and get some money together."

If I could have stayed in Hilo, I would have. I missed my family, but I didn't want to leave the island, for fear that the people who had made Hilo feel like home would move or change by the time I returned.

I hatched more than a few schemes to stay on the island for longer than the one semester.

I first looked into transferring to UH Hilo and finishing my degree there. At my home University, I had one more year to go. If I transferred, however, I'd have to pay out-of-state tuition and depending on the class rotation, stay for at least an extra semester and retake courses that wouldn't transfer. Higher education had me pretty deep into debt already, and sitting in class for longer than four years would push me even deeper into apathy.

Then I decided I'd write a book. Kid Peligro's biography on the Gracie family, *The Gracie Way*, was a success, and most high-profile UFC fighters had published or were in the process of publishing biographies. My newfound optimism mixed with my naiveté, and I decided that I could pitch the project to BJ, find a publisher, and get a book advance to pay for my staying in Hawaii over the summer and longer if necessary—all in the span of about two months. When I contacted the representative of BJ Penn Productions who coordinated my interviews with BJ, he told me to talk with him after BJ fought Sean Sherk. Unfortunately, the bout with Sherk was scheduled to take place long after I returned to the mainland. BJ's representative just shrugged.

When I told Ben that I'd like to stay in Hilo for at least the summer, he said that he had a contact at the newspaper and that he'd talk to him about getting me a job. Before I pushed Ben to pursue that option, I researched renting costs and debated how I'd handle traveling to do interviews without a car. Unless they paid me an exceptionally large amount of money right from the start, my debt would be worse than it already was.

I had to finish school. I had to start a career. I had to make money. Or did I? I'm not sure why I was so pragmatic. Part of me wishes that

I would have dropped out of school and found a cheap room some-where in town. Then again, I had met enough drifters to know that I didn't want to join their ranks.

Before Ethan and I parted ways, we took some pictures. Shakas all around.

Back at Ti's we ate fresh fruit, poi, rice, and some leftover chicken. Britany put in a movie. I fell asleep on the couch (pictures of me sleeping later turned up on Facebook). When I awoke, it was time to go to the airport.

I hadn't seen the Hilo airport since I landed on the Big Island five months earlier. Ti parked in the drop-off lane. Ti and Britany helped me unload my bags. Ti gave me a long hug.

"Marsh, you better come back soon," she said, her voice muffled by my shoulder.

I told her that I'd try.

Britany walked me to the check-in counter. I set down my bags.

She smiled a weak smile and hugged me. "Watch out for those haole girls," she said, turning away quickly, a twinge of remorse in her tone.

I watched her walk to Ti's truck and climb into the cab. I waved as they pulled away.

I turned to the check-in counter. One of my bags exceeded the fifty-pound limit. I sighed and went to pull the suitcases off the scale, wondering what I could move to balance the weight. The large Ha-waiian woman behind the counter shook her head. She wrapped a sticker around the handle to indicate that it had passed the check-in inspection. A Hawaiian man wearing a floral button-up stepped for-ward and lifted the suitcases off the scale.

"Braddah," he said, straining. "You lucky she like you. These suckahs heavy!"

The woman laughed. "Uncle! You strong! No worries!"

He chuckled and set the suitcases on a conveyor belt behind the counter. I thanked them and went to security.

When they scanned my bags, the light flickered and the machine buzzed. Security pulled me aside and they dug through my backpack, the one containing my laptop. They pulled out my digital voice recorder.

"What is this?"

"It's a voice recorder. I'm a journalist."

They stared at me, a cold hard suspicion narrowing their eyes. Then they shrugged.

"Okay. Have a nice flight."

Airport security in Hilo was not at all intimidating.

I settled into a couch near my gate. I called my parents to let them know I was boarding soon. They said they weren't sure if they'd be able to recognize me. I told them I'd be the only one with cauliflower ear.

"Marshal David," my mom said. She didn't appreciate my humor.

When I hung up, I settled into reading *Rant* by Chuck Palahniuk. I absentmindedly ate a protein bar. I checked my phone—no texts or calls. After a time, I stood to stretch. I noticed a familiar face pulling a piece of purple luggage. Shauna. She was also an NSE student, and we had talked a little over the course of the semester, but we never really hung out other than a few dinners in the cafeteria. She was known for being exceptionally nice (and Jake had a pretty serious crush on her), so I rolled my luggage next to her and sat down.

She smiled, and we talked. She was going back to NC State and planned to finish her degree in fashion design, then she wanted to open her own clothing store. She, like me, was sad to be leaving.

"It's just so perfectly beautiful here. And the people I met, I just don't want to leave them," she said.

When we compared itineraries, we discovered that our flights to Maui and then to Phoenix were the same. We were happy that we wouldn't be traveling alone for at least part our trips. Shortly after that discovery, our tin-can of an island-to-island plane was ready to board.

Shauna sat by the window, one row before the last. I sat next to her. The sun was beginning to set as we prepared to take off. I watched Hilo turn to a mismatched checkerboard of greens and browns as we ascended. I watched Mauna Kea shrink. Then the Kona coast. Then purple water, the sun nearly hidden by the horizon. Leaving felt wrong. It ached.

We hit turbulence, bad turbulence. The luggage overhead bounced and slammed. The plane lifted and fell like it was hitting BMX jumps. Shauna yelped and grabbed my hand.

I leaned back and exhaled. I didn't care if the plane crashed. In that moment, as the plane rocked from side to side, I was content. I wasn't afraid to die. If my story ended with a nose dive to the floor of the Pacific, so be it. I had never experienced such a feeling before. It was beautiful. It was like sitting behind Rainbow Falls and knowing that I could stay forever. I smiled.

It was dark when we landed in Maui. Shauna and I ate a cafeteria dinner (I had a salad, concerned about making weight for the Kumite Classic) and wandered through the airport shops. I pitied the tourists buying Hawaii T-shirts and dashboard Hula girls and Kona Coffee mugs. With their noses buried in brochures, they missed the real Hawaii. I was thinking like a local. The salt water from that morning was still on my skin. I could feel it. I could smell it.

Shauna wandered to a jeweler's kiosk. The display cases glittered, a beach of diamonds and emeralds and sapphires. She was just passing the time, admiring the rings out of some unspoken feminine obligation to wish for the biggest one to appear on her finger. I came up next to her right when a saleslady approached.

"Would you like to see any piece in particular?" she asked.

Shauna opened her mouth to speak. I interjected. "We just got engaged," I said.

Shauna looked at me, wide-eyed and confused.

"We need an engagement ring," I said. I couldn't tell if Shauna appreciated the joke or not.

The saleslady grinned. "Well, congratulations, and you're so young. That's beautiful. Would you like to try anything on?"

Shauna looked at me, a smirk curving her lips. "Would you mind?" she asked.

"Whatever you want, sweetie."

"Awe, thanks, *honey*."

The saleslady picked out a few rings and set them on the counter. She started talking about carats and quality and style. I wasn't really listening and neither was Shauna. Shauna slipped each ring on to her finger and studied how the light reflecting off the diamonds played across her fingers.

"What's your price range?" the saleslady asked.

"Money isn't an object," I said. "Whatever she wants."

The saleslady stood up straight. She liked the sound of that. She turned around and unlocked the safe. When she came back to the counter, she set down three rings. Each of them had stones bigger than M&Ms. Shauna smiled, trying to suppress her astonishment. I put my arm around her while she slid one of the rings on to her finger. She savored the weight.

"Which one do you want?" I asked.

"Oh, I don't know," she said with a sense of awe. She tried on the next two.

During all of this, the saleslady looked quite pleased. I felt a twinge of guilt. This honest, hardworking woman thought that she was about to make a huge sale, and I was just getting her hopes up. Then the twinge passed.

I told Shauna that our flight was leaving soon. I asked the saleslady to write down the name of the two rings that Shauna liked the most and to give us her card. She did.

We tried to sit together on the flight from Maui to Arizona, but we both had couples in our row. The couple in my row had just finished their honeymoon. They pawed at each other and cuddled and spoke in hushed high-pitched voices. I was pressed against the window. The space between my seat and the seat in front of me was oppressively small. I couldn't sit in one position for longer than a few minutes without it causing me physical pain.

Before the plane took off, the man started a conversation with me.

"So, were you here for vacation?" he asked.

"Not really. I came here to train, actually."

He looked confused.

"The UFC's lightweight champ is Hawaiian. He has a gym in Hilo on the Big Island. I came here to train."

"Do you fight in a cage?"

"Something like that," I said. I still hadn't figured out an easy way to explain jiu-jitsu. I settled on the easiest way out.

"Well, man," he said, beginning to chuckle, "I'll definitely be nice to you. You could definitely kick my ass."

"Nah, I'm not very good. I couldn't take you," I said. I could.

There was silence for a moment, and then he asked, "So you were there for like what, a few weeks?"

"Since January."

"Jesus," he said, jerking his head. "Was it hard to be away from home that long?"

"At first. Now it's hard to leave."

He shook his head in disbelief. "That's pretty cool, man," he said.

I thanked him. He started fiddling with his overhead light. He wanted to read a John Grisham novel during the flight. He couldn't get the light to turn on. A stewardess apologized and said that it was broken. He looked more hurt than angry. He put his head on his wife's shoulder and started to fall asleep. I put my head against the window and did the same.

In Phoenix, Shauna and I spent an hour waiting for our respective flights to begin boarding. We talked for a bit, and then it was time for me to catch my flight. We hugged and wished each other safe trips. Shauna told me that we should stay in touch. I agreed. I knew that we wouldn't.

I couldn't sleep on my flight to Pittsburgh. A strange sickness tore at my stomach and punched at my chest. Half of me was painfully homesick. Half of me was disgusted with myself for ever walking away from the home I had found in Hilo. Still, I was happy that I would be seeing my family again. They were like the people that I was leaving in Hilo; they loved me for me, for what I was. I looked forward to having their company again.

Before I settled into finishing *Rant* and rereading Truman Capote's *Music for Chameleons*, I turned on my digital camera and cycled through my pictures. I discovered that Britany and Ti had taken a dozen or so self-portraits while I was asleep at Richardson's. The Hilo sun reflected off of their tanned faces. Their hair was wet from the ocean. They were smiling, genuine, loving smiles. I'm glad that they took those pictures.

I looked up from my book a few hours later and glanced out the window.

The trees. I recognized the trees. Oaks. Maples. Birches. Firs. Pines. They were miniatures, like a train set, hot glued to rolling papier-mâché green hills. Hawaii didn't have those kinds of trees or those kinds of hills. This was Pennsylvania. This was home. I couldn't turn on my phone to check the time, so I had no way of knowing just how close I was to landing, but based on those trees, I knew I was almost there.

Not long after that realization, my plane banked for descent. The plane bounced as it touched down on the runway. Home.

It was cold. A chilly rain soaked the pavement. I immediately missed the island warmth.

Being back in Pennsylvania didn't feel real. I had dreamed of returning home. Or did I just dream of being in Hawaii? Was this real? How could I know I had been on the Big Island for five months? It was all so far away now, 4,500 miles. In the Pacific. I felt like I was moving through a fog, some fantasy-distorted vision of an event I had imagined over and over in my mind.

I remembered what Megan had said when she called me in Hilo. "It's like you're dead."

Yes, and I had come back, resurrected as something else. A blue belt in my bag. Cauliflower in my ear. Confidence in my walk. I felt strong enough to take on anyone, or anything. Jiu-jitsu did this for me. The Big Island did this for me.

I dropped my bag and hugged my mom. She squeezed me tight, and held on for longer than usual. I was holding on too. When she let go, she had a look of relief on her face, like she had been up every night, worried about me, waiting for a pair of headlights to turn off the road and up our driveway.

I hugged my father and my little brother.

"You look taller," my mom said.

I wasn't. I was standing straighter.

She grabbed my chin, and turned my head side to side, examining my ears. "They're not as bad as I thought they'd be. If you hadn't told me, I don't think I would have noticed," she said.

"It's not going to get worse, right?" my dad asked.

"As long as I keep training, it will. I like it."

My mom and dad shook their heads. My mom hugged me again.

We collected my bags and went to the car.

The dreary cold made the place seem even more alien. Driving down familiar roads was like moving through a picture book. I had forgotten the depth of this place. My memory had turned each swaying branch into a static representation of what it really was. I felt out of place.

My parents wanted to take me out to celebrate my return, but I declined. I was fighting in a week and had to make weight. I was already expecting a few hours in the sauna and didn't want to spend any more than was necessary.

We drove up our winding driveway. When we came in, the dogs, four of them, began to bark. Our oldest, a shepherd black lab mix, lay on the tile floor. She was aging; standing and walking were painful. She looked at me and looked away. Then she looked back. She stopped barking. Her face softened. Her tail began to wag. She struggled to her feet and hobbled to me, burying her head in my lap as I crouched to greet her.

PART FIVE: GETTING THE TAP

". . .if he fails, at least fails while daring greatly, so that his place shall never be with those cold and timid souls who neither know victory nor defeat."

—*Theodore Roosevelt*

19

HAOLE COUNTRY

or that first week, each morning was startling. I awoke, expecting cinderblock walls, a dirty linoleum floor, and a tropical breeze wafting through the window. But I had a soft mattress and air conditioning. Dry wall. It was 50 degrees instead of 70 degrees. Cold again. I wasn't sharing a bathroom with twenty other people. Dogs. Cats. My little brother, Ryan. No cockroaches. My mom and dad making breakfast in the morning, leaving for work by 7 AM. Sleeping in, and no gym down the street.

At my home on the outskirts of Washington, Pennsylvania, even my high school bus stop was barely within walking distance. A car was a necessity again.

Driving was a bit shaky at first, but the skills came back without any serious damage. I wanted to see the places that filled my head with pictures. Franklin Mall. Claysville. A stretch of Old Route 40 just outside of West Alexander. Ryan and I went to the mall first. I was curious to see if *Ultimate Grappling* had published my articles yet.

They hadn't.

I saw faces from my high school class, working the same retail jobs and serving the same food as they were when I left. But they looked more tired, and their frames softer. As I walked by the food court, passed the Sbarro and the American Eagle Outfitters, I noticed how white all of the faces were. The people all spoke English and dressed the same. Copies of copies of copies.

Claysville, a country town on route 40, just beyond my high school, felt more gray, more run-down, the buildings as worn as the faces in the streets. Long beards. John Deer hats. Empty beer cans in the grass. Confederate flags on the rusted pick-ups. White. White. White.

The stretch of Old Route 40 was more scenic than I remembered. We drove through West Alexander and took Old Route 40 back toward Washington. We crossed Interstate 79 and wove through the houses on the outskirts of West Alexander. We crested the hill.

The cracked asphalt arced downward, bisecting a field of tall green grass. The road ran straight for 150 yards before splitting into a Y, a white farm house at the fork. The grass bowed in the wind, rising, then falling again as another gust swept through. Leafless oaks and maples surrounded the field. Gray clouds lingered on the horizon of the blue sky. When I thought of Pennsylvania, I thought of this road.

My best friend in high school, Nathan, used to drive his black Blazer down this road on aimless summer evenings. Nathan and I were captains of the soccer team and rarely spent time apart. Everyone on the soccer team called him "Pesci" because he smiled and laughed like Joe Pesci. Nathan was also abnormally skinny. Our soccer coach used to tell him that he was a pirate's dream because he had a "sunken chest."

As Ryan and I lingered on the road, I remembered sitting in the passenger seat of Nathan's Blazer, its maroon interior speckled with white paint from when his dad used it for hauling drywall. Stephen, a blond-haired, squeaky-voiced friend of ours, sat in the back.

"We can do it. We can hit 120," Stephen said.

"Dude, how the hell are we going to stop?" I replied, craning my neck around the seat to see Stephen.

"We'll just veer right and go up the hill to slow down."

I looked down the road and then back to Stephen. "There's a stop sign. What if a car comes?" I asked.

Stephen smiled. "They'll move when they see us coming," he said, laughing.

Nathan buckled his seatbelt and smiled. "Here we go," he said.

"Shit. Shit. Shit." I fumbled for my seatbelt and jammed it into the buckle.

The Blazer wasn't much for acceleration, but it was heavy, so gravity propelled us. The engine growled and creaked as Nathan pressed the gas. Soon, we were careening down the hill, the worn-out shocks doing little to cushion the blows of pot holes and cracked asphalt. The tall grass lining the road blurred to a sea of dry brown, us passing between two pulsing waves like Moses and the Israelites. Nathan kept glancing down at the speedometer, announcing our speed each time.

"60 . . . 75 . . . 90 . . ."

We weren't bad kids. We didn't drink. We didn't do drugs. We played soccer, Xbox, and paintball. We spent most of our time in Nathan's basement, sometimes catching the soft-core porn on HBO in the wee hours of the morning. Driving down that road was just a way to push ourselves, to find and peer over the edge, to feel alive. I stopped talking to Stephen once I left for college. Nathan and I were roommates, but halfway through the year we ceased to be friends. I'm not sure why we drifted apart, but we did. Though we lived together we hardly saw—let alone spoke to—each other.

Ryan and I didn't see any other cars on old 40 that day. With the interstate and the new Route 40 nearby, this was the road less traveled. As I looked out over the field, I decided that life was episodic. Some characters stay for two or three seasons and leave. Some characters stay only for an episode. Some may return, but most won't.

ry—all the people I used to know—for one

left my life. I couldn't fault them or myself for

To be happy, to make the most of a character's

story, I had to—

said, grinning mischievously.

the arm, and rolled down the windows as I put the car into drive.

❋ ❋ ❋ ❋ ❋

I was wearing a white belt again. It was my first day back at Steel City Martial Arts, and I made it a point to forfeit my blue belt as soon as I came in the door. I gave it to Sensei Sonny Achille in private and put my white belt back on.

In the martial arts world, and Brazilian jiu-jitsu especially, respect is paramount. In the six months or so that I trained at Steel City before leaving for Hilo, I heard stories of students going to other schools, being promoted, and coming back to Steel City, expecting that belt to be honored. Even if the other instructor was legitimate and respectable (in many cases he wasn't), being promoted elsewhere is a slap in the face to your home instructor. Sensei had invested a great deal of his time and energy in my training. He had gone out of his way to help me. He looked out for me. I was just as much a student of Sensei as I was a student of Charuto or Jay. He deserved a say in my promotion.

Regardless of what fabric was around my waist, I knew that I had the skills of a blue belt. If showing Sensei respect meant wearing my white belt for another year, so be it.

Royce Gracie once said, "A black belt only covers two inches of your ass. It's up to you to cover the rest." I had learned how to cover my ass in Hawaii, blue belt or no.

Cash, my old friend from college who had called me frequently while I was in Hilo, came to Pittsburgh to help me prepare for the Kumite Classic. When Cash and I had trained together before I left, our skill levels were almost perfectly equal. He submitted me as often as I submitted him. Now, even though he had technically been training longer than I had, I dominated him. I picked him apart with ease. My body instinctively moved to the right positions. I caught submissions by reflex.

After half an hour of rolling, Cash sat up. His curly brown hair, soaked with perspiration, lagged a few seconds behind his head as it shook from side to side.

"You're a monster," he said after a deep sigh.

＊ ＊ ＊ ＊ ＊

I kept to my diet for the week leading up to the Kumite Classic. I ate every two hours, proteins and vegetables with minimal carbohydrates, and I took fiber supplement three times a day to flush out any excess waste in my system. When I stepped on the scale in the morning, I consistently came in between 167 and 168 pounds. I had to make 160. I had checked my weight in Hilo, eight weeks away from the fight. I had packed on 17 pounds of muscle during my stay, jumping from 158 pounds to 175. That was all weight that I had to cut.

Weigh-ins were at 3 PM on Friday. I shifted to a mostly liquid diet on the Wednesday evening before so that my body could digest what I consumed quickly and easily. I tried to drink close to a gallon and a half of water a day. On Thursday, I stopped eating and drinking at 7:30 PM. I woke up at 7 AM Friday morning (I always wake up early the day of weigh-ins to make it easier to fall asleep early the night before a fight). I weighed myself. 164.3. I expected to weigh more. I'd need only a few hours in the sauna. I packed a few layers of sweats and went to a nearby health club where my cousin worked as a personal trainer. He arranged for me to have a day pass to use the sauna.

I stepped into the sauna a little after 10 AM. Three wrinkled, balding men were already inside. Their stomachs hung over the white towels wrapped around their waists. I was wearing boxers, a pair of mesh shorts, sweat pants, a pair of windbreakers, short-sleeve Under Armour, a wife beater, a T-shirt, a long sleeve T-shirt, and a hoody. I could have just bought a sauna suit, but I didn't have the money.

I put my hoody up and settled into a corner.

Sitting in the dry heat of a sauna hungry and dehydrated is painful. My body ached. I felt tired, sluggish, and irritable. Beads of sweat pooled on my body. I watched them drip from my nose and chin to the floor and felt them run down my chest and down my legs. I tried not to think about the sauna. I visualized the mat. I mentally rehearsed my game plan. I reviewed each detail of my techniques. I felt myself applying each submission and counter. I saw myself escaping from the worst positions. I saw myself getting the sweep. I saw myself—

"You a boxer or something?" a gruff voice behind me asked.

I looked over my shoulder. The man talking to me had white hair, only on the bottom half of his head, and a jagged nose.

"No, I'm a wrestler," I replied. I wasn't in the mood to explain, yet again, jiu-jitsu. I wanted to be left alone.

I tried to return to visualizing my matches, but water, milkshakes, and tacos occupied my thoughts. I leaned forward and waited for the pounds to drip off.

Two hours later, I was at 159.6, according to my scale and the scale at the health club. My mom and dad picked me up and drove me to Monroeville (near Pittsburgh) to weigh in. I spat into an empty Gatorade bottle on the drive up, just in case the scale was running heavy. I slouched in the backseat, my hoody up and my head down. My parents talked to each other but not to me. They knew that cutting weight was miserable. I had lost so much water that I pissed sand.

The Kumite Classic was held annually at the Monroeville Expo Mart, a convention center on the outskirts of Pittsburgh. The Kumite Classic featured a variety of fitness-related competitions: point karate, jiu-jitsu, power lifting, bodybuilding. The karate competitors and grapplers were both weighing in that Friday. We were split into two lines, and the difference between the groups was stark.

The karate competitors had gelled their hair into spikes and swoops. They looked frail, like toothpicks, their faces were soft, and they had normal ears. They laughed and joked and smiled and bounced in and out of their stances while they waited to register.

Most of the grapplers had shaved heads. Their necks were wide and their cores thick. Their faces were hard, aged from the mat and, for those who trained MMA, by fists and elbows. Many had cauliflower ear. Smiles were intermittent and short.

A grappler somewhere behind me summed up the general emotion of the crowd. He said, "Let's get this line moving. I'm fucking hungry."

And thirsty.

After half an hour of waiting, it was my turn to weigh-in. I handed in my registration form and stepped behind the curtain to the scale. A cute blond was working the scale. I didn't care. Nothing was more important than making weight. I stripped down to my boxer briefs. Grappling destroyed any inhibitions I had about my body. I was completely comfortable in my skin. I hoped she liked what she saw. I stepped onto the scale. The screen blinked. Dash dash. Dash dash. Dash dash. Then 158.2.

The scale was reading way light. Regardless, the battle before the battle was won. Eight weeks of dieting and exercising culminating in three seconds on a scale. Victory. I quaffed two Boost shakes and started sipping on Gatorade to replenish my electrolytes and rehydrate. Downing a whole bottle of water and eating a stomach full of food seems like the right thing to do, but that isn't so. The human body can only digest so much food in a given period of time, and overeating can actually slow the body's metabolism. And water goes through a dehydrated body relatively fast. I assume it does so to expel harmful toxins built up in the kidneys.

The first time I cut weight, for the Kumite Classic the year before, I did not know that.

I had driven to the convention center with Hilary. I weighed-in. As soon as I stepped off the scale, I sucked down two bottles of water. Twenty minutes later, we were stuck in traffic, me in the driver seat, Hilary in the passenger seat, and I had to pee. I really, really had to pee. We were on the interstate, but still within the city limits, half a mile from the tunnels. I didn't know Pittsburgh well enough to take an exit downtown to find a restroom. I'd have to wait until we got through the tunnels, outside of the city.

Traffic wasn't moving.

I shifted in my seat. I shifted again.

"Are you all right?" Hilary asked.

"No. I am not all right."

We inched forward. The dashboard clock read 4:13.

We moved through the tunnels. Keeping myself from peeing now required conscious effort. The dashboard clock read 4:19.

Traffic stopped again. No exit in sight. My groin hurt. Sharp, stinging pain. The dashboard clock read 4:24.

Traffic was creeping. I checked the shoulder. There wasn't room to pull over. I checked the backseat. I had an empty water bottle, but how could I fill it while I drove. I considered having Hilary hold the bottle, but what if someone saw? My Ford Escort was low to the ground, anyone in an SUV could see my girlfriend helping me pee into a water bottle. What if the water bottle couldn't hold all of it? Did I have the fortitude to stop midstream?

Maybe I could pee out the cracked door, I thought. What if a cop saw? How would I explain my need to pee out the door of a moving vehicle?

What was more embarrassing, having my girlfriend helping me pee, a cop catching me peeing in traffic, or wetting myself in my own car? I weighed my options while the pain in my crotch doubled and doubled again. I began vocalizing the pain (and I refuse to describe what that noise sounded like). The dashboard clock read 4:33.

I saw an exit. A Giant Eagle sign. Public restrooms. I sped down the exit ramp. I took the right turn hard. The tires screeched. I thought that I was about to burst—not accidentally wet myself; I thought my groin was going to rupture. I pressed the gas pedal down. I cut through a mall parking lot. I ran a stop sign. I saw the automatic doors of the Giant Eagle. I slammed on my brakes and threw the car into park at the entrance. I jumped out, leaving the door open. The dashboard clock read 4:37.

I stepped through the doors and walked to a woman wearing a brown Giant Eagle apron working a checkout line.

"Excuse me," I said. My voice shook. Sweat ran down my face. My legs quivered. "Where are your restrooms?"

"They're right through there, honey," she said, pointing to a hallway near the pharmacy counter.

"Thank you."

I power walked to the hallway. Once the employees were out of sight, I broke into a run, slamming open the bathroom door. I pulled down my shorts and felt sweet, sweet relief. The nightmare was over. The dashboard clock read 4:42 when I finally walked out.

I never made that mistake again.

This time I sipped my Gatorade on the ride home, and saved the water-quaffing for when I was closer to a toilet.

The cut paid off. I weighed in at 159.6 according to my scale (for the 150–159.9 division). I was 171.4 when I fought the next morning.

* * * * *

The moment you touch hands to begin a match, a thick silent fog surrounds you. You don't hear the crowd gathered around the mat. You don't hear the sound system. For a moment, you hear only the slow thump of your heart, beating like a Mongolian war drum. There's a tension in your chest. A tingling at your finger tips.

Then he grabs your gi.

Everything slows down. You're aware of every detail of his position and yours. You feel the weight. The leverage. The possibilities. You don't think. Thinking takes too long. You trust your body. You trust your training. Your mind calculates the physics of a dozen techniques and picks the right one without you even knowing. Practice breeds instinct, reflex.

It's more than a fight. It's more than simple sport.

Now, after five months of training in Hilo, that thick, silent fog descends. Even the shouting of my opponent's paunchy, bearded coach fades into silence. My opponent's shaggy hair hangs in front of his eyes, and through the sandy blur I see his hesitation, his fear. My back is on the mat. My guard is closed. He grips my lapels with both hands but is not moving to advance his position. I pull down on his head and climb my leg up his shoulder, going to my rubber guard. I wait for him to react, hoping to use his movement to set up an attack, but he doesn't release his grip.

Why is he afraid? Why isn't he attacking?

I break his grip with my left arm and pass his hand to the mat, trapping it with an overhook. I pull my leg over his trapped shoulder and pass it under his chin. I pull down on his head and push up with my leg to drive my shin into his windpipe. He taps to the gogoplata shortly after. My first match of the Kumite Classic is over in forty seconds.

As soon as I let go of the submission, my opponent jumped to his feet and looked to his coach. His coach started yelling at the referee, claiming I used an illegal move. I knew that a gogoplata didn't violate any of the rules, so I let the referee deal with the coach.

My sandy haired opponent turned to me. "What the hell was that?" he asked, a nervous smile on his face. "That was pretty wicked."

I didn't know what to say at first. It didn't make sense. Anyone fighting in the blue belt division should be familiar with a gogoplata. I looked at his waist. He was wearing a yellow belt. I ignored it before. I was focused on the match, but now I knew that something wasn't right. I looked to his coach. His black T-shirt bore a Karate logo. My opponent wasn't a grappler. He was a striker who learned a little bit of ground work. He thought he could hang with guys that live on the mat.

In jiu-jitsu terms, he wasn't even a white belt. I beat up a newbie. The victory was meaningless. It proved nothing.

When I looked at the bracket, I saw that my next opponent was Craig, a Steel City blue belt. He had always been nice to me, and he outranked me. I knew the respectful thing to do; I bowed out, taking second place. Bowing out to a training partner, especially if he outranks you, is common practice among fighters, both in grappling and in mixed martial arts. Fighting a friend in the gym is symbiotic. Both of you are learning and practicing. If one person wins a match in the gym, it does not necessarily mean that he is a better fighter, he just won on that given day. The level of competition may be intense, but it is friendly and private. But at a tournament or in the cage, it's a fight. The victory has meaning, importance. To fight a friend in public can lead to ill feelings. Losing might embarrass him, or he may be offended by your willingness to inflict harm in order to win. So, one person bows out to the other (there is some controversy surrounding this nearly universal practice, especially at high-level tournaments).

I took off my gi and prepared for the no-gi division.

My first opponent in the no-gi division was shorter and thinner. I followed my game plan. I pulled him into my half guard and worked a sweep. I scored a few points taking the top position and controlling, but he rolled me back to guard. After two minutes, we were back in my half guard. I went for the old school sweep, my best move, and he defended by posting his leg out. I transitioned to the electric chair, a position that places me beneath my opponent, forcing his legs into a split. When I had him fully extended he looked down at me.

He yelled, "Fuck!"

He tried to free himself, but I used his movement to trap his foot. I applied a figure-four toe-hold, a submission that torques the ankle. Once the ankle gives, the rotation of the heel can cause damage in the knee.

My opponent's ankle popped once before he tapped, a stabbing grimace on his face. He limped off of the mat. 3:02.

My next opponent had an NCAA Wrestling shirt on. He was taller but skinnier and had a scruffy face. He got the points for the takedown, but he couldn't pass my guard. I kept throwing triangle attempts, and I eventually caught him. He tapped. :55.

My final opponent was smaller too. He wore blue Under Armour. We touch hands.

I circle him for a moment. I grip the back of his neck. I jump into the air. I wrap my legs around his waist and pull him to the ground. Rubber guard. Trap his arm to the mat. He stacks me, posting up on his legs, driving his head and weight into my chest. My knees are touching my face and the mat behind me. I'm flexible. This isn't uncomfortable. I can breathe. In. Out. In. Out.

He pulls his left arm back to set up a pass. I chop it with my leg and look for a triangle choke. He stacks harder, so I transition to a different leg choke: the tepee. He gasps. He gurgles. He shakes back and forth, trying to get free. He's panicking but not tapping. I wonder if he'll go to sleep.

I hear Sensei's voice say, "Triangle! Triangle!"

I grab my foot, check his hip, and close my legs into a figure-four. I wiggle out from the stack. His face is turning red. His gurgles are louder. I pull down on my legs and sink my hips just like Papo taught me. I know that the fight is over. He can either go to sleep or he can tap. He taps. :57. The referee raises my arm. I've won first. When the referee drops my arm, I turn to my family and flex. I'm laughing. I'm happy.

I look to the audience. My family—my mom, dad, little brother, and grandmother—my friends—Sensei and my training partners from Steel City—are clapping and smiling too. I realize that I never had anything to prove to them.

A PROLOGUE MASQUERADING AS AN EPILOGUE

Sensei promoted me to blue belt a few weeks after the Kumite Classic. I took the test. I demonstrated my techniques. I grappled with a Steel City brown belt. The rest of the gym watched while Sensei put his signature next to Charuto's and tied the belt around my waist. Having blue around my waist again and Sensei's blessing was gratifying. I knew that my journey was officially over. Not having a belt whipping to go with the promotion, though, disappointed me.

I resumed my mainland Pennsylvanian life, returning to my old jobs and my old university, but the feeling I had that first week never passed; I didn't belong. I sat through the classes. I ate in the cafeteria. I went to work. I was in the crowd but still on the outside. I was an actor who had walked on to the wrong set, the medieval knight wondering the corridors of a starship. I had my sword, my shield, and my armor. I was battle tested. I had a warrior's sense of honor and respect, but the setting was all wrong, and the other actors just stared.

I did my best to keep in touch with my friends from Hilo. Laura stayed on the Big Island to finish her degree at UH Hilo. Britany and Ti did the same. They called me once a week and texted me frequently to see how their favorite haole boy (or as Ti called me, "her mainland boyfriend") was doing. I wrote Jay a few letters. Though he never wrote back, I heard from other students at the Academy that he was reading them. Chris and Ethan still trained, but a failing economy discouraged them from going to the gym as often as they used to. Papo moved to New York for a few months to teach and to train. He went to Washington DC shortly after and was promoted to brown belt. He eventually returned to the Dominican Republic to start his gym. Poai got married and soon after had a son. I never heard from Iol, Jake, Roke, or Jack again.

I didn't hear much from my old mainland friends either.

If I saw someone from my old circle of friends, they walked by as if they didn't recognize me. If they did say something, they pretended that we were on good terms and always had been.

Hilary moved in with her new boyfriend shortly after I returned. They had a place in town, close to the university. Though she avoided eye contact if we happened to cross paths, she e-mailed and messaged me at random. At first she was just asking how I was and how my family was doing, but she started to say that she didn't like how I had changed. She said that I was less considerate. That I was meaner. That some of my best qualities were being squelched while the worst were becoming more extreme.

I disagreed. I was standing up for myself. I no longer tolerated being mistreated. I didn't hide from anyone or anything, and I didn't back down. Cash would say that I was the best friend that he ever had. He knew that I would die for him, without hesitation, and he would do the same for me (or maybe he liked how easy it was to sucker me into paying for drinks).

The November following my stay in Hawaii, Cash and I were driving back to Pittsburgh from Atlantic City. Lockflow.com had sent me to cover a Ring of Combat card at the Tropicana, and Cash tagged along to keep me company. We were coming up on Harrisburg. The temperature was a few degrees above freezing. Rain made an icy mosaic of my windshield. Cash had his feet up on the dusty dashboard. His jeans and his T-shirt were wrinkled. His ski jacket was unzipped. His brown Einstein hair was flat in some places and puffed in others, the result of a late night in Atlantic City and sleeping on and off in the car.

I had just finished telling him about how hard it was to get an interview with BJ when I was in Hawaii.

"I remember calling you about then," Cash said. "You sounded pretty beat and depressed."

I nodded.

"I know you're not into this sort of thing, but I was praying for you. I want you to know that. I know that things were pretty rough for you for a while, and I'm sorry that I transferred right before all of that went down."

I thanked him.

Cash looked out the window. Headlights shimmered in his glasses. "I know that you've got my back, no matter what. Brother, I've got your back too," he said, pausing. "You're different now. You've changed a lot in the last year, but I guess that much shit will do that to you. You seem happier. You were in a bad place for a long time. I'm glad that you're finally out of it. I know they won't ever really understand what you went through, but it doesn't matter. You're better off."

What I went through? Injuries. Loneliness. Rain. The Red Baron. A hitchhiker named Tim. Cockroaches. Cauliflower ear. A blue belt. A centipede. A really, really big centipede.

I didn't know how to respond. I heard the rain on the windows and the wet sound of passing traffic. The radio was too low to hear.

Cash looked out the window. "I know that they don't like how you've changed. They don't matter. They just wish they could do what you've done. And I appreciate you letting me be a part of it."

I thanked him again for being a good friend.

He turned his head to face me. "So when are we doing our Europe trip?" he asked, grinning.

I had forgotten. Cash and I talked about backpacking around Europe for a few months, exploring the continent and training at every gym along the way. Cash said that it would make the perfect sequel for my book. We'd meet girls in Rome and train. We'd meet girls in Amsterdam and train. We'd meet girls in Berlin and train. We'd meet girls in Paris and train.

"My German has gotten pretty good," Cash continued. "And you can speak jiu-jitsu. Man, that'd be so rad. We'd get in so much trouble."

I laughed and pressed the gas. The mat was calling my name.

ACKNOWLEDGMENTS

'd like to thank everyone that I met in Hawaii. No matter how briefly we may have known each other, your aloha had a profound effect on my life. BJ, Jay, JD, Reagan, Papo, Charuto, Ethan, Chris, Kris, Poai, Ben, Zay, Ro, Iol, Britany, Tiare, JB, Jack, Laura, Jake, Roke, Dr. Panek, Paige, Tom, Jason—I owe you a great deal. If we met on the Big Island, and I did not list your name or you didn't appear in the book, please do not be offended. Every experience was meaningful, but I could not include them all.

Were it not for the guidance and encouragement of my mentor and friend, Alan Natali, this book would not exist. Thank you for going beyond your obligations as a professor and dedicating a great deal of your time to teaching me your craft. I strive to achieve your level of mastery; a feat I fear will take me more than one lifetime.

My mother and father—your unceasing support gave me the tenacity to pursue my dreams. You changed my diapers, you helped me through college, you picked me up each time I stumbled in between. Thank you for your love.

I'd like to thank the following people for helping me edit and fact-check The Cauliflower Chronicles: Adam, Cash, Bryan, Jerod, Ti, Britany, Ryan, Caris, and Nora.

Erich Krauss and Glen Cordoza of Victory Belt Publishing: thank you for giving me this opportunity.

Finally, I'd like to thank Charles Pearson of Lockflow.com and Doug Jeffrey of Ultimate MMA (formerly Ultimate Grappling) for their encouragement and for supporting this book by publishing portions of it as individual articles.

REFERENCES

Bravo, Eddie, Erich Krauss, and Glen Cordoza. *Mastering the Rubber Guard.* Chico, CA: Victory Belt Publishing, 2006.

Doughty, Andrew. *Hawaii: The Big Island Revealed* (4th edition). Lihue: HI: Wizard Publications, 2006.

McKinney, Chris. *The Tattoo.* New York: Mutual Publishing Company, 2001.

Nunes, Keone, & Scott Whitney. "*The Destruction of the Hawaiian Male.*" Honolulu, July1994: 43, 59–61.

Penn, BJ, Glen Cordoza, and Erich Krauss. *Mixed Martial Arts: The Book of Knowledge.* Chico, CA: Victory Belt Publishing , 2007.

BJ Penn: 90 Days (DVD), Kinetic Films, 2009.